LONGMAN LINGUISTICS LIBRARY

Title no 18

THE ENGLISH VERB

LONGMAN LINGUISTICS LIBRARY

General editors
R. H. Robins, University of London
G. N. Leech, University of Lancaster

Title no:

THE LINGUISTIC SCIENCES AND LANGUAGE TEACHING 1
M. A. K. Halliday, Angus McIntosh and Peter Strevens

GENERAL LINGUISTICS 2
AN INTRODUCTORY SURVEY
R. H. Robins

A SHORT HISTORY OF LINGUISTICS 6
R. H. Robins

ESSAYS ON THE ENGLISH LANGUAGE 8
MEDIEVAL AND MODERN
Randolph Quirk

STUDIES IN ENGLISH ADVERBIAL USAGE 9
Sidney Greenbaum

TOWARDS A SEMANTIC DESCRIPTION OF ENGLISH 10
Geoffrey N. Leech

ELICITATION EXPERIMENTS IN ENGLISH 11
LINGUISTIC STUDIES IN USE AND ATTITUDE
Sidney Greenbaum and Randolph Quirk

PHONETICS IN LINGUISTICS 12
A BOOK OF READINGS
Editors: *W. E. Jones and J. Laver*

STRUCTURAL ASPECTS OF LANGUAGE CHANGE 13
James M. Anderson

PHILOSOPHY AND THE NATURE OF LANGUAGE 14
David E. Cooper

SEMANTICO-SYNTAX 15
Frans Liefrink

FROM SIGNS TO PROPOSITIONS 16
THE CONCEPT OF FORM IN EIGHTEENTH-CENTURY SEMANTIC THEORY
Stephen K. Land

SPATIAL AND TEMPORAL USES OF ENGLISH PREPOSITIONS 17
David C. Bennett

THE ENGLISH VERB 18
F. R. Palmer

PRINCIPLES OF FIRTHIAN LINGUISTICS 19
T. F. Mitchell

The English Verb

F. R. Palmer
Professor of Linguistic Science
University of Reading

LONGMAN

Longman
1724-1974

LONGMAN GROUP LIMITED LONDON
Associated companies, branches and representatives throughout the world

First published as *A Linguistic Study of the English Verb* 1965
Fifth impression 1973
Second edition retitled *The English Verb* 1974
Cased ISBN 0 582 52454 7
Paper ISBN 0 582 52458 X

Made and printed in Great Britain by
William Clowes & Sons, Limited, London, Beccles and Colchester

Preface

This book was originally intended to be a revised version of *A Linguistic Study of the English Verb*, which was first published in 1965. In the event it has been largely rewritten and completely reorganized, with different chapters and headings. The overall scope has not been altered.

Although the new version has obviously been influenced by developments in linguistics, an attempt has been made to keep the material as factual as possible but theoretical issues are not avoided. Like its predecessor it is intended both for students of Linguistics and for all who are interested in the description of modern English.

University of Reading FRP
February 1974

Contents

Preface v

1 Introduction 1
1.1 General considerations 2
1.1.1 *Speech and writing* 3
1.1.2 *Form and meaning* 6
1.1.3 *The text* 7
1.2 Linguistic units 9
1.2.1 *Word and phrase* 9
1.2.2 *Sentence and clause* 11

2 The verb phrase 13
2.1 Preliminary considerations 13
2.1.1 *Finite and non-finite* 13
2.1.2 *Concord* 15
2.1.3 *Verb classes* 15
2.1.4 *Simple and complex phrases* 16
2.2 The auxiliaries 18
2.2.1 *The forms* 18
2.2.2 *Negation* 20
2.2.3 *Inversion* 22
2.2.4 *'Code'* 23
2.2.5 *Emphatic affirmation* 24
2.2.6 DO 25
2.2.7 DARE *and* NEED 26
2.2.8 *'Semi-negatives'* 28

3 Tense, phase and aspect 30
3.1 Syntax of the primary auxiliaries 30
3.1.1 *Basic paradigms* 30
3.1.2 *Infinitivals, participials and imperatives* 32
3.1.3 *The four categories* 33
3.1.4 *Arrangement of the analysis* 34
3.1.5 *Outline of the uses* 35
3.1.6 *Time and tense* 36
3.1.7 *Epistemic and displaced time marking* 38
3.1.8 *Auxiliary and full verb* 39
3.1.9 *Adverbial specification* 42
3.2 Tense 43
3.2.1 *Time relations* 43
3.2.2 *Reported speech* 44
3.2.3 *Unreality* 47
3.3 Phase 49
3.3.1 *Time relations* 49
3.3.2 *Non-progressive forms and 'results'* 50
3.3.3 *Progressive forms and 'results'* 53
3.3.4 HAVE *as past* 54
3.4 Aspect 55
3.4.1 *Duration* 55
3.4.2 *Varieties of use* 56
3.5 Future and habitual uses 58
3.5.1 *The problem* 58
3.5.2 *The simple present* 60
3.5.3 *Habitual* 62
3.5.4 *Future: progressive* 64
3.5.5 *Future: non-progressive* 66
3.5.6 *Future and habitual combined* 67
3.6 Aspect again 68
3.6.1 *Limited duration* 68
3.6.2 *Sporadic repetition* 69
3.7 Non-progressive verbs 70
3.7.1 *Private verbs* 71
3.7.2 *Verbs of state* 73
3.7.3 *Use in progressive* 73
3.7.4 *Homonyms* 75
3.8 Phase again 77
3.8.1 *Problem uses* 77

3.8.2 *Displaced phase* 78

4 Voice 81

4.1 The passive 81

4.1.1 *Transformation* 81

4.1.2 *Transitivity* 83

4.1.3 *The meaning of the passive* 86

4.1.4 *Statal passives* 88

4.1.5 GET 89

4.2 Related structures 90

4.2.1 *'Case' relations* 90

4.2.2 *'Pseudo-passives'* 92

5 The modals 94

5.1 Syntax of the modals 94

5.1.1 *The paradigms* 94

5.1.2 *Auxiliary and full verb* 96

5.1.3 *Subject and discourse orientation* 100

5.1.4 *Epistemic and non-epistemic* 102

5.1.5 *Method of analysis* 103

5.2 Basic forms 104

5.2.1 *Futurity* 104

5.2.2 WILL 108

5.2.3 SHALL 113

5.2.4 WILL *and* SHALL *compared* 114

5.2.5 CAN 115

5.2.6 MAY 118

5.2.7 CAN *and* MAY *together* 118

5.2.8 MUST *and* OUGHT 120

5.2.9 DARE *and* NEED 122

5.3 Past tense, negation, passives 123

5.3.1 *Past tense/past time* 123

5.3.2 *Past time – other forms* 125

5.3.3 *Tentative* 127

5.3.4 would, should *and* might 128

5.3.5 *Reported speech* 130

5.3.6 *Negation* 131

5.3.7 *Passives* 133

5.4 Epistemic modals 135

5.4.1 *Basic forms* 135
5.4.2 *Negation* 137
5.4.3 *Past tense* 138
5.5 Conditionals 139
5.5.1 *Tense and modals* 140
5.5.2 *Types of conditionals* 142
5.5.3 *Predictive conditionals* 143
5.5.4 *Other conditionals* 146
5.5.5 *Epistemic modals* 147
5.5.6 WILL *again* 148
5.5.7 *Wishes* 149

6 Marginal verbs 152
6.1 Auxiliaries as full verbs 152
6.1.1 BE 152
6.1.2 HAVE 155
6.1.3 DO 160
6.2 Quasi auxiliaries 162
6.2.1 USED 162
6.2.2 BE GOING 163
6.2.3 BETTER, RATHER and LET'S 164

7 The catenatives 166
7.1 Problems of statement 167
7.1.1 *Basic structures* 167
7.1.2 *Simple and complex phrases* 168
7.1.3 *Aspect, phase, tense and voice* 170
7.1.4 *Verbal nouns and adjectives* 174
7.1.5 *Status of the subordinate clause* 176
7.2 Identity relations 180
7.2.1 *Status of the NP* 180
7.2.2 *Problematic constructions* 183
7.2.3 *Subject complementation* 185
7.2.4 *Other identity relations* 187
7.3 Classification of the catenatives 189
7.3.1 *Semantics and structure* 189
7.3.2 *Preposition in the structure* 190
7.3.3 *Homonyms* 192
7.4 Catenative classes 194
7.4.1 *Futurity* 195

7.4.2 *Causatives* 199
7.4.3 *Reporting* 199
7.4.4 *Perception* 202
7.4.5 *Process* 204
7.4.6 *Effort and achievement* 205
7.4.7 *Attitude* 206
7.4.8 *Needing* 208
7.4.9 *Subject complementation* 208
7.5 Related and contrasting structures 209
7.5.1 *With* to-*infinitive* 209
7.5.2 *With* -ing *form* 211

8 Compound verbs 212
8.1 Grammar and lexicon 213
8.2 Preposition and adverb 214
8.2.1 *Prepositional-adverbs* 215
8.2.2 *Formal contrasts* 216
8.2.3 *Semantic problems* 218
8.2.4 '*Postpositions*' 219
8.3 Phrasal verbs 220
8.3.1 *Formal characteristics* 221
8.3.2 *Accent and position* 222
8.3.3 *Intransitive forms* 223
8.3.4 *Semantics* 224
8.3.5 *Idioms* 225
8.4 Prepositional verbs 227
8.4.1 *Formal characteristics* 228
8.4.2 *Transitive forms* 229
8.4.3 *Semantics* 230
8.4.4 *Idioms* 230
8.5 Related constructions 234
8.5.1 *Verb and particle constructions* 234
8.5.2 *Verbs plus other elements* 235

9 Morphology 237
9.1 The auxiliaries 237
9.1.1 *Irregular forms* 237
9.1.2 *Negative forms* 238
9.1.3 *Weak forms* 239
9.2 Full verbs: *-ing* and *-s* forms 245

9.3 Full verbs: past tense and *-en* forms 246
9.3.1 *Regular* -ed *formation* 246
9.3.2 *Secondary* -ed *formation* 247
9.3.3 *Back vowel formation* 250
9.3.4 -en *suffix* 252
9.3.5 *Idiosyncratic forms* 253
9.4 BE, HAVE and DO 254
9.5 Forms with *to* 254

References 256
Verb index 259
Subject index 265

Chapter 1

Introduction

In recent years interest in English grammar has increased enormously, but there have been far more books and articles on the verb than on the noun, the adjective or any other class of word. One reason, obviously, is that the verb, or rather the verb phrase, as it will be defined in this book, is so central to the structure of the sentence that no syntactic analysis can proceed without a careful consideration of it. Another source of interest is the great complexity of the internal semantic and syntactic structure of the verb phrase itself.

For almost any language the part that concerns the verb is the most difficult. Learning a language is to a very large degree learning how to operate the verbal forms of that language, and, except in the case of those that are related historically, the pattern and structure of the verb in each language seem to differ very considerably from those in every other language. Most of us, as native speakers of a language, are as a result reasonably convinced that our own language has a fairly straightforward way of dealing with the verbs and are rather dismayed and discouraged when faced with something entirely different in a new language.

The verbal patterns of languages differ in two ways, first of all formally, in the way in which the linguistic material is organized, and secondly in the type of information carried.

On the formal side the most obvious distinction is between those languages whose verbal features are expressed almost entirely by inflection and those which have no inflectional features at all, those which, in traditional terms, used to be distinguished as 'inflectional' and as 'isolating' languages. Extreme examples of these are Latin or classical Arabic on the one hand and Chinese on the other. English, in this respect, is much closer to Chinese than it is to Latin; or at least this is true as long as we are thinking about *words*. If we ask how many different forms of the verb there are in Latin, the answer will be over a hundred, and the same is true for classical Arabic. For English, on the other hand, there are only five possible forms; if we consider the verb 'to take', we have only *take*, *takes*, *taking*, *took* and *taken*. But this contrast between Chinese and Latin or between English and Latin is superficial because it is wholly in terms of the word. For if, when we talk about verbal forms in English, we think rather of forms such as *is taking*, *has been taking*, *may have taken*, etc, there are very many more forms in the English verb – well over a hundred. The essential difference between Latin and English is not so much the number of verbal forms but the way in which the verbal forms are divided into words.

Perhaps more important, and certainly more difficult for the learner, is the nature of the information carried by the verbal forms. Speakers of European languages expect that their verbs will tell them something about time, and that we shall have at least a future, a present and a past tense referring to a future, a present and a past time. But there is no natural law that the verb in a language shall be concerned with time. There are plenty of languages in which time relations are not marked at all, and there are some languages in which the verb is concerned with spatial rather than temporal relations. Even in languages where time seems to be dealt with in the verb, it is not always a simple matter of present, past and future; even English does not handle present, past and future as a trio in the category of tense (3.1.6). More troublesome is the variety of other features only indirectly associated with time that are indicated by the verb. In English, for instance, the verb may indicate that an action took place in a period preceding, but continuing right up to, the present moment, as well as simply in the past. In other languages, such as the Slavonic languages, what is important is whether or not the action has been completed. *I read a book last night* will be translated into Russian in two different ways – depending upon whether or not I finished the book.

1.1 General considerations

It is not the aim of this book to raise or to answer questions of linguistic theory for their own sake, though it contains a considerable amount of discussion that is of theoretical relevance. Any book of this kind must, moreover, make assumptions about its subject – that we can, for instance, usefully identify the verb and that statements about the 'meaning' of linguistic items are themselves meaningful. Some general comments, however, on the linguistic standpoint and some of the basic concepts are appropriate.

1.1.1 Speech and writing

It is a reasonable question to ask of a linguist whether he is attempting to describe the spoken or the written language. With a few exceptions most grammarians until fairly recently have been concerned almost exclusively with the written language and their works are often superbly illustrated by copious examples from English literature.[1] This concentration on the written language has sometimes been associated with the assumption that speech is inferior in being ephemeral instead of permanent, and in being often ungrammatical or even corrupt.[2] Not surprisingly, perhaps, there has also been a reaction to this point of view; there have been linguists, especially of the so called 'structuralist' school of Americans[3] who have taken the opposite view and argued that only speech is language.

It is easy to show at the level of the sound and writing systems of the language, the phonology and the graphology, that spoken and written languages are very different. Apart from the fact that they are in different media, one in sound and the other in marks upon paper, there is often no one-to-one correspondence between the units of one and the units of the other, at least in the case of languages that have a long tradition of writing. It is not simply that there are such words as *cough*, *tough*, etc in which there seems to be no relation between the spelling and the pronunciation. The differences go deeper than that. For instance, in English there are only five vowels in the writing, but it would be very difficult to analyse the sound system in any way that would reduce the number of vowels to less than six. More important is the fact that in speech there are the features of stress and intonation, which have only to a very limited degree counterparts in the written language. In this respect the reverse of the traditional belief is true. It is writing that is a very poor representation of speech.

Even the grammar of the spoken language is different from the grammar of the written. In the written language the form *has* is irregular – one would expect on the analogy of *have* to find **haves*, while the form *does* is quite regular – we may compare *go*, *goes* and *do*, *does*; but in the spoken language *does* [dʌz][4] is as irregular as *has* [hæz], for we should expect to find, on analogy with the other forms, *[du:z] and *[hævz]. Conversely, the negative form of *am*, which appears in questions only, is so odd in the writing that we are not sure whether we ought to write it at all – the only possible form is *aren't I?* But in the spoken language this is a perfectly regular form; it is paralleled by *can't I?* and *shan't I?* The negative form differs from the positive in that (i) the vowel is [ɑː] instead of [æ], and (ii) the last consonant of the positive form is missing in the negative form:

can [kæn] *can't* [kɑːnt]
am [æm] *aren't* [ɑːnt]
shall [ʃæl] *shan't* [ʃɑːnt]

However, for the purposes of this book the distinction is not particularly important. We are not concerned with phonology except incidentally, while morphology is dealt with in Chapter 9. For the rest of the grammatical analysis (which is mainly syntactic) the differences between speech and writing are smaller (or, perhaps, one should say, more accurately, that there are greater correlations between the two). In particular, and most fortunately, we can use the writing convention of the language, the orthography, to identify the forms of the spoken language. It will, naturally, not be an accurate indication of the phonology or (to a lesser degree) of the morphology, but it will indicate fairly accurately most of the grammatical structure that we are concerned with. Indeed it is no coincidence that the term grammar is derived from the Greek word meaning 'to write', for an essential part of writing is that it reflects the grammatical system of the language.

It is, therefore, reasonable to claim that this is essentially a study of the spoken form of the language, yet at the same time to use the written form to identify the words and sentences that we are talking about. A fairly recent work on the English verb[5] used as its source material the transcript of a trial. This was essentially the analysis of the spoken form of English, yet the text available was wholly in written form. It need hardly be added that the reader will find the orthographic form of the examples easier to read than if they had been in a phonetic script. This is not simply a matter of familiarity – it is also that a phonetic script supplies details that are superfluous for the grammatical analysis.

It could be argued, however, that the orthography is defective in that it does not mark stress and intonation. This is a just criticism since stress and intonation are clearly grammatical; and it is not only stress and intonation – there are other 'prosodic' features[6] that are left unstated. But these features are grammatical in two different senses. In the first place they often correlate with grammatical features that belong to the written language. For instance we can distinguish:

I didn't do it because it was difficult.
I didn't do it, because it was difficult.

The first sentence means that I did it, but not because it was difficult, the second that I did not do it – because it was difficult. What is negated is *because it was difficult* in the first, *I did it* in the second. The comma indicates this in the written form. In speech the distinction is made even clearer by the use of appropriate intonation (probably a single fall-rise intonation in the first, but two intonation tunes in the second, a rise and then a fall). Secondly, however, intonation involves us in grammatical statements of a different kind. We shall normally regard statement and question as grammatically different in, for instance, *Shall I come tomorrow?* and *I shall come tomorrow.* It is not so clear whether in the written form we must also distinguish *I shall come tomorrow?* where the order of the words is still that of the statement. In speech the intonational difference is obvious, and it would be reasonable to argue that intonation as much as word order indicates the grammatical distinction between statement and question. But there are other distinctions that can be made by intonation. We can also say *I shall come tomorrow* with a fall-rise intonation to mean that I shall come tomorrow but not at some other time that has been mentioned or implied. It is difficult not to conclude that this too is grammatical – there is a difference in both the meaning and the form of the sentence, comparable with the differences between *I come* and *I shall come* or *I shall not come* and *I shall come.*

In spite of this, we shall largely exclude these features from consideration. For if we consider one of them, intonation, we see that we can largely ignore it in the study of the verb. The reason for this is twofold. In the first place, the grammar that belongs to intonation is to a large extent independent of the rest of the grammar of the language. We can, that is to say, deal with most of the characteristics of the verbs of English, we can talk about the tenses, about the other grammatical categories, progressives, perfect, active and passive, the modal auxiliaries, the catenatives, etc, without saying very much at all about the intonation. This point is, however, in itself not a sufficient reason for excluding intonation. The second point is the vital one. It is that it is difficult, if not impossible, to analyse intonation in the kind of framework within which more traditional grammar is handled. The reason for this is that the relation between the intonation tunes that we may recognize and their functions is incredibly complex. For most grammatical features we can talk about specific phonological 'exponents'. For instance, in the case of past tense in English we can talk about the addition of an alveolar consonant, comparing *like* [laik] with *liked* [laikt], and *love* [lʌv] with *loved* [lʌvd], and add the rules for the past tense forms of the kind *took*, *bought*, etc. What we do not find is that an alveolar consonant is sometimes the exponent of past tense, sometimes of future, sometimes of negation, sometimes of a modal auxiliary. Yet in the case of intonation we find that a single intonation tune has a vast variety of different functions, depending on a number of factors, some within the language, others situational and outside the language.

The term 'stress' is, unfortunately, used in several senses. It is used to mean word stress in the sense that different syllables of the noun *convict* and the verb *convict* are stressed. It has also been used to refer to the 'pitch prominent' syllables of a sentence. That these two uses are different is clear from the fact that only in the second sense can we talk about *shall*, *was*, etc (see 9.1.3) as being either stressed or unstressed. We also need to talk about 'tonic' ('nuclear' or 'sentence') stress that will occur once only in a single intonation tune.

Detailed studies of the prosodic features are a most important part of the linguistic analysis of English, but in the study of the English verb little would be gained and a great deal of clarity would be lost if they were always marked. In most cases they are irrelevant for our purposes – *saw* is past tense whatever the intonation or other prosodic features. In fact, we shall seldom need to mark more than the tonic stress, which I shall call the 'accent' – and we can talk about words rather than syllables being accented. This is easily indicated in the orthography by an acute accent:

That's the flag he ran úp.
That's the hill he rán up.

Where there is need to refer to 'pitch prominence', I shall, with some hesitancy, continue to talk about 'stressed' and 'unstressed' syllables.

1.1.2 Form and meaning

As with the controversy over speech and writing there have been disagreements about the relation of form and meaning to grammar. Some older grammarians seemed to assume that grammar was essentially concerned with meaning and defined their grammatical categories in semantic terms, nouns in terms of 'things', gender in terms of sex, singular and plural in terms of counting.[7] More recently some linguists have firmly maintained that grammar must be formal – that grammatical categories must be based on form not on meaning,[8] though at the present time there is once again a school of thought that maintains that grammar *is* semantic.

It is easy enough to show that categories based on form and categories based on meaning are sometimes incompatible. There is an often quoted pair of words in English, *oats* and *wheat*, of which the first is formally plural and the second formally singular. But in terms of meaning there is no difference – no difference, that is to say, in the numerical quantities, 'one' or 'more than one', of oats and wheat.

The argument can become a sterile one, for it is impossible to undertake a grammatical analysis that has in no way been influenced by meaning, and it is equally impossible to undertake an analysis purely based on meaning. The former would result in some kind of statistical analysis of combinations of bits of language, the latter would be impossible because the boundaries of semantic categories are vague. Nor would either exercise be of any value. What we need, and what all grammars have ever provided, is an analysis that is formal in the sense that it illustrates formal regularities and can be justified formally in that formal evidence is always available, but also semantic in the sense that it relies on obvious semantic clues for some of its categorization and also that it accounts for semantic features that correlate with formal distinctions.

It is almost certainly the case than *any* semantic distinction can be matched somewhere in the language by a formal one and that any formal regularity can be assigned some kind of meaning. It is not, then, a matter of form versus meaning, but of the weighting to be given to obvious formal features and to fairly obvious semantic ones. This book will, perhaps, appear to rely more on meaning than the previous one, for that is in accord with the present climate of linguistic thought. But at the same time some new formal features have been introduced – some new formal patterns recognized.[9]

1.1.3 The text

The material for this book is almost entirely the language used by the author, or more strictly the language that he himself believes he uses. This has several disadvantages. First, the native speaker is not always clear or correct about what he actually can say. Secondly, there are many forms that are marginal. It is not possible always to give a Yes/No answer to 'Can you say . . .?' Yet somehow we have to decide whether, for instance, we can allow:

He could have been being examined.

Ideally, it might be thought that such decisions should be based upon the evidence of actual occurrence; grammar then would be based upon recorded texts – preferably, for our purposes, upon spoken texts. But there are two major difficulties in this.

[i] Even with an enormous amount of data some forms will not occur, not because they cannot occur, but simply because of the vast complexity of language. For instance, in Chapter 3 we talk of the non-progressive verbs that do not normally occur with the progressive (BE plus *-ing*) forms – CONTAIN, OWN, etc (**3.7.2**). Under certain circumstances (**3.7.3**) even these may occur with progressive forms. Yet it is almost certain that many hundreds of hours of recorded text would not produce the evidence to establish which are these verbs or the conditions under which they may be progressive.

[ii] In any recorded text there are bound to be a number of anomalous forms – forms that a native speaker would regard as mistakes. This too results from the complexity of language and the difficulty that the native speaker has of always producing what he himself would wish to produce. Yet there is no way that these mistakes can be identified formally. If we rely on recorded data alone they will have to be accounted for in the grammar no less than all the rest of the material.

A grammar based solely on actually recorded data will thus be distorted by the omission of forms that did not actually occur and the inclusion of forms that are not really part of the language at all. Yet the native speaker can quickly rectify both distortions. Appeal to the native speaker is then essential, and is, of course, most convenient if the grammarian is himself a native speaker of the language. Even so there are many points on which even the native speaker is doubtful. It is not the case that some forms are 'in' and others 'out'. There is also a huge area of 'marginality'.

The convention for marking forms that are not accepted is an asterisk:

**He has could been here.*

For forms that are doubtful a question mark will be used.

?He could have been being examined.

We are also sometimes faced with forms that are perfectly acceptable but not in the sense required. For instance in **7.4.1** we have the sentences:

I wish John to meet Mary.
I wish Mary to be met by John.
I persuaded John to meet Mary.
I persuaded Mary to be met by John.

But whereas in the first pair we want to say that they are related in terms of the passivization of the subordinate clause (see **1.2.2**) we do not want to say this of the second pair. Yet the fourth sentence exists – but not as the second member of a formally related pair. To indicate this we shall use the exclamation mark:

!I persuaded Mary to be met by John.

1.2 Linguistic units

We shall be talking in this book about 'words', 'phrases', 'clauses' and 'sentences' – all familiar terms. Some brief comments are appropriate.

1.2.1 Word and phrase

The word is an obvious element in the written language; we can without much hesitation accept it as an element of speech too. Some linguists have been concerned with the precise definition of the word and have even doubted whether it is an essential unit of grammar. The justification is essentially a practical one – that the assumption that the word is a basic grammatical unit works. We can say that the word is precisely the unit that is required for grammatical analysis; its justification lies in its overall grammatical function.

The only alternative that has ever been suggested is the morpheme. But the term 'morpheme' is used in a number of senses that may be arranged along a scale of abstraction. At one end it is used, or was used at least, to refer to the smallest, grammatically relevant, but phonologically segmentable element. For instance, the word *dogs* in this sense of morpheme consists of the two morphemes *dog* [dɔg] and *s* [z]. A refinement on this view of the morpheme treats the morpheme rather as a class of such elements (now renamed 'morphs' or 'allomorphs') such that we classify together the [s] of *cats* [kæts] the [z] of *dogs* [dɔgz] and the [iz] of *horses* [hɔːsiz]. But analysis of this kind breaks down very soon in English. For we cannot easily distinguish the morphemes (or morphs) in *feet*. Similarly it is impossible to establish two morphemes, two distinct segments that is, in *took* the past tense of TAKE, in spite of the ease with which we may establish the two morphemes of *liked*. At the other end of the scale we may dissociate the morpheme from specific phonological segments and use it rather in the sense of an abstract grammatical category so that in *dogs* we have two morphemes, one of which is 'plural', not just *s*. Similarly then we can talk about the two morphemes of *feet*. In the case of *dogs* the 'exponent' of plural may indeed simply be the presence of *s*, but in the case of *feet* the exponent of plural is the occurrence of *feet* rather than *foot*. In this sense we do not segment the elements at all, but the term 'morpheme' is not needed, for it is synonymous with 'grammatical category' or with 'term in a grammatical category'; it is not an identifiable unit, a piece of the language in the same sense as the word is. In this second sense of 'morpheme' the word still remains as the basic unit, the smallest segmentable unit.[10]

Unfortunately the word 'word' is used in two different senses. It may be used to refer to a specific form or to a set of forms that together belong to a single lexical element. For instance 'cat' and 'cats' are two words in one sense but one word in the other. The same confusion is found also with the terms 'noun' and 'verb'. For nouns the 'cat'/'cats' example is again valid. Similarly the verb 'take' might be regarded as being contrasted with 'takes', 'taking', 'took', 'taken', or it might be intended to include all these forms. It is traditional to use the *to*-infinitive (see **2.1.1**) 'to take' to refer to the lexical item that subsumes all the forms, but this does not escape from the difficulty if the form itself is also one of the forms of the verb. For if we talk about the verb 'to take' we might mean either this particular form or (more likely) the set of related forms. What we shall do in this book (and have in fact already done) is to talk about the set of forms as the 'lexeme',[11] and write it in small capital letters, *eg* TAKE, and to write the individual forms in italics, thus *take*, *takes*, *took*, *taking*, *taken*. The lexeme TAKE subsumes all these forms. The term 'verb' will be used to refer to lexemes; forms are 'verbal forms'. But for practical reasons we shall usually restrict this distinction to verbs and verbal forms. Theoretically we should distinguish lexeme and form with adverbs, *eg* QUICKLY, *quickly*, but this would be pedantic since there is but one form. With all words except verbs only the italicized form will be used in this book; this will not lead to ambiguity. It would be pedantic too to distinguish 'word' and 'word forms'; in normal usage 'word forms' are simply called 'words'. We shall follow this usage though it may be theoretically 'incorrect', since it will seldom, if ever, give rise to misunderstanding. However, where other words are closely associated with verbs (especially the particles of Chapter 8), the distinction will be made for them, too, for the sake of consistency.

We shall encounter the term 'phrase' as in 'noun phrase' and 'verb phrase'. The precise definition of verb phrase is left until the next chapter (**2.1.4**). For noun phrase (or NP) it is enough to note that the subjects and objects of sentences are not usually single nouns but nouns modified by adjectives, determiners, etc. The sequence of such elements with a 'head' noun is what is designated 'noun phrase'.

1.2.2 Sentence and clause

The term 'sentence' is used, unfortunately, in modern linguistics in two different but related senses. Consider:

John expected that he would see his father.

In one sense this is a single sentence (and so marked in the orthography by a full stop). In another sense it is two sentences, one of them, *he would see his father*, being both a sentence in its own right and also part of the other sentence. This feature is known in traditional grammar as 'subordination' and in more recent terminology as 'embedding', the embedded sentence being the 'constituent' sentence and the sentence into which it is embedded the 'matrix'.

The use of a single term 'sentence' to refer to both the constituent and matrix has some justification in that, though in one sense the second sentence is part of the first, it is also a whole in its own right – with the same kind of structure. The relation is thus quite different from the relation between sentence and phrase where sentences are made up of phrases (and phrases similarly of words). We have rather the *same* units at different levels of embedding or subordination.

Traditional grammar distinguishes 'clause' and 'sentence' – reserving the latter for the whole such that in our example we have two clauses, but one sentence. This is simple and clear – provided we remember that the relation clause-sentence is not like that of phrase-clause. We shall use the traditional terminology here, in particular distinguishing between 'main' and 'subordinate' clauses. There are two kinds of subordinate clause, one requiring the same kind of verb phrase as a main clause, the other containing no finite form (see 2.1.1):

While he talked, he banged the table.
While talking, he banged the table.

Traditional grammars sometimes used the term 'phrase' for the latter kind of clause. This is, I think, misleading and confusing. If a distinction is to be drawn it is solely in terms of 'finite' and 'non-finite'.

Notes

1 The finest example is Jespersen (1909–49).
2 See Palmer (1971:26–8).

3 *eg* Hockett (1958:4).
4 The phonetic script used is that of Daniel Jones (1958).
5 Joos (1964).
6 See Crystal (1969).
7 Nesfield (1898:8, 20, 21).
8 *eg* Robins (1959).
9 For a more detailed discussion of both speech and writing and form and meaning, see Palmer (1971:26–40).
10 See Palmer (1964:338).
11 Lyons (1968:197).

Chapter 2

The verb phrase

It would have been reasonable to entitle this book *The English verb phrase* since the limits of discussion are set by what is defined as the verb phrase. We shall not deal with the classification of the verbs in terms of the kind of grammatical structure with which they co-occur in the sentence. We shall not, for instance, be concerned, except incidentally, with the fact that 'verbs of reporting' occur with *that* clauses, but we shall be concerned with their function within the verb phrase as defined here.

2.1 Preliminary considerations

There are a few small points of terminology and detail that we should first consider. We must then discuss the status of the verb phrase. The auxiliaries are so important in the definition of the phrase that they are given a whole section to themselves.

2.1.1 Finite and non-finite

Subsumed under the lexeme TAKE are the forms *take, takes, took, taking* and *taken.*

These must be classified in terms of finite and non-finite forms. The first form of the verb phrase of a main clause is always finite; it follows that if there is one form only it will be finite. Hence:

I take coffee.
He takes coffee.
I/He took coffee.
**I/He taking coffee.*
**I/He taken coffee.*

The other forms of the verb phrase are all non-finite as in:

He has taken coffee.
He was taking coffee.
He wants to take coffee.

It is clear from these examples that *takes* and *took* are finite, *taking* and *taken*, non-finite; *take* is both finite and non-finite, or, rather, there are two forms *take*, one finite, the other non-finite.

Subordinate clauses are, as we saw in 1.2.2, of two kinds; their difference lies precisely in whether the verb phrase does or does not require a finite form as its first (or only) element. We need names to identify the forms; but obvious names are not readily available. Let us consider the finite forms first. We can certainly talk about 'present' and 'past tense' forms. The past tense form is, of course, the one that for many verbs (but not all – see Chapter 9) ends in *-ed*. There are two present tense forms one with, one without, *-s*; we will call them the 'simple form' and the '*-s* form'. The non-finite form *take* can be given the traditional name 'infinitive', though we shall wish to distinguish the 'bare infinitive' without *to* and the '*to*-infinitive' with *to*. For *taking* and *taken* the most suitable names are simply '*-ing* form' and '*-en* form'. The former avoids the difficulties about participles and gerunds (see 7.1.4). The latter is justified in that it uses the same kind of label. Many *-en* forms (the traditional 'past participles'), however, do not end in *-en*, but often in *-ed*. But *-en* is an ending confined to these in contrast with the past tense, and thus provides an unambiguous label.

If we distinguish two forms of the infinitive there are four non-finite forms, and we can define four basic structures in terms of them. That is to say, any verb can be classified in terms of the non-finite form it requires to follow it. This is of particular importance for Chapter 7. The four basic structures with examples of verbs that require them are:

(1) Bare infinitive	CAN	HELP
(2) *to*-infinitive	OUGHT	WANT
(3) *-ing* form	BE	KEEP
(4) *-en* form	BE	GET

We shall briefly have to consider in 3.1.2 some verb phrases that contain no finite forms at all. These involve the use of the infinitives and the *-ing* form only and are dealt with under the heading of Infinitivals and Participials. Examples are *having said, to have made* in such sentences as:

Having said that, he walked away.
He cannot be said to have made a success of it.

These sequences occur either in subordinate clauses or as part of a complex phrase (Chapter 7). Also considered in 3.1.2 are the imperatives (the forms used in requests and commands). The imperatives only partly follow the pattern of the other verbal forms.

2.1.2 Concord

There is no place here for the traditional paradigm of the type *I take, Thou takest, He takes,* etc. All that need be noted is that there are certain very limited features of concord or agreement of the verbal form with the subject of the sentence. There are, in fact, three kinds of concord of which only the first is at all generalized.

[i] All the verbs of the language with the exception of the modal auxiliaries (2.2.1 and 9.1.1) have two distinct present tense forms. One of them, the *-s* form, is used with the pronouns *he, she* and *it*, and singular noun phrases. The other, the simple form, is used with all other pronouns, *I, you, we* and *they*, and with plural noun phrases. We cannot define the two verbal forms as singular and plural respectively, unless we treat the first person singular pronoun *I* as plural, since it is found only with the simple form.

[ii] The verb BE alone has two distinct past tense forms, *was* and *were*. These could be regarded as singular and plural respectively, since the first is found with the pronoun *I* as well as the pronouns *he, she* and *it* and singular noun phrases. The other is found only with *we, you* and *they* and with plural noun phrases.

[iii] The verb BE alone in the language has a special form for the first person singular of the present tense – *am*.

2.1.3 Verb classes

The precise classification of the verbs depends on the total analysis. It may be useful, however, to suggest here the basic classes that we shall need to establish.

First, we need to distinguish the auxiliaries. These are marked, but not defined, by some striking characteristics that will be considered in the next section (2.2). The definition depends rather on the definition of the simple phrase (2.1.4). Within the auxiliaries we shall distinguish primary auxiliaries and secondary auxiliaries or modals. These are quite clearly distinguished in terms of the paradigms in which they occur (3.1.1.,

5.1.1), though the modals are morphologically distinct also in that they have no *-s* forms (2.2.1, 9.1.1). The term 'primary pattern' will be used for the forms that contain either no auxiliaries or primary auxiliaries only, and the term 'secondary pattern' for those that contain modals. Secondly, from among the remaining verbs, the 'full' verbs, we need to distinguish the catenatives.[1] These are those that combine with other verbal forms in complex phrases (2.1.4) with regular rules of co-occurrence. We have then:

(1) Primary auxiliaries BE, HAVE, DO.
(2) Secondary or modal auxiliaries WILL, SHALL, CAN, MAY, MUST, OUGHT, DARE, NEED.
(3) Catenatives KEEP, WANT, LIKE, SEE and many others.
(4) The remaining full verbs.

2.1.4 Simple and complex phrases

We shall be considering such sequences of verb forms as *has been running*, *may have run*, *keeps wanting to run* and shall use the term 'verb phrase' to describe them all. However, it is not strictly true that all verb phrases so defined are verb phrases in the sense that they are elements of a single clause. In the last example, for instance, it could well be argued that we have subordination involving three clauses, and therefore three verb phrases *keeps*, *wanting* and *to run*.

Nevertheless, the notion of verb phrase is a useful one here because of the very close and restricted relationships between the verb forms in such sequences. We shall, for that reason, continue to talk about them as verb phrases but distinguish between 'simple' and 'complex' phrases – the latter being those that strictly involve more than one verb phrase, with subordination. We shall, moreover, later want to identify the verb phrases (or VPs) within a complex phrase (see Chapter 7). But there are problems. Let us look at some examples in more detail.

Let us consider first *has taken*. The most obvious way to treat this is to say that this is the perfect form of the verb lexeme TAKE. This is to assign to the two-word sequence the same kind of grammatical status as that of single words in another language (*eg* Latin *amavi* 'I have loved'). To do so we shall have to say that *taken* is a form (in a slightly different sense) of the full verb TAKE, but that *has* is an auxiliary, and that while the full verb indicates the lexical meaning the auxiliary refers to the grammatical category 'perfect' (or rather of 'phase', see 3.1.3). There is, then, only one verb phrase here, and the verb phrase in this sense will contain only one full verb (but it may also contain one or more auxiliaries).

In contrast we should not wish to handle *remembered coming* in the same way. This is not a form of the lexeme COME, but a sequence of forms of the lexemes REMEMBER and COME. Moreover, there is some structural similarity between:

I remembered coming.
I remembered that I came.

In the second of these we clearly have subordination. But subordination involves two clauses and therefore two verb phrases. If then we analyse the first sentence in the same way we have not one verb phrase but two. However, there is enormous restriction on the possibilities of sequence (see Chapter 7) and for this reason the notion of 'complex' verb phrase is useful – the complex phrase consisting of several verb phrases, but in a close-knit construction.

The real problem, however, is to provide means of distinguishing between one verb phrase and two (or more). If we go back to the examples at the beginning of the section we may well decide that *has been running* is one phrase and that *keeps wanting to run* is three, but what of *may have run*? We have to decide whether this is one or two, and thereby whether MAY is an auxiliary and a marker of a verbal category, or a full verb. Part of the evidence must be the very idiosyncratic characteristics of the auxiliaries (2.2). It is simple enough to set them apart by these features alone and so define a simple phrase as one containing any number of auxiliaries but only one full verb.

These characteristics will be used as 'markers' or 'tests' of an auxiliary, but we must also look for characteristics of a more syntactic kind. There are several ways of deciding whether we have one or more verb phrases *ie* whether we have a simple or complex phrase. First, we may assume that the category of tense (or any other verbal category) will occur only once in a simple phrase; if there is double or multiple time marking the phrase will be complex. Secondly, we may make the same assumption about negation – we shall expect a simple phrase not to be negated more than once. Thirdly, if we have a sentence with a single clause we can passivize it (see 4.1.1); passivization thus identifies a single clause and so a simple verb phrase. (For examples see 3.1.8, 5.1.2.)

We shall find that these criteria do not give us an absolute distinction between simple and complex phrases, but they are sufficient to confirm the distinction between primary auxiliaries, modals and catenatives. Phrases involving primary auxiliaries are fairly clearly simple, while those with catenatives are complex (though not all pass all the tests). Phrases with modals lie somewhere between the two, sharing characteristics of both simple and complex phrases.

We shall recognize no grammatical relations between the elements of the verb phrase except subordination (and the 'identity relations' of 7.2). Indeed the notion of verb phrase allows us to avoid many problems of a quite insoluble kind. Some scholars have interpreted the later elements of the verb phrase as being complements, objects, etc of the preceding element, so that *is swimming* is likened to *is happy*, though not, one hopes, so that *has gone* is likened to *has a dog*. Even Jespersen[2] argued that *can* takes the following form as its object; thus *swim* is the object of *can* in *can swim*, in spite of the fact that we cannot say **can cricket*. There seems to be no virtue at all in this line of argument. Nothing is gained by talking of objects, etc; everything that can be said is said in terms of the structure of the verb phrase.

It is rather more tempting to see objects, etc in the complex phrase where *keeps talking* looks like *keeps quiet* and *likes swimming* looks like *likes chocolate*. But even here there are counter arguments (see 7.1.5). The notion of the complex phrase remains a useful one; both the semantics and the syntax of the forms can be fully accounted for in terms of its structure without looking for relationships that are more appropriate to the structure of the clause.

2.2 The auxiliaries

The auxiliary verbs can be listed – and this we shall do in the first subsection (2.2.1). But they stand apart from the other verbs of the language in one striking way – their occurrence in the four syntactic structures that I shall call 'negation', 'inversion', 'code' and 'emphatic affirmation'. These we shall speak of as 'tests' of being an auxiliary, but they are not the final defining criteria which must be in terms rather of the simple and complex phrases. Each of these will be discussed separately (2.2.2, 2.2.3, 2.2.4, 2.2.5). The function of DO and the status of DARE and NEED are subsequently considered in the light of these features (2.2.6, 2.2.7).

2.2.1 The forms

There are eleven auxiliaries, with twenty-eight forms in all:

	finite	non-finite
BE	*is, are, am, was, were*	*be, being, been*
HAVE	*has, have, had*	*have, having*
DO	*do, does, did*	

WILL	*will, would*
SHALL	*shall, should*
CAN	*can, could*
MAY	*may, might*
MUST	*must*
OUGHT	*ought*
DARE	*dare*
NEED	*need*

Only the first three, BE, HAVE and DO, have *-s* forms. The remainder are all modals; the absence of an *-s* form is thus, morphologically, a distinguishing mark of a modal.

Only the first two, BE and HAVE, have non-finite forms. In particular they alone have infinitives. The use of the *to*-infinitive as the label of the verb (the lexeme) is, thus, not always feasible. Reference to the auxiliary verbs 'to will' and 'to shall' is now a linguistic joke;[3] the latter, of course, is non-existent, and the former, though historically related to the auxiliary verb, is synchronically to be considered as a different, and full, verb. Errors of this nature are, unfortunately, still made. Even in a modern grammar there is reference to the auxiliary verb 'to do';[4] yet the auxiliary verb has no infinitive form (in spite of *does go* there is no **to do go*). There are also infinitives 'to can' and 'to must' and the dictionary quotes 'to may', but these are unconnected with the auxiliaries. 'To dare' and 'to need' are certainly closely associated with the auxiliary verbs, but, as we shall see later, we must distinguish between the auxiliary verbs and the full verbs which share the forms *dare* and *need*; the infinitive forms belong to the full verbs. The use of small capital letters to indicate lexemes avoids the difficulty raised by the absence of a *to*-infinitive. As with all other verbs the simple form is available for use – *can* and *will*, for example, to give us CAN and WILL.

Notice also that *had* does not occur among the non-finite forms of HAVE. The full verb HAVE has both a finite past tense form *had* and a non-finite *-en* form *had*, but the auxiliary has the past tense form only. This is clear from:

He's had his lunch.
**He's had gone.*

Having and *being* occur as forms of the auxiliary. *Being* alone occurs within the basic paradigms (3.1.1, 5.1.1). Both occur in initial position in the phrase where they mark 'participials' (3.1.2).

2.2.2 Negation

The first test of an auxiliary is whether it is used in negation, that is to say, whether it occurs with the negative particle *not*, or more strictly, whether it has a negative form (9.1.2). Examples of sentences with auxiliaries used for negation are:

I don't like it.
We aren't coming.
You can't do that.
He mustn't ask them.
They mightn't think so.

Positive sentences may or may not contain an auxiliary form:

I can come.
We must go.
I like it.
We saw him.

An auxiliary verb, then, has forms that are used together with the negative particle – or, to put it a better way, has paired positive and negative forms. The difference between an auxiliary and a full verb in this respect is seen clearly if we consider the negative sentences corresponding to the four given above. The first two are:

I can't come.
We mustn't go.

But there are no similar formations corresponding to the last two. The following are not possible English utterances:

**I liken't it.*
**We sawn't him.*

In modern English it is not even possible to say:

I like not it.
We saw not him.

Instead the corresponding negative sentences, like all negative sentences, contain an auxiliary form – one of the forms of DO:

I don't like it.
We didn't see him.

More striking is the fact that other verbs which notionally might seem to be 'auxiliary' – verbs like WANT and BEGIN – are found only with the forms of DO in negative sentences:

I want to ask you.
I don't want to ask you.
**I wantn't to ask you.*
He began to cry.
He didn't begin to cry.
**He begann't to cry.*

These verbs are catenatives, the subject of Chapter 7.

There are some verbs that have not been included in the list of auxiliaries that may seem to be used with the negative particle. Examples of sentences containing such verbs are:

I prefer not to ask him.
I hate not to win.

These can be excluded if, as suggested early in this section, an auxiliary is marked not by the occurrence of its forms with the negative particle, but by having negative as well as positive forms. For certainly we shall not attest:

**I prefern't to ask him.*
**I haten't to win.*

In fact the two sentences must be regarded as positive sentences, the form *not* being associated not with *prefer* and *hate* but with *to ask* and *to win*. For there are corresponding negative sentences that also contain an auxiliary:

I don't prefer not to ask him.
I don't hate not to win.

The problem is dealt with in greater detail later (7.1.2).

MAY provides a slight problem. There is no negative form **mayn't*. We have only *may not:*

**He mayn't come.*
He may not come.

Mightn't occurs but is not used by most speakers of American English. But although MAY does not, in respect of negation, function like the other auxiliaries, it satisfies the other tests and has the characteristics of the modals as stated in Chapter 5.

2.2.3 Inversion

The second test of an auxiliary is whether it can come before the subject in certain types of sentence, the order being auxiliary, subject and full verb. The most common type of sentence of this kind is the interrogative. Examples are:

Is the boy coming?
Will they be there?
Have you seen them yet?
Ought we to ask them?

In these the auxiliary comes first, before the subject. The verb phrase is discontinuous, divided by a noun phrase, the subject of the clause. The examples given are all questions, but the test of an auxiliary is not in terms of question. For in the first place, a question may be asked without the use of inversion at all, but merely by using the appropriate intonation, commonly (though not necessarily) a rising intonation:

He's coming?
They'll be there?
You've seen them?

Secondly, inversion is found in sentences that are not questions, especially with *seldom* and *hardly*, and in certain types of conditional sentence:

Seldom had they seen such a sight.
Hardly had I left the room, when they began talking about me.
Had I known he was coming, I'd have waited.

There is a different kind of inversion that does not require an auxiliary verb, as illustrated by:

Down came a blackbird.
Into the room walked John.
In the corner stood an armchair.

The essential feature of this (which must be excluded) is the adverbial of place in initial position.

We must restrict inversion, then, as the test of an auxiliary to questions and sentences with initial *hardly*, *seldom*, *scarcely*, *never*, *nowhere* – words that we later shall consider as 'semi-negatives' (**2**.2.8).

If we go back to the four sentences that were considered in the previous section, the test of inversion and its parallelism with negation becomes clear:

I can come.	*Can I come?*
We must go.	*Must we go?*
I like it.	**Like I it?*
We saw them.	**Saw we them?*

Once again the forms of DO are used:

Do I like it?
Did we see them?

The test shows again that WANT and BEGIN are not auxiliary verbs:

Do I want to ask you?
Did he begin to cry?
**Want I to ask you?*
**Began he to cry?*

A rare exception to this, in colloquial speech only, is the verb GO, but only in sentences beginning with *how:*

How goes it?
How goes work?

Alternative forms with little or no difference of meaning are:

How's it going?
How's work going?

These sentences are used as part of a conventional formula for greeting. Sentences using DO – *How does it go?* are not used in this context.

2.2.4 'Code'

The third characteristic of an auxiliary is its use in what H. E. Palmer[5] called 'avoidance of repetition' and J. R. Firth[6] called 'code'. There are sentences in English in which a full verb is later 'picked up' by an auxiliary. The position is very similar to that of a noun being 'picked up' by a pronoun. There are several kinds of sentence in which this feature is found. A type that illustrates it most clearly is one that contains . . . *and so* . . .:

I can come and so can John.
We must go and so must you.
I like it and so do they.
We saw them and so did he.

In none of these examples is the whole verb phrase repeated in the second part. In all of them the only verbal form after . . . *and so* is an auxiliary. Where the first part contains an auxiliary, it is the auxiliary alone that recurs. Where the first part contains no auxiliary, once again one of the forms of DO is used. By the same test WANT and BEGIN are excluded from the class of auxiliary verbs:

I want to ask you and so does Bill.
He began to cry and so did she.

There are other types of sentence in which the auxiliary is used in this way. A common use is in question and answer:

Can I come? *You can.*
Must they go? *They must.*
You saw them? *I did.*

Very often there will already be an auxiliary in the question sentence since inversion is common in questions. But, as the last pair of sentences shows, if a question is asked without inversion and without an auxiliary (being marked only by the intonation) a form of DO is required in the reply.

It is possible to invent quite a long conversation using only auxiliary verbs. If the initial sentence, which contains the main verb, is not heard, all the remainder is unintelligible; it is, in fact, truly in code. The following example is from Firth:

Do you think he will?
I don't know. He might.
I suppose he ought to, but perhaps he feels he can't.
Well, his brothers have. They perhaps think he needn't.
Perhaps eventually he may. I think he should, and I very much hope he will.

The 'key to the code' is *join the army*.

2.2.5 Emphatic affirmation

Finally, a characteristic of the auxiliaries is their use in emphatic affirmation with the accent upon the auxiliary. Examples are:

You múst see him.
I cán do it.
We wíll come.
He hás finished it.

This use of the auxiliaries is not easy to define formally. For any verbal form may take the accent. We may find, for instance:

I líke it. *I can cóme.*
We sáw them. *We must gó.*

I wánt to ask you.
He begán to cry.

What is essential about the use of the auxiliaries is that they are used as emphatic affirmation of a doubtful statement, or as the denial of the negative. In such contexts we should find:

I cán come. (You are wrong to think I cannot)
You múst come. (You do not want to)
We díd see them. (You thought we did not)

Once again forms of DO occur. Often these forms would have occurred in the previous utterance which would be a question or a negation, *I dó like it* being the emphatic affirmative reply to either *Do you like it?* or *You don't like it.* But this is not necessarily so; the previous sentence might have been *You like it?* or *Perhaps you like it?*

There is one further possibility. Any of the auxiliaries may be stressed without having the accent; the stress focuses attention upon the auxiliaries. We may thus attest with the auxiliary stressed:

He will cóme.
He has cóme.
He does cóme.
He did ásk.

With stressed DO attention is drawn to the fact that a simple form (not a progressive or perfect, or a form with a modal) is being used.

2.2.6 DO

We must now collate the uses of DO. It is a special type of auxiliary, in that it is used *only* under those conditions where an auxiliary is obligatory. It occurs only, that is to say, with negation or inversion or code or emphatic affirmation. It is thus the 'neutral' or 'empty' auxiliary used only where the grammatical rules of English require an auxiliary:

I don't like it.
Do I like it?
I like it and so does Bill.
I dó like it.

What does not occur is DO in a sentence such as:

**I do like it.* (with *do* unstressed)

This occurs, however, in some West Country dialects of English instead of the simple form of the verb.

Equally DO does not occur where there is already another auxiliary (which is thus available for negation, etc):

**He doesn't can go.*
**Does he will come?*
**I may go and so does he.*
**He dóes be coming.*

The only exception is in the imperative (3.1.2) where it may occur with BE:

Do be reading when I arrive.

These remarks do not apply to the full verbs BE and HAVE though there are restrictions with them too (**6.1.1**, **6.1.2**).

2.2.7 DARE and NEED

These provide some difficulty because:

[i] if we use the tests we have been discussing, some of their forms are forms of auxiliaries, but others of full verbs;
[ii] the distribution of the auxiliary forms is defective.

DARE and NEED are clearly shown to be auxiliary verbs in negation and inversion:

He daren't go.
You needn't ask.
Dare we come?
Need they look?

Moreover, not only are these verbs used here in negation and inversion, but they also have the characteristic of modal auxiliaries in not having an *-s* form. There are no forms **daresn't* or **needsn't;* nor do we say **Dares he . . .?* or **Needs he . . .?*

At the same time we must recognize that the full verbs DARE and NEED occur in:

He doesn't dare to go.
You don't need to ask.
Do we dare to come?
Do they need to look?

That they are here full verbs and not auxiliaries is clear from the presence of one of the forms of DO in the negative and inverted form.

Another difference between the auxiliary and the full verb is the structure with which it is associated. The auxiliary is associated with structure 1 – it is followed by the bare infinitive (see 2.1.1), while the full verb is associated with structure 2 – it is followed by the *to*-infinitive.

With inversion and negation, then, both the auxiliaries and the full verbs may be used (the latter, of course, with DO). In all other cases only the full verb occurs. This is especially to be noted for the positive non-inverted forms:

He dares to ask me that! *You dare to come now!*
He needs to have a wash. *They need to get a new car.*

The reasons for thinking that these are full verbs and not auxiliaries are:

[i] the forms have a final *-s* for the third person singular;
[ii] the structure is 2 (*to*-infinitive), associated with the full verb, and not 1 (bare infinitive), associated with the auxiliary.

These reasons would not in themselves be sufficient criteria for excluding the forms from the auxiliaries since the primary auxiliaries have *-s* forms and the modal OUGHT is associated with structure 2, but since a distinction between full verb and auxiliary is relevant here they are sufficient to link the forms to the full verbs DARE and NEED, rather than the auxiliaries whose characteristics (no *-s* and structure 1) are shown in the negative and inverted forms.

With code and emphatic affirmation the auxiliary forms do not occur unless there is also negation or inversion:

Dare I ask him? *No, you daren't.*
I needn't come and neither need you.

(There can be no **Yes you dare* or *... *and so need you.*) The full verbs can, of course, occur with DO.

The functions of the auxiliaries and the full verbs are shown in the following table (using only NEED, though a similar statement could be made for DARE):

	AUXILIARY	FULL VERB
positive		*He needs to come.*
negative	*He needn't come.*	*He doesn't need to come.*
inverted	*Need he come?*	*Does he need to come?*
'code'		*He needs to come and so do I.*
emphatic affirmative		*He dóes need to come.*

There are, however, reservations to be made. First, the auxiliaries occur with the 'semi-negatives' (2.2.8):

No one need know.
He hardly dare ask.
He need never know.
Cf: John needs to know.
He even dares to ask.

Secondly, even when the full verb DARE occurs in negative or inverted sentences (with DO) the structure may be I (bare infinitive), the pattern elsewhere associated with the auxiliary:

I don't dare ask. *I don't dare to ask.*
Does he dare ask? *Does he dare to ask?*

The same is true of NEED, but much less commonly:

I don't need ask. (more commonly . . . *to ask*)
Does he need ask? (almost always . . . *to ask*)

2.2.8 'Semi-negatives'

We have twice referred to 'semi-negatives' in the attempt to characterize the modals. The adverbs among these – *seldom*, *never*, *scarcely*, *nowhere* are relevant for inversion (2.2.3). These together with the others – *no one*, *nobody*, *nothing* help to distinguish the auxiliaries and the full verbs DARE and NEED (2.2.7).

It is important to refer to these as 'semi-negatives' not as 'negatives', since they do not function in the negation test of the auxiliary in the way *not* does. Contrast:

He doesn't go.
**He not goes.*
He never goes.
He seldom goes.

There is one other type of structure for which the semi-negative must be recognized – the so-called 'tag-question':

John's coming, isn't he?
John isn't coming, is he?

These are fairly complex in their variety (especially in terms of intonation). For our purpose it is enough to consider the type which merely asks for confirmation of a suggestion (most probably, with a falling and then a rising intonation). With these there is always a reversal of the positive/negative character of the two clauses: if the statement is positive the tag is positive and vice versa. For this purpose too, semi-negatives function as negatives – requiring positive tags:

No one saw you, did they?
He has never tried, has he?
He has scarcely time, has he?
They are nowhere around, are they?

Notes

1 Twaddell (1960: 18).
2 Jespersen (Part v 171).
3 Vendryes (1921: 29).
4 Zandvoort (1957: 78).
5 Palmer and Blandford (1939: 124–5).
6 Firth (1968: 104).

Chapter 3

Tense, phase and aspect

The primary auxiliaries BE, HAVE and DO function within what we have called the primary system of the verb phrase. A phrase of this kind will, it may be recalled, consist of one full verb followed by up to three (including none) of the forms of the primary auxiliaries.

3.1 Syntax of the primary auxiliaries[1]

The primary system is essentially the central system of the English verb – what can be said about the modals and the catenatives is to be based upon it. We shall begin by looking at the basic paradigm, which consists of sixteen (or possibly fourteen) forms (3.1.1) and then some more limited paradigms (3.1.2). This soon leads us to an investigation of the grammatical categories associated with the primary system – tense, phase, aspect,[2] and voice (3.1.3) – though a detailed discussion of the last is left to the next chapter. The next two subsections (3.1.4, 3.1.5) give a general account of the analysis while some particular problems are discussed in 3.1.6, 3.1.7, 3.1.8 and 3.1.9.

3.1.1 Basic paradigms

A basic paradigm in the primary pattern of the simple phrase is set out below. The paradigm stated is one of several. Further paradigms may be set up by taking into account:

[i] the different forms associated with number and person, the paradigm here being for the third person singular (for the first person singular replace *takes* by *take*, *is* by *am*, and *has* by *have*, and for all other forms replace *takes* by *take*, *is* by *are*, *was* by *were*, and *has* by *have*);

[ii] the forms used in negation, inversion, etc (replace *takes* by *does take* or *do take* and *took* by *did take*).

For TAKE the paradigm is:

(1) *takes*			
(2) *took*			
(3) *is*		*taking*	
(4) *was*		*taking*	
(5) *has*	*taken*		
(6) *had*	*taken*		
(7) *has*	*been*	*taking*	
(8) *had*	*been*	*taking*	
(9) *is*			*taken*
(10) *was*			*taken*
(11) *is*		*being*	*taken*
(12) *was*		*being*	*taken*
(13) *has*	*been*		*taken*
(14) *had*	*been*		*taken*
(15) *has*	*been*	*being*	*taken* (?)
(16) *had*	*been*	*being*	*taken* (?)

The columning is deliberate, and is explained in **3.1.3**. Numbers 15 and 16 are marked with a question mark; their validity is discussed later in this section.

There are two important characteristics of the forms that justify their treatment in this paradigmatic fashion. First they are a closed class: there are no other forms that will fit. This depends, of course, upon the way the primary pattern is defined. We are concerned with the auxiliaries BE and HAVE followed by *-ing* and *-en* forms only, plus DO with its very special function in negation, inversion, etc. The pattern is basic to the English verb in that extensions are possible by the addition (with the appropriate morphological changes) of modals or catenatives. BE and HAVE are also followed by the *to*-infinitive:

He is to come tomorrow.
He has to come tomorrow.

With this form the verbs are not primary auxiliaries but belong with the modals or the catenatives (see **6.1.1** and **6.1.2**). The primary pattern, then, forms a coherent system and, as we shall shortly see, is amply justified by its grammatical function.

The second point is that each form in the paradigm is essentially a whole. They cannot be analysed either formally or semantically in terms of the individual (word) forms of which they are composed, except in the morphological description of these (word) forms. Analysis in terms of the syntactical structures with which they are associated (*ie* that BE is followed by the *-ing* form and by the *-en* form and that HAVE is followed by the *-en* form only) is insufficient, since this will not rule out the following, which are not possible:

**is been taking*
**is being been taken*
**was had taken*
**was having taken*
**is being had been having taken* etc

Moreover, the grammatical categories in terms of which the forms of the paradigm are to be analysed (3.1.3) and the semantic features associated with these categories cut right across word division in these forms. The position is very different from that in the complex phrase where the analysis of, *eg: He kept asking her to help him get it finished* may be handled entirely in terms of the semantic and syntactic characteristics of the verbs KEEP, ASK, HELP and GET.

Forms 15 and 16 are marked with a question mark; there is some doubt if they are possible. They are marked in one grammar[3] as 'wanting' but in another (American) book[4] we find:

John had been being scolded by Mary for a long time when the neighbours came in.

There is a place for them semantically, but the non-progressive forms 13 and 14 are normally used instead of them.

3.1.2 Infinitivals, participials and imperatives

The paradigms required for non-finite verbal forms (the infinitivals and participials) and for phrases containing imperatives have fewer forms.

The paradigm of infinitival forms contains exactly half the number found in the basic paradigms, one form corresponding to each consecutive pair (there being no tense distinction – see 3.1.3). For the participials the number is further reduced in that there are no forms containing two consecutive *-ing* forms. The possibilities are, then:

	INFINITIVALS	PARTICIPIALS
(1/2)	*to take*	*taking*
(3/4)	*to be taking*	(no **being taking*)
(5/6)	*to have taken*	*having taken*

(7/8) *to have been taking*	*having been taking*
(9/10) *to be taken*	*being taken*
(11/12) *to be being taken*	(no **being being taken*)
(13/14) *to have been taken*	*having been taken*
(15/16) *to have been being taken* (?)	*having been being taken* (?)

Phrases containing imperatives are still further limited in number in that there are none containing HAVE forms. Semantically there seems no reason to exclude **Have taken*, **Have been taking*, etc, but these forms do not exist. But the four other forms are to be found – *Take*, *Be taking*, *Be taken* and (possibly) *Be being taken*. It might, admittedly, be difficult to attest all the forms with TAKE which is here chosen solely as a model, particularly the last two, but there is nothing odd about *Be dressed* and (with less certainty) *Be being dressed*.

The infinitivals and participials may all be preceded by *not* – these are the negative forms. But the negative and emphatic forms of the phrases with imperatives require special treatment. Neither BE nor HAVE occur in a negative imperative form – indeed there is no negative of the form *be* (**6.1.1**). *Don't* is the only negative form; all the negative forms of the paradigms contain *don't* – *don't take*, *don't be taking*, *don't be taken*, (?) *don't be being taken*. In addition there are the emphatic *dó take*, *dó be taking*, *dó be taken*, (?) *dó be being taken*. Apart from the first, which is 'regular', these are unexpected since emphatic imperatives could simply be marked by accenting *be* – and *bé taking*, *bé taken*, (?) *bé being taken* are possible. Yet it is not surprising that the emphatic forms here, as elsewhere, have the same characteristic (occurrence of DO) as the negatives. A set of examples to illustrate the negative and emphatic forms is:

Don't be reading when I come in!
Do be reading when I come in!
Be reading when I come in!

3.1.3 The four categories

The sixteen forms in the basic paradigm of the primary pattern can be divided into two sets of eight in four different ways, each division being in terms of a formal feature (which is later linked to a semantic one). Each form is thus characterized in four different ways, and distinguished from all the others in these terms. If sixteen forms are admitted there are no 'gaps' – all the possibilities occur; but, as we have seen, only fourteen of them can be positively accepted.

First, the forms may be classified in terms of tense, past and present. Present tense (phrase) forms are defined as those containing present tense (word) forms. The word forms are, of course, defined morphologically, *takes*, *is* and *has* being present and *took*, *was* and *had* past. In the paradigm the odd-numbered forms are present and the even-numbered ones past; the difference of tense is marked in the first column of the table (3.1.1).

Secondly, a distinction in terms of aspect, progressive and non-progressive, may be made, progressive forms being those that contain both a form of BE and an *-ing* form (occurring in column three). Every second pair in the paradigm (beginning with 3 and 4) is progressive. The terms 'continuous' and 'non-continuous' are sometimes used. So too are 'habitual' and 'non-habitual' (habitual = non-progressive) but these are to be rejected as quite misleading (see 3.5.2).

Thirdly, the forms are to be classified in terms of phase, perfect or non-perfect, the perfect forms being those that contain a form of HAVE, which is always followed by an *-en* form (in column two). The first four and the third set of four (9 to 12) are non-perfect, and the others perfect.

Finally, the traditional category of voice, active and passive, distinguishes those forms that contain both a form of BE and an *-en* form (passive) from those that do not (active). The first eight are active and the last eight passive. There is some superficial resemblance between the passive and the perfect since both are defined in terms of one of the two auxiliaries plus an *-en* form. But the place of the *-en* forms in the phrase is different, as is shown by the columning of the paradigm. The form associated with the perfect is always second while that associated with the passive is always last (in column four), with in each case the relevant form of the auxiliary preceding it. Structurally, then, the two are quite different.

This analysis provides a basis, indeed the only satisfactory basis, for more detailed analysis of the forms. In particular it should be noted that there is no place for a 'future tense' (*cf* 3.1.6).

3.1.4 Arrangement of the analysis

The analysis of the primary auxiliaries is very complex and it is necessary to make some clear-cut decisions about the direction to be taken.

[i] Voice is so very different in its function from the other categories that it will be dealt with in a separate chapter – Chapter 4.

[ii] A certain amount of confusion has been created by the fact that time marking may be related either to the time of the action or to the time at which the statement is or was valid. This is dealt with in detail in 3.1.7.

[iii] Most of the forms appear to have three distinct uses. They may be used in what may be called a 'basic' use, but in addition may refer to both future and to habitual activity, the 'basic' use being defined negatively as the one that has neither future nor habitual reference. Examples are:

I'm working at the moment.	('basic')
I'm working tomorrow.	(future)
I'm always working.	(habitual)

A whole section is devoted to the examination of the future and habitual uses (3.5). Previous sections exclude them. Failure to make clear these distinctions, which are formally marked by collocation with adverbs, has been a cause of great confusion.

[iv] The progressive forms create difficulty because, although we must separate the four categories and the habitual and future uses, the progressive forms have two special functions where there is reference to habitual activity. These are dealt with in 3.6.

[v] The use of the progressive forms depends to some degree upon the full verb in the phrase. Most striking is the fact that progressive forms only rarely occur with certain verbs (3.7).

3.1.5 Outline of the uses

[i] The progressive indicates activity continuing through a period of time – activity with duration. The non-progressive merely reports activity, without indicating that it has duration. This is shown by comparison of:

He walked to the station.
He was walking to the station.

The first sentence simply gives the information that he walked to the station; the second indicates that the walking had duration. There is, of course, no suggestion that there are two kinds of activity one without and one with duration, but simply that attention is drawn in the one case to its durational aspect. The reasons for drawing attention to this are various; a common one is to show that the period of time during which the activity took place overlapped a briefer period or a point in time:

When I met him, he was walking to the station.
He was walking to the station at ten this morning.

[ii] Tense and phase are initially best handled together, in order to make the point, not usually made, that both are essentially concerned with time relations. The time features are most simply illustrated by considering progressive forms that indicate activity continuing *throughout* a period of time (they do not always do this – see **3.4.1**):

I'm reading at the moment.
I've been reading since three o'clock.
I was reading when he came.
I'd been reading for an hour when he came.

The present non-perfect refers to a period of time in the present – a vague period that includes both past and future time but overlaps the present moment. The past non-perfect refers to a similar time in the past, which may overlap an indicated point of time in the past; it does not extend to the present. The perfect forms indicate periods of time that specifically began before and continued up to (possibly overlapping) a point of time, the present moment in the case of the present tense, and a point of time in the past in the case of the past tense. The four possibilities may be shown diagrammatically:

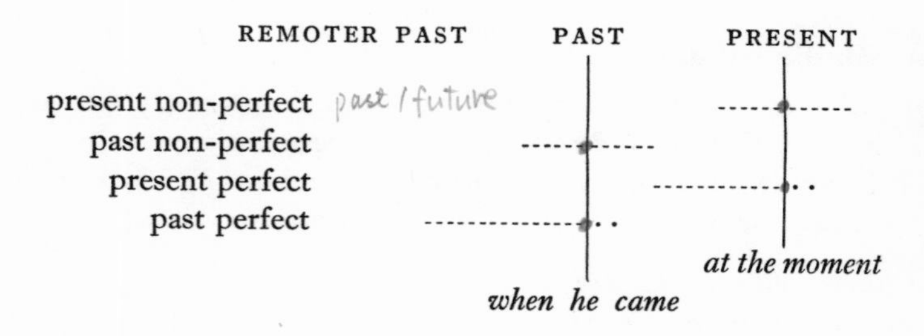

With the perfect the initial point of the period may be indicated, *eg*, by *for an hour*, or *since Tuesday*, as well as the later point.

3.1.6 Time and tense

The traditional statement of tense in terms of present, past and future, exemplified by *I take*, *I took* and *I shall take*, has no place in the analysis presented here. The basic reason for this is quite simply that while *I take* and *I took* are comparable within the analysis, in that they exemplify the formal category of tense as established in the primary pattern, *I shall take* belongs to the secondary pattern and ought not, therefore, to be handled together with the other two.

There are other characteristics of the verb that support the decision to separate future time reference from reference to past and present. First, there is the fact that we have already noted and will examine later in more detail (3.5), that many of the verbal forms of the primary pattern may refer to the future. The second point is that there is really very little justification for the selection of WILL and SHALL as the markers of future tense in English, even if we rely heavily upon time reference. For, in the first place, WILL and SHALL are not the only ways of referring to future time; in fact there are four quite common constructions – as illustrated by:

(1) *I'm giving a paper next Wednesday.*
(2) *I give my paper next Wednesday.*
(3) *I'm going to give a paper next Wednesday.*
(4) *I shall give a paper next Wednesday.*

The first two are examples of the primary pattern forms used with future reference (the subject of the first point made). But the third type – with BE GOING – is very common, indeed, probably more common than sentences with WILL and SHALL in ordinary conversation. A second difficulty about WILL (though not SHALL) is that it often does not refer to the future at all. It may, for instance, indicate probability

That'll be the postman.

or it may refer to habitual activity,

She'll sit for hours watching television.

Even when it does refer to the future it may suggest not merely futurity but willingness as in:

Will you come?

(which is different from *Are you coming?* see 5.2.2).
It is, moreover, characteristic of the other modal auxiliaries that they may refer to the future (though with additional reference to ability, probability, etc) as in:

I can/may/must/ought to come tomorrow.

There is clearly an overriding case for handling WILL and SHALL with the other modal auxiliaries in the secondary pattern and not together with the distinction of past and present tense that belongs to the primary pattern.

3.1.7 Epistemic and displaced time marking

It has been recognized for a long time that a distinction has to be drawn between the epistemic and the non-epistemic modals. The distinction is discussed in **5.1.4**. Essentially the epistemic modals relate semantically not to the content of the sentence but to the status of the sentence (or proposition) itself – its probability, possibility, etc.

It has not been so clearly recognized that precisely the same distinction might be drawn for tense. This to say, though it normally indicates the time of the actions or activity described in the sentence, it may also be used to indicate the time at which the sentence is or was valid.

This notion of epistemic tense is of importance in the treatment of the future use (**3.5**). We must, unfortunately, anticipate. Both the simple form and the progressive are used for future time reference:

John's coming tomorrow.
John comes tomorrow.

But these can also be past tense to refer to 'future in the past':

Yesterday John was coming tomorrow.
Yesterday John came tomorrow.

The last sentence is awkward and it would not be easy to contextualize it, but a more natural example can be found:

At that time he didn't come till next week.

The past tense in these examples is epistemic – there was a time at which the statements that John is coming tomorrow or John comes tomorrow were valid. But notice that *tomorrow* has to be interpreted in terms of the time of speaking – not the time at which the proposition was valid. This is not very surprising – the same is true of reported speech (**3.2.2**).

We may also compare some sentences that relate to the proverbial boasting of the fishermen:

Yesterday the fish was four feet long.
It's always been four feet long.
It had always been four feet long.

Tense (with the adverbial) and phase here indicate not the time at which the fish was four feet long but the time at which the claim was made. This is very clear where there is a contrast:

Yesterday it was three feet long; today it's four.

But there is a difference. There is an implication here that an actual statement or claim was made by someone, not merely that the statement was valid at the time. Moreover, it is not merely tense and phase that can be 'epistemic' in this sense. Other verbs that express time relations may be similarly used (WILL, BE GOING, USED):

Tomorrow the fish will be four feet long.
Tomorrow the fish is going to be four feet long.
The fish used to be four feet long.

Nor is this confined to verbs that indicate time. Verbs of process (7.4.5) may equally be 'epistemic':

When he grew old, the fish began to be four feet long.
When he grew old, the fish stopped being four feet long.

We must, surely, exclude all these – they are related more to reported speech, with the verb of reporting unstated, than to epistemic tense – and label them 'psuedo-epistemic'. The epistemic usage always refers to future events, but the epistemic time is not only past – it can be 'perfect' (*ie* there is epistemic phase too – 3.5.4) and habitual (3.5.6).

Similar in some ways is what we may call the 'displaced' time marking of[5]

The animal you saw was my dog.
The man you'll be talking to will be the Mayor.

The sentences are quite normal even if the animal still is my dog, or the man already is the Mayor. Here we have not only past tense, but also *will* for future time reference (this is discussed further in 5.2.2). BE GOING and USED are not normally used in the same way, though they may be possible if the time is not already marked in a relative clause:

The man next to me used to be the Mayor.
The man next to me is going to be the Mayor.

These are ambiguous. The verbs may refer either to the time of someone being Mayor or of my sitting next to him.

3.1.8 Auxiliary and full verb

The morphology of the primary auxiliaries and their unique function in the primary pattern marks them as quite distinct from the full verbs. This distinction was, however, not made by some of the linguists of the so-called structuralist school that flourished in America in the 1940s and 1950s and more recently it has been questioned in terms of their 'deep structure' function. Some of the recent arguments do no more than show that the auxiliaries share characteristics with the full verbs (in particular that BE functions both as an auxiliary and a full verb – see **6.1**). Both such arguments no more disprove the distinction than an argument in zoology would disprove the distinction between birds and mammals by indicating the facts that birds have four limbs and the platypus lays eggs. All such an argument shows is that full verbs and auxiliaries belong to a larger class (verb) just as birds and mammals are all vertebrates.

Let us consider, however, whether there are any arguments against the auxiliaries being treated as such, in terms of the tests of double tense, double negation and passivization – the tests for simple and complex phrases (**2.1.4** and *cf* **5.1.2** for a clear exemplification of these tests with the modals).

There is no possibility of double tense marking if tense is defined formally in terms of the morphological contrast *is/was*, *takes/took*, etc. But it might be argued that there is double *time* marking, and if this were true we might have to revise our idea of tense as well as of the simple phrase.[6] Consider again:

John was coming tomorrow.

This might be treated as similar to:

John intended to come tomorrow.

For we can separate two time indications by the use of adverbials:

Yesterday John was coming tomorrow.

It becomes attractive, then, to see BE and COME both as full verbs, BE marked here for past time (*was*) as was INTEND, and COME for futurity by the *-ing* form. We shall, however, presumably, see similar double time marking and therefore double tense marking with the present form:

John is coming tomorrow.

This follows by simple analogy – *is* refers to the present, *coming* to the future with collocation with tomorrow. These are forms that we have already considered in terms of epistemic tense (**3.1.7**).

The strongest argument against this interpretation is that we may have double time marking where there is only one verb as in:

John comes tomorrow.

There is the possibility of 'future in the past' with the single verb form. As we saw, it is not impossible to say:

Yesterday John came tomorrow.

Here we have only one verb but two time markers or 'tenses'. This is evidence that double time marking does not need two verbs; where there are two verbs, then, it does not follow that each is separately marked for time/tense, and the argument that the auxiliaries are full verbs no longer follows (unless we want to say that there are two 'underlying' verbs in these examples also).

It has also been suggested that there is a similar situation with the perfect *have* forms. For consider:

In March John had read only two of the books.

This has two distinct meanings – either that in March John was in the situation of having read these books (at some previous time, not necessarily in March) or that John was (at some time) in the position of having read the books in March. We can see a similar distinction between:

Now I've seen him.
I've never seen him.

Now refers to the present time, *never* to the time preceding this. The reasoning is obvious. We have two time markers, one present, one past, giving us thus 'past in the present', and hence two full verbs in a complex and not a simple phrase. HAVE is independently marked for time and is not an auxiliary. Rather we have 'past in the present'.

There is one conclusive argument against this view. Although the past perfect can be 'past past' (3.3.4), the present perfect is never 'present past'. If there are two verbs one marking present, the other past, time, it should follow that we can say:

**I've seen him yesterday.*
**He's read it last March.*

But it is an absolute rule (3.3.1) that the present perfect never occurs with a past time adverbial. Interpretation in terms of two independent tense markers, therefore, fails.

The second test of a complex phrase was that of double negation. It is not normally possible to mark the primary auxiliary and the full verb independently for negation. We shall not allow:

**He isn't not going.*
**He hasn't not gone.*

These are possible only as deliberately and, perhaps, jocularly deviant forms. More importantly we cannot distinguish between negating the auxiliary and negating the full verb – between:

He isn't | going.
He is | not going.

There is no distinction here that is like that found with catenatives, *eg:*

He doesn't prefer to go.
He prefers not to go.

The third test was that of passivization. This is almost always possible with the primary pattern:

John is meeting Mary.
Mary is being met by John.

There are, however, some problems with HAVE and 'current relevance' since we should allow the passive but not the active sentence in:

**Queen Victoria has visited Bath.*
Bath has been visited by Queen Victoria.

For this see **3.3.2**.

3.1.9 Adverbial specification[7]

In the analysis that follows reference will often be made to collocation with adverbials and the examples will frequently contain them. There are basically two purposes in this.

First, the occurrence of adverbials often justifies the semantic analysis of formal distinctions. For instance, it is clear that the present perfect in English is in no sense a past tense since it never collocates with past time adverbials (**3.3.1**):

**I've seen John yesterday.*

An alternative analysis which sees the distinction of past and perfect as of definite versus indefinite[8] cannot account for this; nor can any analysis that sees the perfect as any kind of past, *eg* as a past in the present (see **3.1.8**).

Secondly, the use of adverbials will often justify some of the semantic distinctions that are not formally marked, *eg* between the habitual, the future and the basic uses of the form (**3.1.4**). It equally shows the quite distinct uses of the progressive for limited duration and sporadic repetition (**3.6.1**, **3.6.2**).

It would, of course, be possible to undertake a detailed classification of the uses in terms of all the time and duration categories that can be established in terms of the adverbials. But this would be purely semantic since the adverbials cannot be classified in formal terms, and would be far too detailed and complex for this book.

There is, however, one important point about the adverbials. Some of the uses do not require adverbials, others do. Some, that is to say, require adverbial specification, some do not. In general it is the uses that have been treated here as non-basic that need specification – the habitual and the future uses, the specialized uses of the progressive. But this is not wholly true. A source of some difficulty is that in the present tense the simple form when not specified is usually habitual:

He goes to school.
I go for long walks.

This has led some writers to suppose that the habitual use is the basic use (see 3.5.2).

3.2 Tense

Tense appears to have three distinct functions, first to mark purely temporal relations of past and present time, secondly in the sequence of tenses that is mainly relevant for reported speech and thirdly to mark 'unreality', particularly in conditional clauses and wishes. But we shall have to consider (3.2.3) whether these uses are in fact all distinct.

3.2.1 Time relations

The most important function of tense is to indicate past and present time. The distinction is very clear in:

He's reading the paper at this moment.
He was reading the paper when I saw him this morning.

But there are three reservations to make.

[i] Present time must be understood to mean any period of time that includes the present moment. It includes, therefore, 'all time' as in:

The sun rises in the east.
Water boils at 100° Centigrade.

Past time excludes the present moment. Past time may seem to be the 'marked member' of the pair, in that it specifically excludes the present moment. Present time is any period of time, short, long or eternal that includes the present moment.

[ii] There is one exception only to the statement in (i) – the so-called historic present. There are many examples of this in literary English, but it is also to be found in speech, *eg:*

He just walks into the room and sits down in front of the fire without saying a word to anyone.

The traditional explanation of this usage – that it recalls or recounts the past as vividly as if it were present, is adequate. It seems highly probable that it is not specifically English but a characteristic of many, if not all, languages that make time distinctions in the verb.

[iii] The use of tense is complicated by its relation to the temporal characteristics of phase and by the habitual and future uses of the forms (which are dealt with in later sections).

The adverbials that are used with tense are of four kinds. First, there are those that may be used with past tense only, *last week*, *yesterday*, *last year*, *a long time ago*. Secondly, there are those that may be used with present tense only; *now*, *at this moment*, *at the present time*. Thirdly, there are those that may be used with either, though the period of time to which they refer includes the present moment. These are *today*, *this week*, *this year* etc, as in:

He was working today.
He's working today.

When these are used with the past, the activity is shown as taking place within the period indicated by the adverbial, but before the present moment. Fourthly, there are adverbials that indicate past or present time according to the time at which the utterance is made, and for this reason may be used with past or present forms. Examples are *this morning*, *this afternoon* and *this summer*. *This morning* is present if it is still morning, but past if the morning is over. In the afternoon *this morning* will occur with past tense forms. To complicate matters, these adverbials also function like the previous set. *This morning*, for instance, can be used not only with present tense forms but also with past tense forms, while it is still morning – to refer to an earlier event that same morning.

3.2.2 Reported speech

It is the normal rule in English that a statement in the present tense is reported in the past tense if the verb of reporting is itself in the past tense. Let us consider, for instance, the sentences:

I like chocolate.
I'm reading 'Vanity Fair'.

If we report these with *He said* the normal forms would be:

He said he liked chocolate.
He said he was reading 'Vanity Fair'.

This phenomenon is usually described as the English 'sequence of tenses'. But the sequence of tenses rule is not an absolute one. The present tense form of the original statement can be retained even with a past tense verb of reporting:

He said he likes chocolate.
He said he's reading 'Vanity Fair'.

The explanation is fairly simple. With the reported utterance the tense chosen may either be that appropriate to the time of the original statement (*ie* past) or to the time of the actual utterance in the present. For the latter to be possible, *ie* for a present tense to be used, it is essential that the action being reported is, or can be, seen as still present. It could not, for instance, contain an adverbial that refers to past time. Consider, for instance:

I'm looking forward to the year 1950.
I'm looking forward to the year 2000.

For the first there is only one possible form for the reported speech, but two for the second (if we are reporting after 1950, but before AD 2000):

He said he was looking forward to the year 1950.
**He said he's looking forward to the year 1950.*
He said he was looking forward to the year 2000.
He said he's looking forward to the year 2000.

We can thus 'overrule' the sequence of tenses by choosing a tense appropriate to the time of speaking – what has been called a 'deictic' tense.

There is a difference of meaning if the present deictic tense is selected. It involves the speaker – the time is viewed from his standpoint. In general, then, it implies that the speaker accepts the statement as still valid. If he believes that John will come he may report John's statement *I'm coming* by:

John said he's coming.

The alternative, past non-deictic tense following the sequence of tense rule does not commit the speaker to any view on the matter:

John said he was coming.

Similarly we might find either of the following:

These arguments showed that the world was round.
These arguments showed that the world is round.

But if we do not believe that the world is flat we have only:

These arguments showed that the world was flat.
**These arguments showed that the world is flat.*

Surprisingly, if we have subordination in the original utterance, we can switch to the 'deictic' present tense in both clauses or only in the subordinate one:

I'll visit you when the weather is finer.
He said he would visit us when the weather was finer.
He said he will visit us when the weather is finer.
He said he would visit us when the weather is finer.

In the first of the reports there is no deictic tense. In the second the deictic tense is used for the whole of the reported speech. In the third it is confined to the clause *when the weather is finer*.

The account given so far is oversimplified. We have been talking about 'reporting' and about the 'original statement'. But the notion of reported speech must also apply to verbs like SHOW, BELIEVE, etc, where there were no 'original statements'. Nevertheless the sequence of tense rule still applies and deictic presents are still possible as in the examples with SHOW above. But there is a restriction on 'verbs of thinking and knowing', in that they always follow the sequence of tense rule alone and do not permit deictic tense. We cannot say:

**I knew you aren't coming.*
**I thought you don't like it.*

Let us now return to the 'basic' reported speech forms and note what happens when the original statement was not in the present tense.

If the verb of the original statement is already in the past it is normally reported in the same form:

I was reading when she came.
He said he was reading when she came.

But a past non-perfect tense form may also be reported by a past perfect form which then functions as a 'past-past' (see also **3.3.4**):

I saw him yesterday.
He said he had seen him the day before.

This again is a matter of using the deictic tense – the past non-perfect for the action is past in relation to the speaker – or of the sequence of tense rules which require a 'past of a past'. But in this case the use of the deictic (past non-perfect) is the more normal.

The past perfect also, of course, reports the present perfect, and it is the only form available to report the past perfect:

I've already seen him.
I'd already seen him.
He said he'd already seen him.

There are, then, only two possible forms for past time reporting related to four possible forms in the original:

ORIGINAL	REPORTED
I see	
I saw	*he saw*
I have seen	*he had seen*
I had seen	

3.2.3 Unreality

The use of the past tense to refer to 'unreality' is very common with the modals (5.3, 5.5). But it is also found with primary pattern forms:

[i] It is used to express a tentative or polite attitude in questions and requests:

I wanted to ask you about that.
Did you want to speak to me?

These are a little more tentative or polite than:

I want to ask you about that.
Do you want to speak to me?

[ii] It is always used in the *if* clause of 'unreal' conditions (see 5.5 for more details):

If he came, he would find out.

The 'real' condition is:

If he comes, he will find out.

Similar to this are clauses introduced by *supposing* and some relative clauses that must be regarded as also being part of 'unreal' conditions:

Supposing we asked him, what would he do?
Anyone who said that would be crazy.

Belonging to this pattern is the almost fossilized *If I were you*. Only in this form is *were* used regularly with *I* in spoken English. *If I was you* would be regarded as substandard English, but in other cases *was* or *were* are both possible. There is a choice between:

If I were rich . . . *If I were to ask him . . .*
If I was rich . . . *If I was to ask him . . .*

But it is only in unreal conditions that this form *were* occurs. In past real ('implicational') conditions (see 5.5.2, 5.5.4) only *was* will occur with *I*, *he*, *she*, *it* and singular nouns:

If he was here, he was in the garden.
**If he were here, he was in the garden.*

[iii] It is found in wishes and statements of the type *It is time* . . .:

I wish I knew.
It's time we went.

Sentences beginning *If only* are perhaps to be handled here, though they might equally be treated as unreal conditions:

If only I understood what you are saying.

It has been suggested[9] that the use of unreality and the past time use of the past tense are essentially the same – that the past tense is the 'remote' tense, remote in time or in reality. There is some attractiveness in this idea, for tense could then be seen to have but a single use (for the sequence of tenses, too, can obviously be easily explained in terms of time and time-shifting).

There are, as far as I can see, no positive arguments against this thesis. Traditional grammarians would object that the unreality use is essentially the subjunctive, but the notion of a subjunctive mood is a simple transfer from Latin and has no place in English grammar, since all the potential subjunctives turn out to be past tense in form (or to be the simple uninflected form as in *God save the Queen*). Even the formal *If I were you* does not prove the existence of a subjunctive. For those speakers of English who insist on *were* the 'subjunctive' is exactly like a normal past – the same form throughout the paradigm – *were* just like *took*, *loved*, etc. The unique feature of the past tense of BE is that when it marks past time it has the two distinct forms *was* and *were* – unlike any other verb in the language. *Were* in *If I were you* is thus more 'regularly' past than the *was/were* forms of past time!

Nevertheless semantically the 'subjunctive' is quite different from the past time/past tense and this is enough for us not to identify them. But that does not mean that we shall talk of 'subjunctive', but only that we shall distinguish the past time and unreality uses of the past tense.

We have already considered the sequence of tense rule for past tense as a mark of past time only. But the rule applies also to past tense for unreality as illustrated by:

You might think he'd finished it.
I could say I was coming.
You might think he's finished it.
I could say I'm coming.

These do not seem to involve deictic tense and committing the speaker to a view; it is merely that the sequence of tense rule is optional with tense for unreality.

3.3 Phase

As has already been suggested, the perfect is used to indicate a period of time that began before, but continued right up to, a point of time (either present or past, according to the tense).

3.3.1 Time relations

There is no problem as long as we are concerned only with activity going on throughout the period of time as in:

I've been reading for an hour.
I'd been reading for an hour when he came.

With the first (present tense) the activity began an hour before, and continued right up to, the present; in the second (past tense) it began an hour before, and continued right up to, the past point of time indicated by the adverbial clause.

The adverbials associated with tense are the same with the perfect forms as with the non-perfect. That is to say *last week*, *yesterday* occur with past (perfect) tense forms, *now*, *at this moment* only with present (perfect) tense forms, *today*, *this week* with either, while the use of *this morning*, *this afternoon* etc depends upon the actual time of speaking. What is important here is that the adverbials that are collocated only with past tense forms are collocated only with the past (perfect) and never with the present perfect, even although the present perfect appears to have reference to the past – it refers to activity that began in the past. We cannot say:

**I've been reading yesterday.*

In addition to the adverbials collocated with tense, there are some that are specifically associated with the perfect. These are the adverbial clauses and phrases beginning with *since* – *since Tuesday*, *since we met*. They indicate the starting point of the period of time.

The adverbials beginning with *since* are collocated only with perfect forms (except rarely with progressive forms used for limited duration – 3.6.1):

I've been reading since three.
I'd been reading since three o'clock.
**I'm reading since three o'clock.*
**I was reading since three o'clock.*

Adverbials beginning with *for* (*for an hour*, etc) are often used with perfect forms, but they are not restricted to them. The restrictions on adverbials of this kind are to be stated in terms of aspect.

3.3.2 Non-progressive forms and 'results'

In spite of the simple picture set out in the previous section there is a problem where it is clear that the activity does *not* continue throughout the relevant period of time. This is likely with action verbs, since their activity is without marked duration:

I've cut my finger.
He's painted his house.
Have you seen him?

A common explanation of such examples is that the perfect is used where the activity has results in the present. This is, however, rather misleading unless we interpret results to include 'nil results' as is shown by:

I've hit it twice, but it's still standing up.
I've written, but they haven't replied.

A more accurate explanation is in terms of 'current relevance'[10] – that in some way or other (not necessarily in its results) the action is relevant to something observable at the present. The past perfect may be treated in a similar way – activity occurring before, but relevant to, a point of time in the past.

But examples such as these in no way refute the suggestion made earlier that phase refers, like tense, to features of time, and that the perfect indicates a period of time preceding but continuing up to a later point of time (present or past). To make this point, we will again consider only the present perfect; but similar considerations hold for the past perfect too. Examples of present perfect (non-progressive) forms are:

I've seen John this morning.
I've mended it three times today.
He's written the letter.

In all three cases, the activity took place in the past. The same actions could have been reported by past tense forms:

I saw John this morning.
I mended it three times today.
He wrote the letter.

What this proves is that the periods of time indicated by the present perfect and the past (non-perfect) overlap, and that an action performed in the past may be included in either of them. The interpretation in terms of time reference that accounts for *I've been reading* equally accounts for the perfect forms exemplified here; the actions all took place in a period of time that began in the past and continued right up to the present.

The problem that remains is to establish what determines the choice of the present perfect rather than the past in these cases, but the question is best asked in the form, 'Why is the activity placed in the period of time indicated by the present perfect rather than the period indicated by the simple past, since it occurred within them both?' It is here that we must refer to current relevance. A period of time that includes the present is chosen precisely because there are features of the present that directly link it to the past activity. The temporal situation being envisaged by the speaker is one that includes the present; the present perfect, is, therefore, used. Examples are:

I've bought a new suit.
I've finished my homework.
They've left the district.

In all of these there are features of the present which form part of the whole relevant situation set out in time. The new suit may be displayed at the time of speaking, or the implication may be 'I shan't be untidy any more'. The child who says 'I've finished my homework' is probably asking to be allowed to go out to play now. The information 'They've left the district' tells us that we shan't find them, that it's no use calling on them any more. Other examples, with comments, are:

I've cut my finger. (It's still bleeding)
He's broken the window. (It hasn't been mended)
I've told you already. (You are stupid *or* I won't tell you again)
They've fallen in the river. (They need help *or* Their clothes are wet)
You've had an accident. (I can see the bruises)

The insistence on the interpretation of phase in terms of periods of time is partly justified by the fact that it makes possible a single statement for all the perfect forms, and does not need to handle current relevance as a special meaning of the perfect, unrelated to its other uses. But it is wholly confirmed by a consideration of the adverbials that are collocated with the present perfect and past tense forms, for an adverbial that indicates purely past time is never used with a present perfect. We cannot say **They've come last Monday*, though an adverbial that indicates a period that includes the present is possible – *They've come this week.* An explanation simply in terms of results or current relevance cannot account for this, for that would not exclude **They've come last Monday*, meaning that they came on Monday and are still here. English would be the richer if this were possible, for as it is we cannot in a single phrase combine the two pieces of information about (i) their arrival at a specific time in the past and (ii) the current relevance of this. It is because the present perfect indicates a period of time that includes the present that it is not possible further to specify by an adverbial a past time at which the activity took place.

Indeed, often it is only the choice of the adverbial that determines the choice between present perfect and past. There is no question of current relevance, but only whether the period of time being indicated includes the present moment or not. Thus we may say *I've seen him three times today*, but *I saw him three times yesterday* and not **I've seen him three times yesterday*. Similarly *I've seen him this morning* is a possible utterance only if it is still morning; if the morning is over, the period of time indicated is wholly in the past and a present perfect form cannot be used.

There is one fundamental difficulty about 'current relevance' – that it is not easy to define what is and what is not relevant. British speakers of English seem to use the perfect wherever there seems to be any kind of relevance, but some American speakers at least, use it more sparingly. For a British speaker it would not be normal to ask a child coming to the table:

Did you wash your hands?

But for many, if not most Americans, this is quite acceptable. There is no evidence that the function of phase is different in American speech, only that the interpretation of 'relevance' is stricter.

It is, naturally, unusual to use the perfect when talking about the dead:

**Queen Victoria has visited Brighton.*
**Shakespeare has written a lot of plays.*

Yet there is nothing odd about the passive:

Brighton has been visited by Queen Victoria.
A lot of plays have been written by Shakespeare.

The reason is obvious. In the first set we are talking about people who are dead – and there can be no current relevance. In the second set we are talking about present-day Brighton or the presently extant quantity of plays. But we must be careful here. Subject position does not necessarily indicate what we are 'talking about' and so what may be relevant. There would be nothing odd about:

Even Queen Victoria has visited Brighton.
Shakespeare has written most of the best plays we know.

Here we are 'talking about' not Queen Victoria or Shakespeare but Brighton and the best plays and the perfect is not at all abnormal.

We have been concerned so far in this subsection with present perfect forms. Exactly the same remarks are true of past perfect forms – with a past point of time, the point at which there was current relevance:

I'd cut my finger. (It was still bleeding)
He'd broken the window. (It hadn't been mended)
I'd already told you. (I wouldn't tell you again), etc

3.3.3 Progressive forms and 'results'

Where progressive forms are used, they often, as we have seen, refer to activity going on throughout the period of time. But this is not always so. There is a problem with such sentences as:

Someone's been moving my books.
Who's been eating my porridge?

The position is exactly the same as with the non-progressive forms, provided only that it is accepted that the use of the progressive does not necessarily imply that the activity continues *throughout* the relevant period of time, but merely that it has duration *within* the period. Someone had been moving my books (continuing activity) within a period of time that began in the past and continued up to the present; this period of time rather than a wholly past period is chosen because the present disorderly state of the books is linked to the past activity. So, too, the three bears ask, 'Who's been eating my porridge?' because they can see that some of it has gone. Other examples are:

I've been working in the garden all day.
I've been cleaning the car.

Both activities continued for some time and both are to be related to the present (even if they did not continue up to the present). The man who has been working suggests that he is tired and has a right to be, while the man who has been cleaning his car is probably apologising for the state of his hands and clothes. It would be an error to regard these examples as essentially different from those in which the activity is clearly shown to continue right up to the present, usually by the adverbials *since* . . . and *for* . . . The period of time is the same; it is the adverbials, not the progressive form itself, that show the activity continued throughout. Other examples are:

You've been working too hard. ('You need a rest' – to someone now in bed, certainly not still working)
You've been playing with fire. (I can smell it)
I've been drinking tea. (That's why I'm late)
He's been talking about you. (I know something now)

The same kind of remarks are valid for the past perfect:

You'd been working too hard.
He'd been talking about you. etc

3.3.4 HAVE as past

In spite of the clear distinction of perfect and past noted in **3.3.1** HAVE marks past tense rather than perfect phase in two kinds of structure.

[i] The formal 'past perfect' is used also as a 'past past'. This is clearly shown in the contrast of:

I had already seen him when you arrived.
I had seen him an hour before you arrived.

The first is clearly past perfect – I saw him in a period of time preceding but up to the time of arrival, and there is current relevance. But the second merely places seeing him before the arrival – previously to a past point of time, *ie* 'past past'. There is a clear contrast with present perfect which cannot be interpreted as a past:

I've already seen him.
**I've seen him an hour ago.*

We have already noted a similar use in reported speech (3.2.2); there is another similar use in unreal past conditionals (5.5.1).

[ii] Non-finite forms of HAVE may mark tense or aspect. This is clear from the adverbials that are possible with the infinitivals and participials:

To have finished already/yesterday.
Having finished already/yesterday.

This is equally valid of HAVE used with modals (see 5.1.2, 5.3.2, 5.4.3, 5.5.1 for further examples):

He may have finished already/yesterday.
He ought to have finished by now/yesterday.

But these remarks in no way invalidate the very clear distinction between phase and tense with the finite forms.

3.4 Aspect

It has already been suggested that the progressive indicates duration.[11] There are, however, some rather special uses of the progressive that are linked either to its habitual use or to particular verb classes (the non-progressive). These are dealt with later.

3.4.1 Duration

The duration that is associated with the progressive is clearly indicated by collocation with such adverbials as *all morning*, *for a long time*, *continually:*

I was reading all morning.
He's been working for a long time.

The progressive together with these adverbials may be used with verbs that indicate single momentary actions with the necessary implication that the actions were being repeated throughout the time:

He was hitting him for several minutes.
He was jumping up and down for a long time.

It does not follow from this, however, that a verb that necessarily indicates activity over a period of time such as READ or WORK must always occur in the progressive – even when collocated with such adverbials:

I read all morning.
I worked for a long time.
He slept all night.

Nor does it follow that verbs of momentary action must be in the progressive if the action is repeated:

He hit him for several minutes.
He jumped up and down for several hours.

The progressive is thus not directly related to the actual duration of the activity but rather to the indication of that duration. The non-progressive form merely reports the action as if it were replying to the question *what did he do?*, whereas the progressive specifically indicates its duration, as if it were a reply to *How did he spend his time?* The use of the non-progressive, that is to say, does not deny duration; it simply does not indicate it.

For non-activity over a period of time the progressive is not required. The denial of the action is enough, for if it did not take place it did not take place over a period of time. Thus we find:

I haven't met him for years.
I didn't open it for a week.

The positive forms would be unusual here unless they were marked as habitual and repeated (see **3**.5.3):

I've met him every day for years.
I've opened it every morning for a week.

3.4.2 Varieties of use

Although in general we may point to duration as the feature marked by the progressive, there are several points to make:

[i] The progressive is used with such adverbials and adjectivals as *more and more, faster and faster:*

It's getting bigger and bigger.
More and more people are buying television sets.
He's working less and less.

The adjectivals and adverbials indicate an increase or decrease in the activity or some aspect of the activity, and therefore imply duration. But perhaps this is 'limited duration' – see **3**.6.1.

[ii] Where a point of time is indicated by an adverbial, the progressive and non-progressive differ in their temporal relations to that point of time. The progressive always indicates activity continuing both before and after the time indicated. The non-progressive indicates either simultaneity or, more commonly, immediate succession. A contrast may be made between:

When I saw him, he was running away.
When I saw him, he ran away.

In the second clearly the act of running away was preceded by (and probably an effect of) my seeing him. Simultaneity is possible, however, as in:

As the clock struck ten, he died.
He died at ten o'clock.

The non-progressive specifically excludes overlap, as is shown where a number of actions are reported:

When I arrived, he shouted three times.

All three shouts followed my arrival here. In fact, English has no simple way of showing that there were three shouts and that the shouting both preceded and followed my arrival. There is no logical reason why the non-progressive should always indicate successive activity rather than, for instance, immediately preceding activity; it is merely a fact of English that it does.

[iii] The progressive often suggests that the activity was unfinished, while the non-progressive normally suggests its completion. We may compare:

I painted the table this morning.
I was painting the table this morning.

It is more likely that in the first case the painting of the table has been completed. This is not a completely clear distinction. It is possible to say:

I painted the house this morning.

without meaning that I completed the painting, but simply to report the activity. But such a statement might imply the completion of the activity and invite the reply:

What? The whole of it?

Where the present progressive is used, the activity is not complete, since it indicates activity continuing into the future. If I say 'I'm reading a book', it follows that I have not finished it.

[iv] The use of the progressive does not necessarily imply unbroken activity, as shown by:

I'm reading 'The Mayor of Casterbridge'.

This may suggest either that I am at this moment sitting with a book in front of me, or that I have read part of the book and intend to read some more, but that at the moment I am not actually reading it. We may similarly compare:

I'm writing a letter.
I'm writing a book.

It is at least likely that the letter is actually being written at the time of speaking, whereas the book has merely been begun.

[v] With the perfect progressive it is not necessarily the case that the activity continued throughout the period of time indicated (this has already been noted in 3.4.1).

3.5 Future and habitual uses

The fact that many of the forms are used to refer to the future or to habitual activity is a source of great confusion. All too often comparison is made between forms in their basic uses and forms in their habitual or future uses. Up until now we have been concerned only with the basic uses.

3.5.1 The problem

We have already seen that a single form, *eg* the present progressive non-perfect, may be used to refer to an action in the future, or an action that is habitual, as well as to an action going on at the present time:

He's reading at the moment.
He's reading a paper tomorrow.
He's reading, whenever I see him.

The future and habitual uses are normally marked by adverbials (*tomorrow*, *next week*, etc, and *always*, *whenever* . . .) while the basic use is normally not marked in this way.

A common and misleading statement of the uses of the forms is one that treats the non-progressive non-perfect present form (henceforth to be called the 'simple' present) as 'habitual' and the present progressive as referring to action taking place at the present moment[12] – making the distinction between habitual and non-habitual present action:

He reads the paper every day.
He's reading the paper at the moment.

But this is merely to compare incomparables. For the progressive as well as the simple form may be used in a habitual use:

He's always reading at meals.
He always reads at meals.

The difference between the two is, as usual, one of duration (or statable in terms of one of the other features associated with the progressive that are still to be described). But in *both* cases the activity is habitual. The contrast habitual/actual present is a false one.

Another, slightly less misleading, interpretation is that the present tense form is timeless, while the past tense alone specifies time – past time. There is some truth in this, for the 'present' is the period of time that includes the present moment, but extends into the past and the future without any specified limits. This may account for its use for 'timeless' truths such as:

Oil floats on water.
The sun rises in the east.

But if this is to be taken to imply that only present tense forms may refer to habitual actions, while past tense forms refer to actions in the past, it is false, for we may certainly attest habitual actions in the past:

I meet him every day.
I was meeting him every day.

And in any case we must distinguish between habitual actions and timeless truths (see 3.5.3). Nor does this fact account for the use of the present tense for reference to the future. For why is it not equally used to refer to the past, by the same argument? Moreover it would not account for the fact that the progressive and non-progressive forms have a considerable difference in meaning when used for future reference, a difference that is not otherwise associated with aspect (see 3.5.5).

It is clear that future and habitual reference must be treated separately, and not as characteristics of any one of the forms or of any one of the terms in the four grammatical categories.

3.5.2 The simple present

One of the reasons why the simple present is often designated 'habitual' is that it is rarely used in its basic, non-habitual, non-future use. But this fact ought not to obscure the overall pattern, especially since there are reasons for its rarity in its basic use.

There are two reasons why the simple present is rarely used in its non-habitual sense. First, a non-progressive form merely reports an activity, but it is rarely that we need to report a present activity, for the simple, but non-linguistic, reason that if the speaker can observe it (at the present time) so too in most circumstances can the hearer. Past activity on the contrary is often reported by a speaker who observed it (or heard about it) to a hearer who did not. With the past tense, therefore, unlike the present, non-habitual activity is commonly referred to, as well as habitual activity:

I saw my mother yesterday.
I saw my mother every day.

A second point is that present activity is usually incomplete and therefore even when there is no specific reference to the duration of the activity, its incompleteness implies the use of the progressive. In, for instance, *What are you doing?* the speaker avoids the suggestion that the activity is complete.

The progressive is, thus, the commoner form for reference to present activity. We can, indeed, treat it as the norm, and say that unless there are obvious reasons to the contrary the progressive is used. (With the 'non-progressive' verbs, as we shall see (3.7), the reverse is true.) But there are a number of situations in which the non-progressive, the simple present, is used.

First, it is the form normally used in a commentary, especially on the radio where the commentator is reporting something that the listeners cannot see. This use is exactly parallel to the use of the simple past to report past activity:

. . . and he passes the ball to Smith, and Smith scores!
He bowls, and he just misses the wicket.
He hits him again, right on the jaw.

Secondly, it is used in demonstrations, where the audience can see what is happening, but the demonstrator reports it as well to make sure there is no misunderstanding. Once again he is merely reporting the activity, he is not indicating its duration; the simple present is the only appropriate form:

(Conjuror) *I place the rabbit in the box and close the lid.*
(Cookery demonstration) *I take three eggs and beat them in this basin. Then I add sugar . . .*

A third use is where the words themselves form part of the activity they report. These are the so-called 'performative' verb forms.[13] Again they merely state the occurrence of the activity:

I name this ship . . .
I pronounce you man and wife.
I declare the meeting closed.

A rather similar use is of verbs of statement which are used merely to reinforce the fact that the speaker makes his statement:

I say he should go.
I call it an outrage.

These utterances imply not 'I am saying . . .' or 'I am calling . . .' but '. . . that's my opinion' and '. . . that's my name for it.'

Less easy to explain are:

He talks like an expert.
Look at the way he walks!
Why do you say that?

The common characteristic of all these utterances is that they contain an adverbial to indicate either the manner or the cause of the activity. It is in the manner or cause that the speaker is interested; the duration of the activity is not in question. Again the simple present is appropriate. In some cases it might be argued that we are concerned with habitual activity:

Why do you cut it like that?

But it is equally clear that in many cases the activity is not habitual, that the speaker is concerned only with a single present activity. There can be contrast between a present and a past activity, neither of them apparently habitual, as in:

Yesterday he talked nonsense. Today he talks like an expert.
He walked all the morning. Look at the way he walks now.
You said something different a few minutes ago. Why do you say that now?

Similar considerations hold for:

John enters through the window. (Stage directions)
It says in the Bible . . .

The stage directions are similar to a commentary; the play simulates present activity. The words in the Bible are simply statements; we are concerned only with the fact of statement and there is no indication of any duration. It must be admitted that the present is timeless in some cases but only in so far as present *time* is timeless, in that it extends without limit on both sides of 'now'. This may partly account for the use of the simple present in stage directions and in the report of written statements. More will be said on this point in dealing with the habitual. But what has been shown here is that most of the non-habitual uses of the simple present fit quite normally into the pattern, and ought not to be treated as 'special' uses of the form. On the contrary there is more plausibility in treating habitual usage as secondary to the basic use, in spite of its much greater frequency with this particular form.

The simple present does, however, cause difficulty to the teacher of English, at least if he tries to illustrate the verb forms situationally; for in order to illustrate the use of the present progressive, he is likely to perform actions and describe them:

Now I am opening the door.
Now I am writing on the blackboard.

The natural reaction of a native speaker in these situations would be to use the simple form, not the progressive, but teachers are warned not to use this form, as it will confuse the pupils. What is wrong here is not the form – but the situation. For the teacher *is* demonstrating and ought to use the simple form; but he is pretending not to be demonstrating, but acting in a 'normal' non-demonstrating type of situation. The classroom unfortunately creates a situation (that of demonstration) in which the progressive would not normally be used, and, therefore, cannot be taught naturally. It is obviously necessary to use artificial situations in teaching, but in this case the difference in the forms used in the pretended situation and those likely to be used in the actual situation (in the classroom) can only create confusion.

3.5.3 Habitual

Every one of the forms may be used in a habitual (as well as a non-habitual) sense. Examples of all of them (active only) are:

(1) *He bowls, and . . .*
He always bowls well.
(2) *He's writing a book.*
He's always writing a book.

(3) *He went to work yesterday.*
He always went by bus.
(4) *He was reading when I arrived.*
He was reading, whenever I saw him.
(5) *He has come to see me.*
He has come to see me every day.
(6) *He had called on them, when I saw him.*
He had called on them every week, when they died.
(7) *He's been reading since three.*
Whenever I've seen him, he's been reading.
(8) *He had been reading all day.*
Whenever I saw him, he'd been playing golf.

As the examples show, the distinction made by progressive/non-progressive is valid for the habitual use no less than the non-habitual – the activity may or may not be durational. The points made in **3**.4.2 are still valid too, though there are some complications with the perfect that are considered separately in a later section (**3**.8.2). Especially to be noted is the distinction made by the progressive/non-progressive with respect to simultaneity and successivity where a point of time (or in the case of the habitual, a series of points of time) is indicated:

Whenever I see him, he runs away.
Whenever I see him, he's running away.

On each occasion the activity of running follows (non-progressive) or overlaps (progressive) my sight of him.

We saw earlier that the simple present is used for 'timeless truths'. This is explained by the fact that the 'present' extends without stated limits on both sides of the present moment and may then refer to a few minutes, years, or eternity.

There is no very clear line between 'timeless' truths and statements of habitual activity – the distinction is not a linguistic one. This may be shown by the following list, graded, as far as possible, in varying approximations to completely timeless truths:

I always take sugar in tea.
The milkman calls on Sundays.
The Chinese grow a lot of rice.
Cows eat grass.
Birds fly.
The Severn flows into the Atlantic.
The sun rises in the east.

Oil floats on water.
Water boils at 100°C.

The last three might seem timeless truths (or perhaps the last two only). But what about the Severn? Did it always flow into the Atlantic? (Did the sun always rise in the east?)

It might, however, be feasible to distinguish:

(1) habitual, iterative activities,

I go to work every day,

(2) inductively known facts,

Oil floats on water,

(3) 'general' truths,

The Severn flows into the Atlantic.

A distinguishing feature of (1) is regular collocation with adverbials such as *every day*, while (2) is to be compared with (and is replaceable by) a form with *will* (*cf* 5.2.2).

What is important is to contrast these simple present forms in their habitual/timeless truth usage with the progressives. With the removal or addition of relevant adverbials and with progressive forms the sentences refer to activity going on (with duration) at present:

I'm going to work.
The oil is floating on the water.
The Severn is flowing into the Atlantic. (I can see it moving)

An interesting trio is (the third refers to habitual activity with duration):

The bucket leaks. (It has a hole)
The bucket's leaking. (You can see the water coming out)
The bucket's always leaking. (In spite of countless repairs)

Among the adverbials used with the habitual use are *every day*, *always*, *whenever*. There are some, such as *continually* and *for ever*, which occur almost exclusively with progressive forms, but with these the progressive usually indicates not duration but sporadic repetition (3.6.2).

3.5.4 Future: progressive

The progressive is commonly used to refer to future activity:

I'm reading a paper to the conference tomorrow.

This use of the progressive is very common with verbs that indicate or imply motion:

I'm meeting him next week.
He's coming to see me soon.
They're taking the children to the theatre this evening.
He's joining the army next week.

But there is no restriction to such verbs:

I'm watching the play on television this evening.
We're having turkey for lunch tomorrow.

Epistemic tense – marking the time at which the statement was valid, *ie* at which the event was envisaged as future, is very common with the progressive. With past tense we find:

I was reading a paper to the conference tomorrow.
I was meeting him next week.
He was coming to see me soon.

The combination of past tense and a future adverbial makes clear here the two different times – one of the validity of the statement, the other of the proposed activity. Without the future time adverbial the past validity meaning can be marked by accent and the appropriate intonation – normally a fall-rise on the auxiliary:

I wás reading a paper.
I wás meeting him.
He wás coming to see me.

With the perfect and past perfect we find similarly such sentences as (and here adverbial specification seems necessary (3.1.9)):

I've been coming to see you for ages.
He's been going abroad for years.
I'd been coming to see him the next day (but he died).
We'd been going to Paris for years (but never went).

The third sentence here is an example of the past perfect used for past past (3.3.4). But all the others have past perfect time marking – the time at which the activity is or was proposed is the period of time preceding and continuing up to the present or to a point of time in the past. There are, thus, examples of epistemic phase (3.1.7), but it seems that it is restricted to this habitual use.

3.5.5 Future: non-progressive

The non-progressives are also used with future reference. The simple present is exemplified in:

I start work tomorrow.
He goes to Paris next week.
Exams begin on Monday.

We have already seen that there can be epistemic tense indicating that the past is the time of the validity of the statement:

At that time I didn't see him until tomorrow.

There is little possibility, it seems, of similar epistemic phase (contrast the perfect progressive in 3.5.4):

**I've read my paper tomorrow.*

The progressive is used for 'simple' futurity to indicate a prediction or in the case of activity by the speaker an intention. The non-progressive, however, indicates that the activity is in some way scheduled – that there is a fixed decision or plan. This accounts for the difference between:

I'm starting work tomorrow.
I start work tomorrow.

The first suggests that the speaker now expects or intends to start work – he may, perhaps, have been ill. The second indicates that tomorrow is the time fixed for him to start, *eg* by his firm or by the doctor. It is for such reasons that we would normally expect the first but not the second of:

Examinations start tomorrow.
Examinations are starting tomorrow.

The non-progressive future use is common with verbs such as START, BEGIN, FINISH, END, etc, simply because beginnings and ends of activities are often scheduled.

Still within the same meaning is the notion of total commitment by the speaker – refusal to accept any other possibility, a firm threat to act as in:

Either shé leaves or Í leave.
If he does that again, he goes to prison.

The second sentence could be said under two different sets of circumstances. It could be said where a prison sentence inevitably followed from an action (*eg* where it constituted contempt of court) or it could be said by a judge as a firm threat. These are not, I think, two distinct meanings.

The essential point about both of them is the inevitability – the fixed nature of the course of events.

Not very different is the use of the simple present to confirm future arrangements:

You meet us at the station this evening.

There is hardly a plan or schedule here – merely an agreed arrangement. The present is also used to give directions:

You take the first on the left and then . . .

There is futurity, but not prediction. Rather there is just the one possible inevitable course of action, if you want to arrive at your destination.

3.5.6 Future and habitual combined

There are two ways in which future and habitual uses may be combined.

[i] The simple present is used to refer to a future event that is part of a habitual pattern:

You get tea at five tonight.
The baker calls on Saturday.

This use is not very different from the one we have already considered except that there is reference not to a decision but to a regular pattern. In the second example *on Saturdays* (plural) would have indicated habitual activity. The singular *Saturday* may be taken to indicate the application of the habitual to a single future date.

[ii] The progressives may be used epistemically to refer to habitual intended activity. Examples in the present non-perfect are:

He's always coming to see me (but never does).
She's usually writing in a few days.
He's always taking them on holiday (but hasn't yet).

The other progressive forms may be similarly used epistemically, though this usage is not common and the following examples are a little artificial:

Whenever I wanted to visit him, he was going away the next day.
Whenever I've wanted to visit him, he's been going away the next day.
Whenever I'd wanted to visit him, he'd been going away the next day.

With the first of these two kinds of habitual-futures the adverbials used are of the type that refer to the future – *The baker calls tomorrow.* We can even allow:

I've always read my paper tomorrow.

This could be said at a conference where the speaker always read a paper on a certain day that (at the time of speaking) is 'tomorrow'. With the second kind, the adverbials are mainly of the type that indicates the habitual nature – *He's always coming to see us*, though adverbials that refer to the future, such as *the next day*, are also possible.

3.6 Aspect again

There are two uses of the progressive that, though related to its use to indicate duration, do not directly follow from it. Except with the 'non-progressive verbs' (considered in the next section) both are habitual uses referring to (i) habitual activity over a *limited* period of time, and (ii) habitually repeated but *sporadic* activity.

3.6.1 Limited duration

The progressive is used to indicate habitual activity in a limited[14] period of time in:

He's going to work by bus.
We're eating a lot more meat now.
We've been getting up early this week.
I'd been visiting him every day.

The activity is habitual, but it is over a limited period. In the first example the inference is probably that the man's car has broken down, and that he is now forced (temporarily) to take the bus. If he always went by bus, the non-progressive would be normal:

He goes to work by bus.

The period of time is normally shown to be limited by adverbials, especially *these days* or *in those days.* We may contrast:

We eat a lot of meat. (And always have)
We're eating a lot of meat these days.
I went to work by bus. (All my life)
I was going to work by bus in those days. (Now I have a car)

The present progressive often differs very little in its use from the present perfect, and may even be used with *since*, in spite of the fact that adverbials of this kind mark a period of time characteristic of the perfect:

We're eating more meat since the war.
He's going to work by bus since his car broke down.

In both cases a perfect would equally be possible – *we've been eating*, *he's been going*. With the perfect the period of time is, of course, often limited; *since* marks the limitation. But one important difference is that the present progressive implies the continuance of the activity, even though for a limited period, through present time into the future. The perfect does not.

In the case of the man whose car has broken down then, if the car is now back at his disposal we will expect *He's been going* rather than *He's going*. The latter suggests that the activity, though limited in its duration, is both future and past.

A special use that can, perhaps, be treated under the heading of limited duration is that of showing increasing or decreasing activity, or increase or decrease of some feature of the activity; this has already been mentioned (3.4.1):

More and more people are buying television sets.
They are visiting us more and more often.
They were stealing more and more of his money.
I've been giving him less and less every week.

Non-progressives could be used in all these sentences, but they are far less likely. Adverbials such as *more and more* suggest limited duration.

3.6.2 Sporadic repetition

The progressive is also used to indicate habitual activity that is repeated and sporadic:

She's always breaking things.
The car's always breaking down.

What is happening happens very often, but it does not happen at set times. If there is reference to repeated points of time, indicating regularity, the non-progressive is used:

The car always breaks down when I start for home.

We may contrast:

I always break the eggs first.
I'm always breaking the crockery.

The progressive carries with it too a hint of the speaker's disapproval, especially with adverbials such as *for ever* or *everlastingly*. Some more examples of this use, which is quite common, are:

I was continually falling ill.
They were for ever leaving the gate open.
He's always asking silly questions.
He's for ever losing his money.
They're always getting in the way.
You're continually making poor excuses.
She's been dropping things recently.
He'd been continually stealing from his friends.

In most of these examples there is no suggestion that the activity is continuous – the progressive is used because it is repeated and sporadic. But the activity may be both continuous (at every occasion) and repeated sporadically:

He's always grumbling.
She's for ever writing letters.

Indication of the sporadic nature or the speaker's disapproval of the activity may be carried by the intonation, by *eg*, a high fall on the adverbial or by a 'stepping head' (the first stressed syllable on a high pitch, each succeeding one a step lower) and a low fall.

3.7 Non-progressive verbs

There are some verbs that are commonly not used in the progressive form at all, even where they seem to indicate duration:

I forget his name.
I see my brother over there.
It contains sugar.
They own a lot of property.

These verbs differ from the other verbs of English in that they usually, even in the present tense, occur with the non-progressive. The non-progressive is, in fact, the norm, and progressive forms are used only where there is specific reference to duration or one of the special features indicated by the progressive. There are some fairly obvious reasons why these verbs are used with the non-progressive form, but the reasons apply to them *as a class* and are not valid on each occasion of use. This may be clearly shown by placing together the exactly comparable:

What are you doing?
What do you see?

In neither of these is there specific indication of duration nor is duration specifically excluded. In such circumstances most verbs occur in the progressive form, but the 'non-progressives' in the non-progressive.

There are some verbs such as READ, SLEEP, WORK that refer to non-momentary actions and sometimes occur in the non-progressive with adverbials that indicate duration (3.4.1). These are, perhaps, marginally non-progressive verbs and deserve a separate mention, but they occur quite commonly in the progressive form, and for this reason are not treated in this section as 'non-progressive' verbs.

The verbs fall into two subclasses – verbs of 'state' and 'private' verbs. The reason why these do not normally occur with the progressive is different for each subclass.

3.7.1 Private verbs

Private[15] verbs are those that refer to states or activities that the speaker alone is aware of. These are of two kinds, those that refer to mental activities and those that refer to sensations. Both commonly occur with non-progressive forms.

Examples of verbs referring to mental activities are:

THINK *I think that's mine.*
IMAGINE *I imagine he'll be there.*
HOPE *I hope it's true.*
PLAN *I plan to go to London tomorrow.*
FORGET *I forget what you said.*
BELIEVE *I believe that it's true.*

In all these examples the subject is *I*. But though it is common for the subject to be the first person, this is not always so:

You think you're clever!
Do you remember what he said?

Examples of verbs referring to sensations are:

SEE *I see my brother over there.*
SMELL *I smell something burning.*
HEAR *I hear music.*
TASTE *I taste salt.*
FEEL *I feel something hard.*

Once again these verbs are most common with the first person, but they may occur with other subjects:

He smells something burning.
Do you see that tree over there?

It must be noted here that these verbs very commonly occur with CAN, with no apparent difference in meaning – *I can see . . ., I can smell . . ., Can you feel . . .?*, etc. (5.2.5).

The frequent occurrence of these verbs with first-person subjects gives a clue to the reason why they are so common in the non-progressive. For when these verbs are used, the speaker is in exactly the same position as the commentator – he is reporting something that is not perceived by the hearer (*cf* 3.5.2). Just as the radio commentator uses the non-progressive because his main aim is merely to report, so too the person who reports on his own mental activities or sensations is simply reporting and so uses the non-progressive form. As we have already seen, with most verbs we seldom need simply to report in the present. If we refer to a present activity it is only with reference to its duration, for there is no need to report what can be perceived by the hearer as well as the speaker. But the private verbs have the special characteristic that they refer to activities available for perception by the speaker only. He alone can report them and in so doing uses the appropriate form – the non-progressive.

The verbs can, of course, be used with second or third person subjects, but only to ask about the activity, or to report it at second hand or by inference. *Do you think* . . . is looking for the answer *I think* . . . while *He thinks* . . . is either a report of *I think* . . . or merely a guess. But in all these cases we are merely concerned with a bare statement; duration is not at issue.

The characteristics of the non-progressive verbs apply to them as a class, and, indeed, a class that is formally definable in terms of regular occurrence in the non-progressive. A verb that does not belong to the class will not occur in the non-progressive even if it is reporting a sensation. The verb SUFFER, for instance, does not belong to the class of non-progressive verbs at all – mainly, no doubt, because sufferings are so often observable by both speaker and hearer. Even when a purely private sensation is being reported, the progressive form is used:

I'm suffering from a headache.

There are some other verbs which occur with little or no difference of meaning with progressive or non-progressive forms. These are to be regarded as optional members of the class, *eg*, ACHE, ITCH:

My foot itches/is itching.
My arm aches/is aching.

3·7·2 Verbs of state

There are many verbs which refer not to an activity but to a state or condition. The sense of duration is an integral part of the lexical meaning of the verb, and there is for this reason no need for a progressive form to indicate duration. Examples are:

CONTAIN	*It contains sugar.*
BELONG	*It belongs to me.*
MATTER	*It doesn't matter.*
DESERVE	*He deserves something better than that.*
CONSIST	*It consists of little but water and colouring.*
PLEASE	*It pleases me no end.*
DEPEND	*It depends on what you mean.*
OWN	*I own my own house.*

A rather special subgroup is that of the verbs which indicate the quality of creating sensations, those that may be treated as the intransitive forms of the verbs of sensation:

It smells sweet.
It tastes nice.
It feels soft.

The verbs of sensation SEE and HEAR have no similar intransitive forms. The problem of these is dealt with in the section on homonyms (3·7·4).

3·7·3 Use in progressive

The characteristic of the non-progressive verbs is that they are not normally used in progressive forms, *ie*, that unless there is some specific reference to a feature marked by the progressive, the non-progressive is used. But they are used in certain circumstances with progressive forms. We may contrast the sentences at the beginning of the section with:

I'm forgetting names nowadays.
I'm seeing things.

The private verbs are used with the progressive where there is simply emphasis upon the duration:

I'm actually hearing his voice!

He's seeing stars.
She's hoping all the time that he'll come back.

A more common use is to indicate habitual activity over a limited period (3.6.1):

I'm feeling the cold these days.
He's forgetting names nowadays.
I'm thinking now that we ought perhaps to go.

The progressive is also used for sporadic repetition (3.6.2):

I'm continually forgetting names.
He's always feeling ill.
You're always imagining you'll win a prize.

In other words, the private verbs function in very much the same way as the other verbs, with the sole exception that they are commonly used merely to report and in reporting occur in the non-progressive. But wherever there is specific indication of one of the features associated with the progressive, they too occur with progressive forms.

With the verbs of state the position is a little different. With them there is never emphasis on the duration and they cannot normally be said to have a habitual sense at all since they refer to permanent or semi-permanent states. Yet they are used with progressive forms where there is reference to limited duration, but it is not the limited duration of *habitual* activity:

He's looking better since his operation.
I'm feeling all right now.
We're living in London at the moment.

We may contrast the last of these with:

We live in London.

The progressive form suggests either that we have moved there recently, or that we intend to move soon, or both. The non-progressive indicates that London is our permanent home.

Similarly examples that indicate increasing or decreasing activity are to be found:

He's looking more and more like his father.
It's mattering less and less now.
It's tasting nastier and nastier.

Again these differ from those dealt with previously only in that there can hardly be reference to *habitual* activity.

3·7·4 Homonyms

We have already seen that the verbs SMELL, FEEL and TASTE have two different uses, the one transitive with the sense of having the sensation, the other intransitive with the sense of having the quality to produce the sensation. The verbs are non-progressives in both their senses, but in one sense they belong to the private verbs, in the other to the verbs of state. There is yet a third use, with the meaning 'to act to achieve the sensation'. In this sense the verbs are not non-progressives. Examples of all three uses are:

I smell flowers.
The flowers smell lovely.
I'm smelling the flowers.
I taste salt in the soup.
The soup tastes salty.
The cook is tasting the soup.
I feel something rough.
The cloth feels rough.
I'm feeling the cloth.

The verbs SEE and HEAR are not similarly used in three senses. In comparable senses different verbs are used:

	I see my brother.
(LOOK)	*He looks well.*
(LOOK AT)	*I'm looking at my brother.*
	I hear music.
(SOUND)	*It sounds beautiful.*
(LISTEN TO)	*I'm listening to the music.*

Diagrammatically we have:

(1)	(2)	(3)
SMELL	SMELL	SMELL
TASTE	TASTE	TASTE
FEEL	FEEL	FEEL
SEE	LOOK	LOOK AT
HEAR	SOUND	LISTEN TO

where (1) is a private verb with the sense of 'acquire the sensation', (2) is a verb of state with the sense of 'produce the sensation', and (3) is not a non-progressive verb with the sense of 'act to acquire the sensation'.

In view of the differences of the functions of the verbs and especially in view of the fact that the verbs SEE and HEAR are not used in all three senses, it is as well not to treat these as the same verb (lexeme) at all, but rather to speak of homonyms. It would, of course, be possible to handle them as a special class with a grammatical statement accounting for the three different uses (transitive non-progressive, intransitive non-progressive and transitive progressive). But SEE and HEAR would need to be included; *sound*, *listen to*, *look* and *look at* would have to be treated as forms of these verbs, not lexemes in their own right, in the way that *went* is a form of GO.

Treating these as homonyms (separate lexemes) avoids any suggestion that *I smell the flowers* and *I'm smelling the flowers* can be accounted for simply in terms of the durational characteristics of the progressive versus the non-progressive. For it is more than that. In the first SMELL belongs to the class of non-progressive verbs, in the second SMELL does not. But there are many other forms that raise problems. The difficulty arises from the fact that there are many contrasts of progressive and non-progressive forms in which there is clearly a difference of durational aspect, but in which this is not the only difference of meaning. With these there is reason for suggesting that we have again cases of homonymy; this accounts not only for the difference in the progressive/non-progressive category (for one only is a non-progressive verb), but also for the difference in meaning:

I imagine he'll come.	(think)
You're imagining things.	(having hallucinations)
I plan to go tomorrow.	(intend)
I'm planning my holidays.	(making arrangements)
I think he'll come.	(believe)
I'm thinking about it.	(pondering)

It will obviously be difficult in some cases to decide whether to treat the differences of progressive and non-progressive in terms of verb classes (the non-progressives versus the rest) or to handle them purely in terms of the uses of the progressive/non-progressive category. Consider:

Now I'm remembering.

We might say that the progressive form is used because it emphasizes the duration, or perhaps indicates limited duration. Alternatively we might argue that REMEMBER here has the meaning of 'make a conscious effort to remember' and that with this meaning it is not a non-progressive verb at all. We are at the borderline of lexis and grammar, and some of our decisions will have to be arbitrary.

3.8 Phase again

3.8.1 Problem uses

There are three uses of the perfect that need some comment.

[i] Very recent activity is indicated by *just* with the perfect:

I've just seen him.
He's just gone.
I've just been waving goodbye to him.

These are, presumably, 'current relevance' perfect form – the activity does not continue up to the present time. The use of *just* here can only be accounted for if it is seen as a present time adverbial – to mean in a brief period of time preceding, but up to the present moment. The adverb is, in fact, used unambiguously as a present time marker in:

They're just arriving.

But it is also used as a past time adverb:

I just saw him leave.
He just went out of the door.

The function of *just* is thus like that of *today*. Yet semantically it is a little odd for there is little or no current relevance in the examples we first quoted – the sentences are no different from:

I saw him a moment ago.
He went a moment ago.

Here the present perfect cannot be used. It is, then, to some degree a formal fact that *just* is used with the present perfect. In British English there is a much greater tendency to use the present perfect than in American English where the simple past is common. The problem does not arise with the past perfect since this is both 'past perfect' and 'past past' (3.3.4).

[ii] The perfect with accent on the auxiliary (and usually with a fall-rise intonation) is used to refer to past experiences:

I háve read Oliver Twist.
She hás visited Paris.

The use of the perfect is to be explained on the grounds that past experiences are part of a person's present make-up – that reading 'Oliver Twist' is included among the experiences that make me what I am.

[iii] The verb BE is used with a special meaning with the perfect, and with the perfect alone occurs with *to:*

I've been to London.
He'd been to my house.

We will not attest, however:

**I am to London* (or **I was to London*).
**He was to my house.*

With the perfect and followed by *to* the verb has the meaning of having gone and returned. There is a difference, then, between:

He's gone to London.
He's been to London.

In the former he is still in London; in the latter, he has returned. Quite commonly the verb occurs in the use mentioned in (ii), to refer to past experiences:

I hàve been to London (but it was years ago).

3.8.2 Displaced phase

In spoken English forms occur that are not strictly 'correct' in terms of what we have already said about phase. Phase sometimes seems to be doubly marked as in:

I should have liked to have seen him.

We would expect rather:

I should have liked to see him.

The former would be marked as 'incorrect' by some speakers of English who are even unaware that they themselves produce such forms.

There is also sometimes sequence of tense (or sequence of phase, rather) as in:

He's always said he's been willing.

When we look to more complex sentences the phase marking becomes a little obscure. Consider:

Every time I've seen them, they've been swimming.

This is most likely to be interpreted to mean that they were swimming at the time at which I saw them – the perfect indicating that the period of time that includes my series of visits and of their swimming goes right up to the present time. But the sentence might also mean that at the time of each of my visits they had (previously) been swimming. The ambiguity arises from the fact that the perfect may be used to refer either to the overall period of time that we are talking about, or in addition about each repeated period. The overall period of time is clearly shown by *Every time I've seen them* to be one that began in the past and continues up to the present moment. But the successive periods of time that are to be related to the series of points of time – my seeing them – may either be periods that simply overlap these points of time (non-perfect type), or they may be periods that began before and continued up to the points of time. This may be shown diagrammatically:

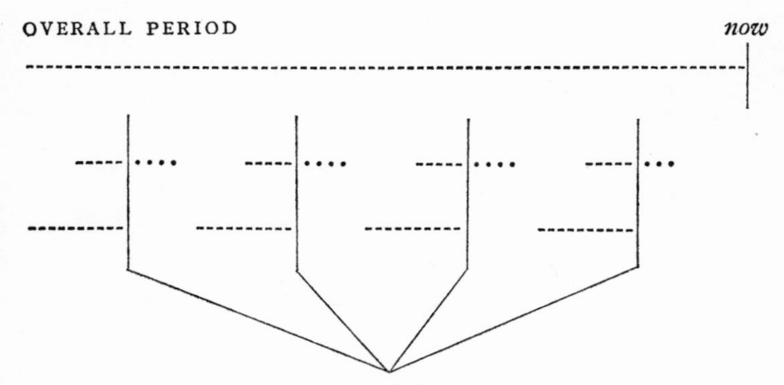

Every time I've seen them

The second interpretation is unlikely unless clearly marked. But there are situations in which the distinction is very clear:

Whenever I've tried carpentry, I've cut my finger.
Whenever I've had to go to the doctor, I've cut my finger.

Clearly in the first the finger-cutting and carpentry are simultaneous, in the second the finger-cutting is previous to the visit to the doctor (but related in terms of current relevance).

In the second interpretation the perfect form is 'doubly' perfect. We want to say the impossible:

**They have been having been swimming.*
**I have been having cut my finger.*

The past perfect is, perhaps, also possible here (for this meaning only):

Whenever I've seen them, they'd been swimming.
Whenever I've had to go to the doctor, I'd cut my finger.

But we are in an odd area of uncertainty of usage.

Notes

1 For the auxiliaries an important work is Twaddell (1960).
2 For 'phase' and 'aspect', see Joos (1964: 126, 138).
3 Palmer and Blandford (1939: 131).
4 Hill (1958: 220).
5 Lakoff (1970: 839).
6 Huddleston (1969: 787) who, however, sees two distinct tenses here.
7 See Crystal (1966).
8 Diver (1963); see Palmer (1967: 189–91).
9 Joos (1964: 121).
10 Twaddell (1960: 6).
11 See also Hatcher (1951).
12 Hill (1958: 207–11).
13 Austin (1962: 4).
14 See Twaddell (1960: 8).
15 Joos quoted in Hill (1958: 207).

Chapter 4

Voice

A complete chapter is devoted to voice, not because of its importance in the system of the verb, but because it is syntactically so very different from the three other verbal categories.

The first section will deal with voice proper – with the passive.[1] The second considers some related structures that are active in form yet have close semantic and syntactic relations with the passive.

4.1 The passive

At the most formal level the passive is defined in terms of the last eight forms of the primary pattern. It should be recalled, however, (3.1.1) that perfect progressive forms in the passive are rare and improbable. To passivize the active perfect progressive we should normally use the corresponding non-progressive passive (even though the progressive is then no longer marked):

The doctors have been examining him all morning.
He has been examined all morning by the doctors.
? He has been being examined all morning by the doctors.

There are, however, syntactic features that have to be taken into consideration.

4.1.1 Transformation

The passive is par excellence the grammatical structure that exemplifies the concept of transformation.[2] For let us consider:

John plays the piano.

We can change the tense, aspect or phase (or any combination of these) to produce:

John played the piano.
John is playing the piano.
John has played the piano.
John had been playing the piano.

But we cannot change the voice to give:

**John is played the piano.*

Rather we need a transformation that involves a change in position of the subject and the object (as well as the addition of *by*):

The piano is played by John.

It follows from this that the passive is possible only with transitive verbs (*ie* those that may have objects). There is no similar restriction on the other verbal categories.

It is possible to write a simple and general formula for the formation of the passive from the active:

$NP_1\ V_{act}\ NP_2 \rightarrow NP_2\ V_{pass}\ \textit{by}\ NP_1$

Here V_{act} and V_{pass} stand for 'active verb' and 'passive verb' respectively.

It was thought, before the idea of transformation was proposed, that active and passive sentences are related semantically only. But a little consideration will show that voice (with transformation) is no less formal than tense (or aspect or phase). For, first, transformation must take place to preserve the grammaticality of the sentence, and, with rare exceptions, every active sentence has a corresponding passive one. Secondly, however, we can see that the same collocational relations hold between the noun phrases and the verb, though with a change in the position of these noun phrases. This is no more problematic than establishing the grammatical relationship between past and present. For morphological shape alone will not establish that *took* is the past tense of TAKE, rather than of TALK. But the collocational relations soon make this clear (as do the semantics, of course):

He took the money.
He takes the money.
**He talks the money.*

The active/passive relationship is, in principle, no different.

There is one very important syntactic point about the passive – that there may be no second NP (the one preceded by *by*). The NP that is the subject of the active sentence may, that is to say, be omitted:

The boy was killed.
The thieves were caught.

There are no actual corresponding active sentences, though for some purposes it may be useful to postulate them, using the symbol △ for the 'dummy' subject:

△ *killed the boy.*
△ *caught the thieves.*

4.1.2 Transitivity

The passive rule in formulaic terms mentioned only NP_1 and NP_2 – *ie* noun phrases designated solely by their position in the sentence. Yet at the same time it was said that passivization was possible with transitive verbs, *ie* those that have objects.

It is clear that not all noun phrases that follow the verb may become the subject of the passive. We shall not passivize:

The baker comes every day.
**Every day is come by the baker.*

The reason is obvious – *every day* is an adverbial, not the object of *comes.* But we cannot merely say that it is only the object of the verb that becomes the subject of the passive sentence. There are two clear exceptions to this.[3]

[i] A very common passive form is that exemplified by:

The boy was given a present by the teacher.
We have been told lies.
The children were left a small fortune.

The corresponding active forms are:

The teacher gave the boy a present.
△ *told us lies.*
△ *left the children a small fortune.*

Our formula in terms of NP_1 and NP_2 is perfectly valid for all these sentences – the second NP takes initial position when the sentence is passivized. But NP_2, *the boy, us, the children* is in traditional terms the 'indirect' object while the third NP, *a present, lies, a small fortune* is the 'direct' object. This is to some degree verified by the fact that these direct objects can equally be the subject of the passive:

A present was given to the boy by the teacher.
Lies were told to us.
A small fortune was left to the children.

However it could be argued that these are the passives of active sentences containing *to* (which appears in the passive):

The teacher gave a present to the boy.
△ *told lies to us.*
△ *left a small fortune to the children.*

Moreover, it is not simply *to* that may be involved in this syntactic complex. *For* also occurs with exactly the same set of sentences:

He bought John a book.
John was bought a book.
He bought a book for John.
A book was bought for John.

Perhaps the simplest way of handling the sentences is to say that GIVE, TELL, LEAVE, BRING are 'di-transitive' verbs – that they may take two objects, as well as a single object plus *to*/*for* and noun phrase. With passivization the object still becomes the subject of the passive (the first object where there are two). The two active constructions thus account for the passives.

[ii] There are many sequences of verb and preposition that may be passivized even though the second NP is clearly not the object of the verb but part of the prepositional phrase:

He looked after the old man.
The old man was looked after by him.
They had sat in the chair.
The chair had been sat in.

Many, but not all of these are 'prepositional verbs', which are discussed in detail in **8.4.4**. There is a similar situation with the 'phrasal prepositional verbs':

This noise cannot be put up with.
She was done away with.

It is true also of similar constructions of the type (**8.5.2**):

The matter was taken care of.
The house was set fire to.
The rubbish was soon got rid of.

In all these examples it is clear that the verb plus the following element is treated, for the purposes of passivization, as a single unit – and there are semantic reasons for this (see Chapter 8).

There are also verbs that seem to be transitive and to have objects that nevertheless never, or rarely, occur in the passive, *eg* RESEMBLE, LACK:

John resembles his father.
**His father is resembled by John.*
The car lacks a mirror.
**A mirror is lacked by the car.*

With some verbs the passive is possible with one meaning where there is activity, but not in another where there is indication only of a state:

The jar holds oil.
**Oil is held by the jar.*
The thief was held by the police.
The king possessed great wealth.
**Great wealth was possessed by the king.*
The city was soon possessed by the enemy.

Other such verbs are CONTAIN and HAVE (see **6.1.2**). More idiosyncratic are the different meanings of MARRY and EQUAL:

Jack married Jill.
**Jill was married by Jack.*
They were married by the priest.
Two and two equals four.
**Four is equalled by two and two.*
He is equalled in strength by no one.

There is a slight problem with noun phrases indicating quantity ('How much?'). These will not normally occur as the subject of the passive, as illustrated by:

The book weighs a pound.
**A pound was weighed by the book.*
The boy grew six inches.
**Six inches were grown by the boy.*

We should, I think, wish to say that these verbs were intransitive, though they also have transitive functions (see below **4.2.1**). When transitive they passivize:

The greengrocer weighed the plums.
The plums were weighed by the greengrocer.

The gardener grew the beans.
The beans were grown by the gardener.

If this is correct, *a pound* and *six inches* are not the objects of the verb while *the plums* and *the beans* are. Their precise status is unclear – but they function as a kind of adverbial. They are, however, borderline. Notice that we can use *what?* with WEIGH, but not with GROW (in the first sense):

What did it weigh?
! What did he grow?

With verbs that explicitly indicate measurement – WEIGH, MEASURE, TOTAL, COST, etc *what* may be used; with others a form that indicates the kind of measurement is needed:

What does it measure?
How long did the session take?
How far does it stretch?

Although the possibility of *what* might seem to indicate that these are transitive verbs with objects (as opposed to *how far* which is clearly adverbial), it does not correlate with the possibility of passivization.

Slightly different is the contrast illustrated by:

He ran a mile to work.
**A mile to work was run by him.*
Bannister first ran a mile in four minutes.
A mile was first run in four minutes by Bannister.

We must, presumably, distinguish between two kinds of RUN A MILE. Only in the sense of running on the race track is passivization possible.

4.1.3 The meaning of the passive

It is far from clear why or when the passive is used. There are, perhaps, three points.

[i] The passive is used when the 'agent' (see below 4.2.1) – the subject of the active verb – is unknown or unspecified:

He was killed.
That work was soon completed.
The water was quickly boiled.

For this reason, it is very common in scientific writing – especially in reports on research, for the work may be described impersonally –

without indicating who did it.[4] 'Agentless' passives, as these are called, are a most useful device for not providing irrelevant or undesirable information.

[ii] The use of the passive often permits 'thematization',[5] *ie* the placing of a certain noun phrase in subject position for the purpose of prominence. This is particularly useful in narrative to retain the same subject in successive sentences (or in a sentence with coordinate clauses):

John came in. He was immediately welcomed by the committee.
John came in and was immediately welcomed by the committee.

[iii] One difference has already been noticed – that related to perfect and current relevance. We have to contrast (if Queen Victoria is no longer alive):

Bath has been visited by Queen Victoria.
**Queen Victoria has visited Bath.*

This is, perhaps, closely related to 'thematization'.

There is a useful sense, however, in which it can be said that the passive has no meaning. We often wish to say that a sentence may be passivized without change of meaning. The test of passivization is used to distinguish simple and complex phrases (**2.1.4**, **3.1.8**, **5.1.2**), where the lack of meaning change is one criterion (though it can always be supported, with the right examples, by collocational restrictions). What is meant is that there is no true difference in the truth conditions – that if the active is true so is the passive. Where this is so we shall talk of 'voice neutrality'.[6]

There appear to be other more formal explanations for the use of the passive.

[i] It is rarer with the progressive than with the perfect or the modals (and this may account for the near-impossibility of the passive perfect progressive).

[ii] It is common where the agent is long (in terms of number of words, and especially when the agent is coordinate (two or more noun phrases joined by *and*)).[7] The passive is to some degree a device for placing long (and 'weighty') agents in final position.

[iii] Reflexives and parts of the body of the subject that occur as objects in the active will not occur as subjects of the passive:

John blamed himself.
**Himself was blamed by John.*

John washed his face.
**His face was washed by John.*

4.1.4 Statal passives

There is a clear distinction between *were married* in:

They were married last year.
They were married when I saw them.

In the first we have a past passive (verbal) form. In the second there is a form of the full verb (copula) BE plus an *-en* form that functions as an adjective.

Forms of the second kind have been the subject of considerable discussion, but their status is in no real doubt. Semantically the *-en* adjectival form carries the time relation of the perfect:

The glass has been broken.	(verbal)
The glass is broken.	(adjectival)
My bags have been packed.	(verbal)
My bags are packed.	(adjectival)
They have been divorced.	(verbal)
They are divorced.	(adjectival)

Ambiguity is, of course, inevitable. All of the verbal examples above could be interpreted as adjectival (*ie* that the glass was once broken but no longer is, that my bags were once packed but are now unpacked, that they were once divorced but are together again). In practice such ambiguity is easily resolved.

There are a number of arguments to show the adjectival nature of these *-en* forms:

[i] They occur with *already* with a present tense verb (*already* normally requires the perfect):

My bags are already packed.
They are already divorced.
**I pack my bags already.*
**He divorces her already.*
I have already packed my bags.
He has already divorced her.

[ii] They may be coordinated with adjectives:

They were happy when I saw them.
They were married and happy when I saw them.

[iii] They occur with verbs other than BE:

They look married.
My bags will stay packed.

These forms raise no problem within the analysis of voice.[8]

4.1.5 GET

This is a suitable place to look at GET. For although it is also handled among the catenatives (7.3.3), it could be argued that it is an alternative to BE in the formation of the passive:

He was killed by the bus.
He got killed by the bus.

GET here is unlike BECOME, LOOK, etc, the verbs that are sometimes called 'linking verbs' in that they occur only with adjectival *-en* forms. For we cannot say:

**He became killed by the bus.*
**He looked killed by the bus.*

GET does not, therefore, substitute with BE in the statal passive type – but in the normal passive.

However, semantically, forms with GET have much in common with statal passives. GET always suggests that the person or object designated by the subject NP has undergone some change or has been in some way affected – with lasting effect. It could not be used, for instance, in such sentences as:

**The lesson got read by the choirboy.*
**The letter got written by the poet.*

We are not here reporting some change in the state of the lesson or the letter – and though BE is appropriate, GET is not. But we can quite naturally say:

The ball got lost.
The child got punished by the teacher.

GET, unlike the passive, implies that the person or object was in the state of having been killed, punished, lost, etc after the event. Semantically, GET reports both the action and the resultant state. *The ball got lost* says both *The ball was lost* (passive) and *The ball was lost* (statal passive). It can thus be seen either as a process verb with an *-en* form while BE is purely statal, or as combining the two functions of BE.

4.2 Related structures

There are several types of active sentences that are both semantically and syntactically like the passive.

4.2.1 'Case' relations

It has long been known that many verbs in English function both as transitives and intransitives, *eg* RING and BREAK in:

He rang the bell.
The bell rang.
The wind broke the window.
The window broke.

The significant point is that the object of the transitive verb is the subject of the intransitive. Syntactically, and to some degree semantically, the intransitive is like the passive:

The bell rang.
The bell was rung.
The window broke.
The window was broken.

There is more than this, however. Consider OPEN:

The door opened.
The boy opened the door.
The key opened the door.
The boy opened the door with the key.

The last sentence illustrates the maximum number of noun phrases that appear to be directly associated with the verb. In semantic (and fairly traditional) terms we may refer to *the boy* as the 'agent' (or 'actor'), *the door* as the 'goal' and *the key* as the 'instrument', or describe them in terms of three 'cases'[9] – 'agentive', 'objective' and 'instrumental'. The sentences we considered show that agent, goal and instrument may all function as the grammatical subject. But there are some severe restrictions. First, the goal must always be present. We cannot say:

**The key opened.*
**The boy opened.*

Secondly, priority for subject place is given to agent, instrument and goal *in that order*. *ie* (*a*) the goal can be subject only if the other two are absent, (*b*) the instrument can be subject only if the agent is absent. Hence we cannot say:

**The door opened with a key.*
**The door opened by the boy.*
**The key opened the door by the boy.*

(For *The door opens with a key* see 4.2.2.) The goal can, as we know, occur as subject if the verb is passive:

The door was opened with a key.
The door was opened by the boy.

It is clear from this that the transitive/intransitive functions of verbs like OPEN must be handled together with voice.

Generally the instrument is marked by the preposition *with*, but there are some sentences in which it could be argued that it is marked by *by:*

The steel was heated by the fire.

The corresponding active sentence is:

The fire heated the steel.

Alternatively, of course, it could be argued that *by* indicates the agent. This has some semantic plausibility since the sentence suggests that there was no active participation by human agents. They are thus different from:

The steel was heated with the fire.
The men heated the steel with the fire.

We can compare too:

The wind rustled the leaves.
The leaves were rustled by the wind.

Is *the wind* the agent or the instrument? It has been suggested that agents must always be animate.[10] But more plausibly we should perhaps distinguish agent and instrument only where both are syntactically (and perhaps semantically) present. Where they are not both present we have simply a 'causer' that may be animate or inanimate and indistinguishably either 'agent' or 'instrument'.

The statements concerning 'instruments' are valid also for some noun phrases that seem rather to be 'locative' – indicating the 'place where':

The article shows that . . .
He showed in his article that . . .

Semantically there is not a great deal of difference; *in his article* means something like 'by what he wrote in his article'. But formally *in* functions like (and raises the same problems as) *with*.

The semantic relations between the transitive and intransitive are of a variety of kinds. The examples we have considered are close to that of active and passive – the intransitive like the agentless passive merely leaving the 'agent' unstated. But this is not enough for:

The soldiers marched.
The sergeant marched the soldiers.

For in the first *the soldiers* is surely the agent since marching is a voluntary action. *The sergeant* semantically represents a further 'causative' element – the one who caused someone else to act. The passive as a result is very different semantically from the intransitive:

The soldiers were marched.

There is, however, little or no causation in:

He walked the children across the road.
I'll run you to the station.

Both have rather the same sense of accompaniment. The first means 'walked with the children'. The second is semantically more complex; it relates presumably to running a car, *ie* to mean 'run the car with you in it'. But the syntax is clear enough – and it is syntactically that these intransitive/transitive forms resemble voice.

4.2.2 'Pseudo-passives'

Many verbs can be used in a 'passive' sense in such sentences as:

These shirts wash well.
The meat cuts easily.
Oranges are selling cheaply today.

The contrast of active and passive meaning is clear enough in a much quoted pair of sentences:

They're selling like experts.
They're selling like hot cakes.

But there is also a clear distinction between these 'pseudo-passives' and the intransitives that were discussed in the previous subsection. This is illustrated by the ambiguity of:

The door doesn't open in wet weather.[11]

This can either mean that it stays shut (intransitive) or that it cannot be opened ('pseudo-passive'). There is, however, no ambiguity in:

The door opens with a key.

The intransitive interpretation is ruled out here (see 4.2.1) *ie* to mean that it is regularly opened with a key. It can only mean that it can be opened with a key.

There is, perhaps, also a special use of WILL with these pseudo-passives (see 5.2.2).

These uses of the active in the 'passive' sense are 'adverbial' in that they normally occur with adverbs and indicate how the items are or are being washed, cut, sold, etc. *The shirts wash well* means that they can be or are washed successfully. *They're selling like hot cakes* means that they are being sold as quickly as the proverbial hot cakes. The non-progressive seems to indicate potentiality – they can be washed, cut, sold, etc, or, perhaps, a quality rather than an action. This usage seems to be confined to action verbs. For we cannot say:

**These people like easily.*

This ought, one might think, to be possible – to mean that it is easy to like them, but it is an impossible sentence.

Notes

1 For one of the most complete modern works see Svartvik (1966).
2 See Chomsky (1957) and a vast amount of subsequent literature.
3 Joos (1964:94) refers to these as 'secondary' and 'tertiary' passives.
4 Svartvik (1966:70) notes that one of his scientific texts has four times more passives than either of two novels that he examined.
5 This is a subject largely neglected in American and British linguistics, but discussed in detail by the Czechs. See *eg* Firbas (1964) but also Halliday (1967) and Huddleston (1971:315ff).
6 Huddleston (1969:258).
7 Svartvik (1966:71).
8 Svartvik (1966), curiously, hardly recognizes the distinction at all, while Huddleston (1971:97–104) devotes a great deal of discussion to it. But I can see no need for extensive justification of such an obvious distinction.
9 Fillmore (1968).
10 Fillmore (1968:24).
11 Halliday (1968:167).

Chapter 5

The modals

The modal auxiliaries WILL, SHALL, CAN, MAY, MUST, OUGHT, DARE and NEED function in what we have called the 'secondary' pattern of the 'simple' verb phrase.

5.1 Syntax of the modals

The modals raise a number of problems of syntax. In particular, their status as auxiliaries (and so as forms functioning within the simple phrase) is a matter for investigation. The distinction auxiliary/full verb is a useful one, but in no way absolute.

5.1.1 The paradigms

If we take WILL as an example, the possible forms (again sixteen – see 4.1.1) are:

(1)	*will*	*take*			
(2)	*would*	*take*			
(3)	*will*	*be*		*taking*	
(4)	*would*	*be*		*taking*	
(5)	*will*	*have*	*taken*		
(6)	*would*	*have*	*taken*		
(7)	*will*	*have*	*been*	*taking*	
(8)	*would*	*have*	*been*	*taking*	
(9)	*will*	*be*			*taken*
(10)	*would*	*be*			*taken*
(11)	*will*	*be*		*being*	*taken*
(12)	*would*	*be*		*being*	*taken*

(13) *will*	*have*	*been*		*taken*
(14) *would*	*have*	*been*		*taken*
(15) *will*	*have*	*been*	*being*	*taken* (?)
(16) *would*	*have*	*been*	*being*	*taken* (?)

This is essentially an extension of the paradigms of the primary pattern – by the addition of the forms of WILL, *will* and *would*. The finite forms of the primary pattern are replaced by the corresponding infinitive (second column). The infinitive does not, of course, mark tense; this is marked instead by the forms of WILL. As in the primary pattern, therefore, the first form is finite and marks tense; all the other categories are marked in exactly the same way as in the primary pattern.

There is only a 'basic' paradigm; there are no participials, infinitival or imperatival phrases, since the modals have no participles, infinitives or imperatives.

SHALL, CAN and MAY have a similar set of sixteen possible forms. MUST, OUGHT, DARE and NEED make no distinction of tense and, therefore, have paradigms of only eight (these are in most respects present rather than past tense, as we shall see). OUGHT is idiosyncratic in that it alone of the modals (unless we include BE – **6.1.1** (iii)) is followed by the *to*-infinitive rather than the bare infinitive. But the close association of *to* with the preceding auxiliary is shown by the fact that there is, in normal conversation, a single not a double ('geminate') [t] – [ɔːtə] rather than [ɔːt tə] (see **9.5**).

Numbers 15 and 16 are again marked with a question mark. They are even more unlikely to occur than the corresponding forms of the primary pattern. Numbers 11 and 12 are also marginal and are marked as 'wanting' in one grammar.[1] Where the semantics might seem to require these progressive forms (duration of the activity) non-progressive forms would be normal. The following is not impossible, but unusual:

?He'll be being examined, while we are there.

More normal is:

He'll be examined, while we are there.

It is assumed in the paradigm that *will* and *would* are the present and past tense forms of WILL and that similarly *shall* and *should*, *can* and *could*, *may* and *might* are the forms of SHALL, CAN and MAY. This interpretation is, I believe, basically correct though the function of tense has a very different set of emphases from that of the non-modal forms.

To begin with, the most obvious function of past tense is to mark tentativeness – which is comparatively rare with the non-modal forms (3.2.3) *eg:*

Will you help me?
Would you help me?
I can do that for you.
I could do that for you.
He may come tomorrow.
He might come tomorrow.

The second of each pair is less positive, more tentative. (But we cannot pair *shall* and *should* in the same way – see 5.3.4.)

In only a very small number of uses of the modals does past tense, in fact, mark past time:

He can run ten miles with ease.
When he was young he could run ten miles with ease.

This function of tense is not only rare, but there are also considerable restrictions.

The most important argument for the treatment of *would*, *should*, etc as past tense forms is found in their function in reported speech. It will be recalled (3.2.2) that with a past tense form of reporting, a present tense in the original speech is reported by its corresponding past tense form. This is exactly what happens with the modals:

I'll come.	*I said I'd come.*
I shall come.	*I said I should come.*
I can come.	*I said I could come.*
I may come.	*I said I might come.*

This is a clear grammatical test and establishes the tense relationship beyond all doubt.

There will be a more detailed discussion of tense and the modals in 5.3.

5.1.2 Auxiliary and full verb

The treatment of the modals as auxiliaries was based initially upon their functions with relation to negation, inversion, code and emphatic affirmation (2.2).

A second argument is provided by the paradigms. The paradigm for the modals shows that there are severe restrictions of combination with other forms. For the modals have no finite form and as a result of (or perhaps because of) this can occur only in initial position. They cannot, therefore, combine with each other. There is no possibility of **is shalling* or **has would*. With other verbs, the catenatives, there is much greater freedom. Nor can they change their position when combined with other verbs. Hence:

I ought to begin.
**I begin to ought.*

No such restrictions exist for the other verbs – the catenatives. We have:

I want to begin.
I begin to want.

It is, moreover, possible to have sequences of almost any length (*cf p* 166).

Yet there are some respects in which the modals are more similar to full verbs, *ie* catenatives, than they are to the primary auxiliaries. Let us again consider the tests for simple and complex phrases (2.1.4), comparing the primary auxiliaries as characteristic of simple phrases (3.1.8), and the catenatives as typical of complex ones (7.1.2).

[i] Tense is a feature that is present once only in a simple phrase. In a complex phrase it may be marked twice, as the following examples show:

He happens to live there.
He happened to live there.
He happens to have lived there last year.
He happened to have lived there the year before.

In these examples the second verb is marked for past tense by *have*; the fact that it is past tense and not perfect is clear from the adverbials, *last year* and *the year before* (see 3.3.4). The pattern is the same with some of the modals. The clearest set is provided by the negative forms of CAN:

He can't be there now.
He couldn't be there yesterday.
He can't have been there yesterday.
He couldn't have been there the day before.

It may be apparent that this set of four forms combine some quite different uses of the modals; in particular we have both 'epistemic' and 'non-epistemic' (5.1.4). But the point concerning the marking of tense is still valid.

[ii] Negation may be present once only in a simple phrase. In a complex phrase it may be marked at least twice:

I prefer to come.
I don't prefer to come.
I prefer not to come.
I don't prefer not to come.

Both PREFER and COME may thus be negated. This is not, of course, possible with a simple phrase. Negation is marked once only:

He has come.
He hasn't come.
He is coming.
He isn't coming.

With the modals it seems that we can in fact mark negation twice as in:

We can go with them.
We can't go with them.
We can not go with them.
We can't not go with them.

The third and fourth examples need a few comments. The fourth is certainly possible and indeed fairly normal, with the meaning that we cannot refuse to go with them. The third is perhaps more easily understood if we add *always:*

We can always not go with them.

This has the meaning that we can always refuse to go with them. But it is not possible to find all four possibilities with all the modals in all the meanings – not, for instance, for the WILL of future (5.2.1), or for the generalizing CAN or MAY (5.2.7).

For MUST there is a different argument in favour of recognizing the possibility of double negation. For although there is a form *mustn't*, this does not negate the modal (as *can't*, for instance, does), but the following verb. To negate the modal, the formal negative of NEED, *needn't*, is used (or perhaps *may not*, see 5.3.5). If we compare these forms with the first three of the PREFER examples the pattern seems to be:

I prefer to go.	*I must go.*
I don't prefer to go.	*I needn't go.*
I prefer not to go.	*I mustn't go.*

Possibly there are also the forms *I needn't not go* and *I mustn't not go* (=*I needn't refuse to go, I mustn't refuse to go*). The first parallels *I don't prefer not to go;* the second actually suggests that there is a complex of three verb phrases. But this shows how imprecise is any attempt to establish phrasal structure of this kind.

[iii] With a simple phrase the whole may be passivized with no change of meaning. There is 'voice neutrality' (4.1.3):

John has seen Mary.
Mary has been seen by John.
John is visiting Mary.
Mary is being visited by John.

This would not be the case with a catenative such as WANT:

John wants to meet Mary.
!Mary wants to be met by John.

These are not related in terms of passivization; the most obvious reason is that *wants to meet* is not a simple phrase. We then have a problem with:

John will meet Mary.
Mary will be met by John.

If WILL is taken to refer to simple futurity (5.2.1), these are related in terms of passivization. If, however, WILL is used for volition (5.2.2) to mean (roughly) 'is willing to', the position is exactly the same as with the WANT examples above; it does not follow that if John wants or is willing to meet Mary, Mary wants or is willing to be met by John. Again this provides evidence that with the modals we do not strictly have a simple phrase. However, it could be argued that this test is not proof of the simple or complex nature of a phrase. For the following pair are also related in terms of passivization:

John happened to see Mary.
Mary happened to be seen by John.

Is *happened to see* then a simple phrase? Voice neutrality is a characteristic of the 'subject complementation' catenatives, which are almost 'pseudo-modal' (7.2.3, 7.4.9).

All of these tests suggest that the modals are in some respects more like the catenatives than the primary auxiliaries, and that the phrases in which they occur are complex. But they lack the freedom of combination that the catenatives have, and are still best regarded as part of a close-knit sequence. Whether the term 'simple phrase' is still appropriate is little more than a matter of terminology.

5.1.3 Subject and discourse orientation

Most scholars who have considered the semantics of the modals have seen that they appear to be paired: WILL and SHALL, CAN and MAY, MUST and OUGHT, DARE and NEED.

This pairing relates to what I shall call 'subject orientation' and 'discourse orientation'. Strictly, this is a classification not of the modals themselves but of their uses; but with certain qualifications (see end of this subsection) WILL and CAN are subject oriented, while SHALL and MAY are discourse oriented. It is these four that we shall use for illustration here; but the distinction is also relevant to OUGHT and MUST (5.2.8), and perhaps obvious, but less important, for DARE and NEED (5.2.9).

The subject oriented modals relate semantically to some kind of activity, quality, status, etc of the subject of the sentence, while the discourse oriented modals relate rather to the part played by one of the participants in the discourse (the speaker in statements, the hearer in questions). This is well illustrated by WILL and SHALL in:

John will come tomorrow.
John shall come tomorrow.

In the first it is John who agrees to come, while in the second it is the speaker who agrees and guarantees that John will come. There is a similar contrast in:

Bill can run a mile in four minutes.
Bill may go now.

In the first it is Bill who has the quality that permits him to run a mile. In the second it is the speaker who permits him to go.

I have referred to these as 'discourse oriented' modals rather than 'speaker oriented' modals because, although in statements such as those illustrated here the modal relates to the speaker, in questions it relates to the hearer. In statements it is the speaker who guarantees, gives permission, etc; in questions it is the hearer from whom a guarantee or permission is sought. This is illustrated by:

Shall I come tomorrow?
May John go now?

There is a further point to notice with *we*. *We* refers to *you and I* or *he/she/they and I*. But with discourse oriented modals it is usually the speaker alone (*I*) who guarantees or permits the action, though the action is undertaken by all those indicated by the pronoun (*we*). Thus in *we shall*, *we may*, the speaker says, in effect, 'I guarantee/promise that we . . .'.

There is a sense in which the discourse oriented modals (together with the epistemic modals that are soon to be discussed) are the 'true' modals, those that mark 'modality' as opposed to providing information or being part of the propositional content of the sentence. They are part of the 'speech act', have 'illocutionary force'[2] in that they are not used to state or question but to promise, permit, etc or to seek promises or permission. The subject oriented modals are not in this sense true modals and so are much more like full verbs, *ie* catenatives; they seem to belong more to complex than to simple phrases. They provide information about the subject who is (in a loose sense at least) the actor – the one who 'can' or 'will'.

There are some formal distinctions (that have semantic explanations) related to the distinction between subject oriented and discourse oriented modals.

[i] The subject oriented modals alone have past tense forms for past time. The discourse oriented modals SHALL and MAY have no such forms – for one cannot guarantee or permit action to take place in the past. There are, however, some restrictions on the subject oriented modals too (see 5.3.1).

[ii] The discourse oriented modals usually allow passivization:

John shall meet Mary.
Mary shall be met by John.
John may meet Mary.
Mary may be met by John.

This is not so with all the subject oriented modals:

John won't meet Mary.
!Mary won't be met by John.

The semantic explanation is obvious – with the subject oriented modals the modal relates to characteristics of the subject and the subject is changed with passivization, but with the discourse oriented modal it is unrelated to the subject or any other element within the sentence. (But for the conditions under which subject oriented modals permit passivization and discourse oriented ones do not, see 5.3.7.)

[iii] Formal negation of the modal negates the modal itself with the subject oriented modals:

John will come.
John won't come. (is not willing)
John can run a mile.
John can't run a mile. (is not able)

With the discourse oriented modals the position is more complex. With SHALL the full verb is negated – the speaker positively undertakes that the action will not take place:

He shall not go.

With MAY, however, it is the modal that is negated; the meaning is that permission is not given, not that permission is given that the action shall not take place:

He may not go.

We can now see the difference between SHALL and MAY (and similarly between WILL and CAN). SHALL and WILL are essentially 'initiative' – they refer to the initiation of the action. MAY and CAN are essentially 'permissive' – they indicate that the action is in some sense possible.

As was noted at the beginning of this subsection there are some qualifications to the classification of the modals themselves in terms of subject and discourse orientation. First, for most speakers of English MAY is replaced by CAN for the giving of permission. Instead, therefore, of having a contrast between MAY and CAN in terms of orientation we have two quite distinct kinds of CAN, one subject oriented, the other discourse oriented. The discourse oriented CAN has the formal as well as the semantic characteristics of MAY. For instance it allows passivization:

John can meet Mary.
Mary can be met by John.

Secondly, the distinction is often 'neutralized' – the orientation is not specified (see 5.2.4, 5.2.7).

5.1.4 Epistemic and non-epistemic

There is yet another distinction that must be made – between what has been called the epistemic and non-epistemic[3] uses. This chiefly involves WILL, MAY and MUST (though some of the other modals have epistemic uses too). The distinction is clear in two sentences that we have already considered (in the discussion of tense marking with modals (5.1.2)):

He couldn't be there yesterday.
He can't have been there yesterday.

In the first example the modal itself is marked for past tense (past time); in the second it is the full verb that is so marked. But the two sentences reveal two quite different uses of the modal. The first refers to lack of ability in past time, the second to the (timeless) impossibility of an event in the past. The latter is the epistemic use, *can't* indicates impossibility; other modals relate to the certainty, possibility, probability of the proposition.

The epistemic uses, or for convenience the 'epistemic modals', are independent of the distinction of subject and discourse orientation. If a modal is epistemic it is not relevant to ask about its orientation, and we may describe these subject and discourse oriented modals as 'non-epistemic'. Yet the concept of epistemic modal has some similarity to the concept of discourse orientation, since it is the speaker who is certain, uncertain, etc (or the hearer whose certainty, uncertainty is questioned in the question forms). But both the syntax and the semantics are different. (It could, as noted in 5.1.3, be argued that the discourse oriented and epistemic modals are true modals in this respect, whereas the subject oriented modals are semantically like the other verbs of the language – but there is little to be gained from this.)

The three types of modal are most clearly distinguished in terms of tense marking:

discourse oriented – no tense marking;
subject oriented – modal may be marked for tense (some exceptions);
epistemic – full verb may be marked for tense.

The epistemic modals alone permit tense marking of the full verb with *have*; OUGHT, DARE and NEED seem *prima facie* to be exceptions but are strictly not (see 5.3.2). Only very rarely is an epistemic modal itself marked for tense. Passivization is always possible.

5.1.5 Method of analysis

In the sections that follow we shall naturally take into account the discourse oriented/subject oriented and epistemic/non-epistemic distinctions as well as the features of tense, negation and passivization.[4]

There is one further point that will be mentioned – the possibility of future time reference and collocation with future time adverbials. We can contrast:

She'll visit us tomorrow.

She'll sit for hours doing nothing.

There is some relevance too in collocation with other adverbials, *for hours* or *at times* in:

He can be very unkind at times.

The complexity of the modals makes it difficult to know how to arrange the analysis. The simplest way, perhaps, is to ignore, to begin with, the problem of negation, tense and the epistemic modals. The first section (5.2) is therefore headed 'basic forms', with tense and negation discussed next (5.3) and the epistemic modals after that (5.4). Within the first section the problem of the future use of *will* and *shall* has to be discussed first. Then WILL and SHALL are discussed separately and then together, and CAN and MAY are treated similarly. Single subsections deal with MUST and OUGHT, DARE and NEED.

A final section deals with a syntactic feature that deeply involves the modals – the conditional sentences (5.5).

5.2 Basic forms

We will begin by considering only the 'basic' forms of the modals – those that are present, positive and active. However, it is impossible to deal with the classification of these forms without constant reference to their corresponding past tense and negative forms – these are often the criteria for the classification. But a detailed and comprehensive discussion of the other forms is left to the next section.

5.2.1 Futurity

As we have already noted, *will* and *shall* are treated in many grammar books as the markers of future tense, *ie* as tense auxiliaries. Although I have argued that strictly English has no future tense, there are respects in which *will* and *shall* are 'tense like' in that they sometimes function more like the primary auxiliaries than the modals. We will therefore begin with a reconsideration of *will* and *shall* when used simply to refer to future time.

Reference to future time is clearly shown by collocation with future time adverbials:

It'll rain tomorrow.

The letters will arrive in a few days.
I shall be ill tomorrow.
We shall see them next week.

It would be enough simply to indicate that this is one of the several uses of the two modals. There are, however, a number of points that make this use rather different from the others, and that, therefore, to some degree, justify the traditional treatment.

[i] In this use *shall* occurs only with the pronouns *I* and *we*. It is for this reason, of course, that the grammar books have set up paradigms of the kind *I shall*, (*thou wilt*), *he/she/it will, we shall, you will, they will.* A particularly important piece of evidence of the close relationship between *will* and *shall* is shown by their function in reported speech. For the choice of *will* or *shall* is not dictated by the form in the original sentence but by the pronoun. We have then:

I shall see him tomorrow.
He says he will see him tomorrow.
You will see him tomorrow.
He says I shall see him tomorrow.

I shall, that is to say, is reported by *he will*, and *you will* by *I shall* (or with a past tense verb of reporting by *he would*, *I should*). But the traditional paradigm is not wholly correct. First, *will*, and especially the weak form *'ll* (see 9.1.3) is regularly used not only with *he*, *you*, *they*, etc, but also with *I* and *we*:

I will be seeing her this afternoon.
We'll be seeing her this afternoon.

The position is, then, that both *will* and *shall* occur with *I* and *we*. Secondly, it would be incorrect to talk about *shall* occurring as the 'first person' form. For it does not occur with such sequences as *John and I* or *you and I* even though these are in traditional terms 'first person plural':

**John and I shall be there.*
John and I'll be there.

[ii] Passivization is always possible, as we have already seen (5.1.2). Here the WILL of futurity contrasts very clearly with the WILL of volition (5.2.2). Passivization is, it is to be recalled, normal with the simple phrase type with no auxiliaries or merely primary auxiliaries – those that mark tense, aspect and phase alone. Moreover, with passivization

we can see the relationship (*ie* interchangeability according to the pronoun) of *will* and *shall* again:

I shall meet Mary at the station.
Mary will be met by me at the station.

[iii] A particularly important point is that *will* and *shall*, as markers of futurity, do not occur in conditional clauses (see 5.5.2, 5.5.6). Hence we must relate:

I shall be ill tomorrow.
If I'm ill tomorrow.
He'll be ill tomorrow.
If he's ill tomorrow.

It is not the case that *will* cannot occur in conditional clauses. There is nothing odd about:

If he'll come tomorrow.

But here we have the WILL of volition with the meaning 'If he agrees to come . . .'. The contrast is perhaps well seen in:

It'll rain tomorrow.
If it rains tomorrow.
?If only it'll rain tomorrow.

The first is likely to be simple futurity – there is no obvious 'it' that can agree to rain and the second is thus its conditional counterpart. The third is a jocular or semi-jocular suggestion that 'it', the weather, might agree to bring some rain. It is not an impossible sentence, but is deliberately unusual. In conditional clauses, then, the modal form with WILL of futurity is replaced by the non-modal, the present tense, form. This is completely unrelated to the uses of present tense forms to refer to future events that were discussed earlier (3.5.4, 3.5.5) in relation to:

I'm going to London tomorrow.
I start work tomorrow.

These indicate intention or plans. The sentences we have been considering are not comparable. For the following sentences would be decidedly odd:

**It's raining tomorrow.*
**I'm ill tomorrow.*

Even if they could be contextualized they would not be the non-conditional counterparts of:

If it's raining tomorrow.
If I'm ill tomorrow.

The corresponding non-conditionals will contain *will* or *shall*.

[iv] We have seen (3.1.7) that *will* may be used in exactly the same way as past tense to indicate displaced time marking.

The man you were talking to was the Mayor.
The man you will be talking to will be the Mayor.

However, we should not find with the same implication (*ie* that he still is the Mayor):

!The man you used to talk to used to be the Mayor.
!The man you've been talking to has been the Mayor.
!The man you're going to be talking to is going to be the Mayor.

Here *used to*, *has been* and *is going to* in the main clause carry the normal time indications. It might, then, be argued that WILL here functions like the past tense and so should also be regarded as a tense marker.

[v] There appears to be some restriction in the use of WILL and SHALL for past time reference. They occur quite regularly in the *would* and *should* forms for reported speech:

He said he would be better soon.

But they are not commonly used for simple past (*ie* for future in the past), except in literary English:

I should see her again the next day.
He would die within a month.

In colloquial English *I was going to . . .*, *He was to . . .*, etc would be more normal. Some forms of *would* and *should* that are *prima facie* indicators of past time are probably to be treated in terms of pseudo-epistemic usage or of a verb of reporting that is unexpressed:

I decided not to telephone. I should see him the next day.

There are several points in which SHALL and WILL differ from the other modals (but not from all other uses of WILL, especially the WILL of volition). First, there are no tentative forms *would* or *should* with futurity. Secondly, there can never be double negative marking (5.1.3). There is one way only of negating the verb phrase:

He won't come tomorrow.

There is no possible syntactic or semantic distinction between negating *will* and negating *come* in:

He won't come tomorrow.
He'll not come tomorrow.

These differ formally and stylistically, but not semantically, in terms of what is negated. The negation of the futurity of an act seems not to be distinct from the futurity of the negation of an act!

There are some reasons, then, for regarding the WILL and SHALL of futurity as closer to the central system of the verb than WILL and SHALL in their other uses and the other modals. But they are still clearly not wholly 'tense auxiliaries' and little is to be gained by divorcing them from the other modal uses and setting up future tense paradigms.

5.2.2 WILL

Let us now look at the other uses of WILL. We must distinguish at least four.

[i] *Volition.* We have already noted the WILL of volition in the previous subsections. Like the WILL of futurity it refers to the future and collocates with future adverbials. But there are major differences.

In this use, WILL is clearly a subject oriented modal, and whereas the WILL of futurity functions very like a primary auxiliary to produce what functions more like a simple than a complex phrase, the WILL of volition is more like a catenative in a complex phrase. We have already noted several points:

(*a*) There is no association with SHALL. This is limited to the WILL of futurity.

(*b*) Passivization is not possible. There is no voice relation between:

John won't meet Mary.
! Mary won't be met by John.

(*c*) The WILL of volition regularly occurs in conditional clauses. Indeed its occurrence there is a clear distinguishing feature. For although *He'll come tomorrow* is ambiguous between the two uses, the ambiguity is resolved in:

If he comes tomorrow.
If he'll come tomorrow.

(*d*) There is a past tense form *would* that is regularly used in the tentative sense. Indeed there is no other difference between:

I'll do that for you.
I'd do that for you.
Will you pass the salt?
Would you pass the salt?

Would is also used for past time, except where there is reference to a single agreed and subsequently executed action in the past. It is exemplified by the negative (5.3.1):

I asked him to come but he wouldn't.

But we cannot say:

**I asked him to come and he would.*

It can be argued that this gap may be filled by forms of BE WILLING as BE ABLE fills a similar gap for CAN (5.2.5, 5.3.2). They are available not only for past time, but also to indicate future willingness:

I asked him to come and he was willing.
He'll be willing to come tomorrow.

Except, then, for the absence of *would* for single past time actions, these features all indicate the extent to which WILL here functions like a full verb in a complex phrase. Negation, however, does not support this interpretation. Let us consider what is negated in:

He won't come with us.

It could be argued that this is equivalent to 'He will not-come with us', *ie* that he has made a definite decision not to come. Or it could be said that it is equivalent to 'He not-will come with us', *ie* that he refuses or is unwilling to come. The point is that there is one simple Yes/No choice – to 'will' not to come and to 'not-will' to come are the same (see also 5.3.6).

The volition use is a very common use of WILL – probably the most likely with verbs that refer to activities that can be willed or agreed. With such verbs reference to the 'simple' future is more likely to be made by BE GOING or the non-modal progressive. WILL normally suggests willingness or agreement. This is especially true in questions where it would be assumed that agreement was being sought rather than that a factual question was being asked. The following sentences would usually be interpreted as invitations:

Will you read a paper tomorrow?
Will you come with us this evening?

If the questioner is merely seeking information, more appropriate sentences are:

Are you going to read a paper tomorrow?
Are you coming with us this evening?

Naturally, if the verb does not permit of the invitation interpretation, WILL may be used for a simple enquiry without fear of ambiguity or misunderstanding as in:

Will you feel better tomorrow?

Under this heading, perhaps, we ought to include such sentences as:

The books will all fit here.
The board will bear his weight.

These might seem *prima facie* to be no more than examples of futurity with certain conditions implied:

. . . if you put them here.
. . . if he stands on it.

But formally the occurrence of *wouldn't* (but not *would*) for past time places these with volition:

The books wouldn't fit here.
The board wouldn't bear his weight.

We must also include here the 'pseudo-passives' (4.2.2):

This shirt won't iron.
This shirt wouldn't iron.

Semantically these seem odd. The subjects are inanimate – there can be no volition. Perhaps we need a wider term than volition to include the qualities of inanimate things that permit them to act or undergo actions. There is one point that supports this view – that even with inanimates the verb REFUSE may be used:

The door won't open.
The door refuses to open.

With some of the examples we have considered REFUSE is less likely, but not impossible:

The books refuse to fit there.
The shirt refuses to iron.
? The board refuses to bear his weight.

If inanimates can 'refuse', it is plausible to argue that they can also 'will'.

[ii] *Insistence.* We could, perhaps, have included under 'volition' the WILL of 'insistence' where WILL is always accented as in:

He wíll act the fool.
If you wíll do these things.

There is, here, the notion of deliberate, willed action – the difference in meaning could, perhaps, be attributed to the accent. In terms of relation with SHALL, passivization and occurrence with *if*, this use of WILL is wholly consistent with that of volition. However, there is one major difference. The past tense *would* may refer to a single action in the past (whereas the *would* of volition never does):

I asked him to stop but he woúld do it.

Semantically too the negatives clearly negate the main verb ('insisted on not . . .'):

He wouldn't stop fooling about.

This is less crucial, since it is not clear where negation is focused in the volition use.

We might also include the unaccented *will* of *Boys will be boys* but this is a non-productive use restricted to the proverbial saying.

[iii] *Characteristic.* There is another use of WILL that has some resemblance to the WILL of volition. It indicates characteristic activity as in:

She'll sit there for hours doing nothing.

It could be argued that semantically this is very close – it refers to habitual willed activity. But there are sufficient differences to warrant treating it as a different use:

(*a*) No futurity is indicated and collocation with future adverbials is not possible.
(*b*) The past tense form *would* is used for past time reference in the non-negative form:

She'd sit there for hours doing nothing.

But it does not seem to occur in the 'tentative' use.

(*c*) It may be replaced with little or no change of meaning by the non-modal form:

She sits there for hours doing nothing.

Notice, of course, that the converse is not true – not every non-modal form can be replaced by a form with WILL. There is a clear difference between:

I go to work every day.
I'll go to work every day.

In particular this use seems not merely to refer to characteristic activity, but also to do so with some disapproval or condescension. Further examples are:

He'll come in and sit down without speaking.
She'll keep talking so that no one else can get a word in.

In this use WILL will seldom, if ever, occur with *I* or *we* since we do not normally state disapproval of our own habitual actions.

[iv] *Inference.* There are at least two uses of WILL which do not refer to future events, but to what will occur if certain conditions are met.

(*a*) WILL is used for 'timeless truths' that may be proved inductively such as:

Oil will float on water.
Pigs will eat anything.

There is the possibility here of replacement of the modal form by the non-modal:

Oil floats on water.
Pigs eat anything.

But this use of WILL is not possible with general truths of the kind:

The sun rises in the east.
The Severn flows into the Atlantic.

The distinction is, perhaps, rather obvious. The inductive truth can be proved by experimentation: the event will take place, if conditions are met – if you pour oil on water it will float; if you give pigs anything, they will eat it (see **3.5.3**).

(*b*) Not very different is the WILL used for deductive conclusion as in:

Bill is John's father and John is Tom's father. So Bill will be Tom's grandfather.

As with the WILL of induction the non-modal 'simple' form may be used with little change of meaning:

. . . So Bill is Tom's grandfather.

But an alternative is MUST:

. . . So Bill must be Tom's grandfather.

It could, however, be argued that this is epistemic MUST (but not epistemic WILL since epistemic MUST and WILL differ in meaning – 5.4.1).

5.2.3 SHALL

There is only one other use of SHALL.

Obligation. Apart from its use with WILL for futurity, SHALL has a use that Jespersen called 'obligational'. This is our first clear example of a discourse oriented use. SHALL has future time reference and collocates with future time adverbials:

Shall I come tomorrow?
You shall have it next week.
He shall be rewarded for this.

In the first of these, a question, the speaker asks whether the hearer expects or wishes him to come; in the second two the speaker is, in some sense, the initiator of the action. The first is, *prima facie*, ambiguous between the two meanings of SHALL, but as with volitional WILL the futurity meaning would normally be excluded if the action is one that can be deliberately undertaken. Thus the question could normally be interpreted as one about the hearer's wishes and not a simple query about a future event. If the question is simply whether I am going to come (simple future), the form would be:

Am I coming tomorrow?

It might seem that SHALL has two different meanings, one for statements, the other for questions. But this is characteristic of a discourse oriented use. For in statements the speaker is indicating the part he himself is playing – he is promising or guaranteeing, but in questions he is asking about the hearer's part – whether he will promise or guarantee.

Hence the apparent reversal in question and statement. As with all discourse oriented uses the past tense form (*should*) does not refer to past time – one cannot promise or guarantee past actions. *Should* is not used in a tentative sense either (though there is a use which might seem not too far removed from it – 5.3.4).

The negative form *shall not* or *shan't* negates not the modal, but the full verb; it is a promise or a guarantee not to act. In this respect it is like MUST (5.2.8), but not like the other discourse oriented modal MAY (5.2.6).

Formally this use is clearly distinct from the futurity use in the occurrence of SHALL with pronouns other than *I* and *we*.

5.2.4 WILL and SHALL compared

If we look upon volitional WILL and obligational SHALL as 'central' uses, WILL and SHALL relate to each other as subject oriented and discourse oriented modals in precisely the same way as do CAN and MAY (5.2.7). WILL is subject oriented – it refers to activity that is initiated by the subject. SHALL is discourse oriented – it refers to activity that is initiated by one of the participants in the conversation. In statements it is the speaker who initiates – he guarantees or promises; in questions it is the hearer – it is from him that the guarantee or promise is sought.

In statements with *I* speaker and subject are the same and it ought, therefore, to follow that SHALL and WILL have little or no difference in meaning, both being speaker = subject oriented. The same would be true of *you* in questions since there subject and hearer are the same. In such cases WILL seems to be preferred to SHALL.

With *we*, however, there is a clear distinction, since with *shall* it normally refers to initiation by the speaker alone of an action that 'we' undertake (see 5.1.3), whereas with *will* it refers to the willingness of the plural subject *we*.

We are now moving away from the distinction of subject and discourse oriented modals to the idea of initiation by means of a 'speech act' – to ask how do we give or request an undertaking to act. We could (substituting WILL for SHALL as argued above) set up 'initiation' paradigms of the kind:

I will	*Shall I?*
You shall	*Will you?*
He shall	*Shall he?*
We will/shall	*Shall we?*
They shall	*Shall they?*

These bring out clearly the function of *Shall I?*, *Shall we?*, *Will you?* – that none of these, as we have already seen, can be requests for information, but are always to be interpreted as seeking advice or agreement, in spite of the apparently parallel *I shall*, *We shall*, *You will*.

If we now turn to the SHALL and WILL of futurity we are concerned not with a speech act of the kind we have just considered, but with the use of the modal for part of the linguistic information, for the 'propositional content' of the sentence. It is not surprising that the paradigm for WILL and SHALL of futurity are almost (but not quite) the converse of those we have been considering. The converse forms would be:

I shall	*Will I?*
You will	*Shall you?*
He will	*Will he?*
We shall/will	*Will we?*
They will	*Will they?*

The statement paradigm is almost exactly the paradigm found in the traditional grammar books, and it differs from what is proposed in 5.2.1 only in that it does not include *I will*. One could, possibly, argue that both *I shall* and *I will* occur by analogy with *We shall* and *We will* (these are equally available because both occur equally in the 'initiation' paradigm). In the questions *Will I?* and *Shall you?* are rare – BE GOING or a progressive form being normally preferred, but it is important to note that *Shall I?* and *Will you?* do *not* occur here – for we have already seen that these are to be avoided as questions of fact if there is any possibility that they may be interpreted as requests.

5.2.5 CAN

The relationship between CAN and MAY is very like that between WILL and SHALL. However, there is no single common use like the futurity use of WILL and SHALL in which they are combined. Rather there are several uses that they appear to share and in which they are largely interchangeable. It is convenient, then, to look first at some of the more specific individual uses of CAN (and later of MAY) and to leave the combined or overlapping uses to another subsection.

[i] *Ability*. The most familiar use of CAN expresses ability to perform an action:

He can lift a hundredweight.
I can read Greek.

In this use CAN is more like a full verb than any other modal.

(*a*) There is a past tense form with past time reference:

When he was young, he could lift a hundredweight.

However, this is not used for a single achievement in the past:

**He put a lot of effort in and could lift the weight.*

This is similar to the use of *would* in 5.2.2; both are further discussed in 5.3.1. The past tense is not used in the tentative use – in such a use it would normally be interpreted as the CAN of willingness (see below).

(*b*) There is a special relationship with BE ABLE which seems to supply the 'missing' modal forms. Thus we have, in contrast to the asterisked form above:

He put a lot of effort in and was able to lift the weight.

Similarly we can refer to future ability only with BE ABLE:

When he's older, he'll be able to lift a hundredweight.

There are no other modals for which another form may so clearly be regarded as suppletive (except possibly BE WILLING for WILL of willingness, but that too was, as we saw, the use most like that of a full verb – see 5.3.1).

(*c*) The negative *can't* negates the modal – inability to act, not ability not to act, as in:

He can't lift a hundredweight.

(*d*) Passivization is not normal except with no agent or with unspecified agent (*cf* 5.3.7):

**A ton can't be lifted by John.*
A ton can't be lifted by anyone.
A ton can't be lifted.

Closely associated with ability is the use of CAN to express willingness. Here it is similar to that of the WILL of volition as in:

Can you pass the salt?
I can do that for you.
cf: Will you pass the salt?

These, like comparable sentences with WILL, are requests or offers. The past tense form is commonly used in its tentative sense:

Could you pass the salt?

It could be argued that this tentative use of CAN marks it as distinct from the ability use. But it is, naturally, precisely in requests that the tentative use is likely to occur most. Using the past tense form in the tentative use implies, therefore, that the statement of one's ability is to be interpreted as an offer. *I could do that* means not only that I can, but also that I am willing to if requested. It would be difficult to draw any clear line between the ability and willingness uses of CAN.

[ii] *Sensation*. Another very similar use is with verbs of sensation where the modal seems often to add nothing that is not indicated by the non-modal form:

I can see the moon.
I can hear music.
I see the moon.
I hear music.

It could be argued that saying that one can see something usually means that one does see it. But a distinction between this use of CAN and the ability use is possible. The following sentence is ambiguous:

I can see the tiniest dots on the paper.

This could refer either to my present seeing of the dots or to my potential ability to see them if the occasion arose.

There is a past tense (past time) form *could:*

I could see the moon last night.

This also suggests that this use is not to be identified with the ability use, for there is reference to a single occasion here, where the *could* of ability is not used.

[iii] *Characteristic*. There is also a use of CAN to refer to characteristic, but sporadic patterns of behaviour, often in a derogatory sense:

He can tell awful lies.
She can be very catty at times.

There is a past tense form *could*, but there are no suppletive forms with BE ABLE:

She could be very catty when she was younger.
**She'll be able to be very catty when she's older.*

The use of CAN is, perhaps, related to the basic ability use in the same way as the WILL of characteristic is related to the basic volition use. The difference, however, is that CAN refers to possible or sporadic action rather than habitual behaviour. In particular it collocates with such adverbials as *at times* whereas WILL does not.

5.2.6 MAY

MAY is used to give or request permission:

You may go.
You may come tomorrow.
May I come in?

It is important to notice that in the statement the speaker gives permission, in the question he requests permission from the hearer. There is then a complete parallel with SHALL; we have discourse oriented permission (instead of discourse oriented initiation), the relevant participant being again the speaker in statements and the hearer in questions.

The past tense form *might* is rarely used in this sense. It never occurs as a past tense form or as a discourse oriented tentative, except in question form:

Might I come in?
* *You might come in now.*
* *You might come to see him yesterday.*

The negative form *may not* negates the modal – a refusal of permission unless *not* is accented, in which case it may negate the full verb – permission not to act:

You may not go. (Permission to go is refused)
You may nót go. (Permission not to go is given)

However, this use is now very formal – CAN is more normal in ordinary speech. The story of 'Can I come in?' – 'You can, but you may not' belongs to a different age.

5.2.7 CAN and MAY together

We have already seen that MAY in its permission sense is discourse oriented. It is obvious, too, that CAN in its ability sense is subject oriented in that the possibility of the action stems from the subject. It was also suggested that WILL and SHALL are essentially 'initiative', while CAN and MAY are essentially 'permissive' (although neither of these terms quite accurately suggests what is meant).

A better interpretation for CAN and MAY is the negative notion of 'no obstacle' – *nil obstat*;[5] for subject orientation there is nothing about the speaker that prevents him, for discourse orientation there is no prevention emanating from the discourse participants. This negative notion may explain why CAN and MAY are so often interchangeable, for the orientation of the *nil obstat* is often irrelevant – there is little need to specify whether it is the subject or the participant for whom there is no obstacle to allow the event. This probably accounts both for the discourse oriented CAN and the frequent neutralization (see below).

[i] CAN – *permission.* The forms of MAY for permission are today rather formal and are normally replaced by CAN:

You can go.
You can come tomorrow.
Can I come in?

Could similarly is used only in tentative questions while *cannot* and *can nót* are used in exactly the same way as *may not* and *may nót.* This use of CAN is clearly discourse oriented – formally and semantically equivalent to the rarer MAY.

[ii] CAN/MAY – *generalization.* Both modals are used to refer to actions that sometimes happen – the orientation is neutralized:

A situation like this may occur from time to time.
A situation like this can occur from time to time.

With CAN this is not far from our 'characteristic' use – but that is, of course, very clearly subject oriented (it is talking about behaviour that is characteristic of the subject). Negation is interesting here. With MAY it would normally be interpreted to negate the full verb, but with CAN it will almost always negate the modal:

A situation like this may not occur from time to time.
A situation like this cannot occur from time to time.

The first sentence says that sometimes it does not occur, the second that it never occurs (*ie* it not-sometimes occurs). In this respect the use of MAY and CAN is very like the epistemic use (5.4.1), and probably not always clearly distinct from it. However, even with MAY the negative can negate the modal. The first sentence could also but less obviously be taken to mean 'never occurs'. Moreover, if we have a choice stated (a disjunction) the probability of interpretation is reversed:

The flowers may be red or blue.
The flowers may not be red or blue.

The second sentence would usually be taken to mean that the flowers are never red or blue, and much less obviously that they are sometimes colours other than red or blue.[6] The past tense form *could* and *might* are used both as tentatives and for past time (for general habitual activity).

[iii] CAN/MAY – *general possibility*. The modals are also used for vague general possibility as in:

We can/may take this as our starting point.
We can/may now prove that . . .

The subject/discourse orientation distinction is here neutralized. The negative would normally be interpreted to negate the modal (as would be expected with the CAN of ability). Past tense forms for tentative and past time are possible.

5.2.8 MUST and OUGHT

Both verbs refer to obligation – to some kind of moral duty as in:

I must go now.
I ought to go now.
You must come again.
You ought to come again.

The distinction is not in terms of the strength of the obligation, and it would be wrong to see OUGHT as the tentative form of MUST (though this may be valid for the epistemic uses (5.4.1)). In particular notice that the last pair could both be used as invitations. Yet with MUST the invitation is formal and could be quite insincere; with OUGHT there is some suggestion that the host would like to see his guest again. To understand the relation between MUST and OUGHT there are three points to be considered:

[i] MUST has no past tense forms – the past tense form of HAVE, *had*, can often be used, but they are not related (see 5.3.2). OUGHT, however, has a past time form in *ought to have*:

You ought to have gone yesterday.

This clearly marks past time for the modal (duty in the past) rather than for the full verb – for it is not easy to understand how one can have a duty in the present to act in the past. Moreover, as we have seen (5.1.4), it is normally only with the epistemic modals that the full verb may be marked for past tense.

[ii] The negative forms *mustn't* and *oughtn't* negate the full verb – duty not to act. To negate the modal the forms *needn't* or *may nót* are to be used for both MUST and OUGHT (see 5.3.6). It would seem that if obligation is denied it is irrelevant what kind of obligation is being denied – the distinction between MUST and OUGHT is lost.

[iii] More importantly, however, there is a difference in that OUGHT allows for non-action while MUST does not. Hence:

He ought to do it, but he won't.
**He must do it, but he won't.*

The first point clearly suggests that the distinction between MUST and OUGHT is once again in terms of discourse and subject orientation. MUST like SHALL and MAY is discourse oriented. It is a performative – laying the obligation on someone just as MAY gives permission and SHALL guarantees. OUGHT on the other hand is subject oriented; it merely indicates that the subject has a duty just as he has a wish (WILL) or ability (CAN). For that reason MUST has no past tense – one can no more impose a duty to perform an act in the past than give permission or a guarantee; but OUGHT has a past time form – because people can have duties in the past as well as the present.

The second point – that the two modals have identical negative forms – supports this conclusion. For if the obligation is denied it is no longer relevant whether it was subject or discourse oriented, and it is thus neutralized. But it must be pointed out that in this respect MUST and OUGHT appear to be closer than the other modal pairs, for there is no single form that regularly negates both WILL and SHALL or both CAN and MAY – with these the orientation is preserved in the negative.

The third point, too, seems to support the conclusion. For if the speaker imposes the obligation he obviously cannot at the same time admit that he conceives of non-action. But the same constraint would not apply to the subject oriented OUGHT. Notice again, however, that this is not paralleled by WILL and SHALL, for not only SHALL (as we might expect by analogy with MUST), but also WILL does not permit non-action:

**He shall do it, but he won't.*
**He'll do it, but he won't.*

Yet we can say:

He is willing to do it, but he won't.

However, not all the purely formal characteristics of OUGHT are those associated with the subject oriented modals – see 5.3.6 and 5.3.7.

The relation of MUST and OUGHT is complicated by the fact that there exists a third verb in the same semantic area – HAVE. It is clear enough that HAVE is not discourse oriented – the obligation does not come from the speaker but from some external source. Consider:

You have to come again.

This does not say that the speaker imposes the obligation, but that there are some other forces that oblige you to come again. Indeed it would be possible, even if slightly odd, to say:

You don't háve to come again, but you múst.

In some ways, MUST pairs as much with HAVE as with OUGHT. In particular, if the orientation is irrelevant, the two verbs may be mutually substitutable (see also 5.3.2). Often the meaning is no more than something like 'There is no possible alternative course'. This is particularly clear if we wish to state the necessary conditions for an event to take place as in:

If you want to be fit, you must take exercise.
If you want to be fit, you have to take exercise.

It is also clear in the 'weak' obligation of:

I must admit that . . .
I have to admit that . . .

In these examples MUST and HAVE are interchangeable, but OUGHT would mean something different. It would still carry the notion of personal duty, which is lacking from these.

More problematic is the use of HAVE with WILL where it seems to have the meaning of a discourse oriented modal:

You'll have to go now, I'm afraid.
He'll have to do it whether he likes it or not.

It could be argued that HAVE is suppletive here, as are BE WILLING and BE ABLE (since neither MUST nor WILL nor CAN may co-occur with WILL). But we can say rather that the MUST/HAVE distinction is neutralized here too.

HAVE involves, it seems, a third kind of orientation – from an external source, neither the subject nor the speaker or hearer; but orientation is often neutralized vis-à-vis discourse orientation.

5.2.9 DARE and NEED

As we have already seen (2.2.7) these verbs function as auxiliaries only in their negative forms or where there is implied negation, and in questions.

We need to recognize one meaning only for each. For DARE it is roughly a matter of having (or not having) the courage to act. For NEED it is merely a denial of an obligation or duty:

I daren't ask him about that.
You needn't bother about that.

The negative form negates the modal with both. Both seem to have past tense forms with HAVE:

I daren't have asked him.
You needn't have bothered about it.

But, in fact, the discourse/subject orientation distinction is valid here too. DARE is subject oriented. This is obvious semantically, but is also shown formally by the existence of a past time form (*cf* 5.3.1). NEED, however, is both subject and discourse oriented according to whether it is the negation of MUST or OUGHT (see 5.2.8). It is only when it is subject oriented that past tense forms occur. In the sentence above the meaning is 'You did not have a duty' not 'I do not impose on you the obligation' (to act in the past) – it reflects subject oriented OUGHT not discourse oriented MUST.

5.3 Past tense, negation, passives

The previous section dealt primarily with the present tense forms of the modals, though some reference was made to past tense and negative forms for the purpose of classification. In this section it will be possible to consider the modals together in relation to past tense for past time, tentative and reported speech, and to negation. Only WILL, SHALL, CAN and MAY, of course, have past tense forms; for the others we must ask how past time reference can be made.

5.3.1 Past tense/past time

The past tense forms *would*, *should*, *could* and *might* seem often to have no past time reference and even to be quite different in meaning from the present tense forms (see 5.3.4). For this reason some scholars have treated them as quite distinct modal auxiliaries. The argument for so doing is to some extent supported by the fact that the other modals have no past tense forms at all.

There is, however, a pattern in the function of these four forms that can be expressed by three simple rules:

[i] The futurity forms of WILL and SHALL have no past tense/past time forms. There is no future in the past.
[ii] Only the subject oriented modals WILL and CAN have past tense forms for past time.
[iii] Even these are not used where there is reference to a single past action (with specific exceptions).

The first point has already been discussed in detail (5.2.1) and no more need be said.

The second point makes it clear that *would* and *could* are used for past time reference, but not *should* or *might*. This is explainable in semantic terms. The discourse oriented modals refer to speaker or hearer participation (promising, permitting, etc) at the time of speaking and it is not possible to promise, permit, etc actions in the past.

The third point is illustrated by sentences such as the following:

**I asked him and he would come.*
I asked him and he wouldn't come.
Whenever I asked him he would come.
**I ran fast and could catch the bus.*
I ran fast but couldn't catch the bus.
Whenever I ran fast I could catch the bus.

Would and *could* are not used, then, where there is the implication that a single action in the past actually took place, but can be used to refer to the denial of such action or to habitual activity. They are quite normal, therefore, in the characteristic uses:

She'd sit there for hours doing nothing.
She could be very catty at times.

The only exception to this general rule are the WILL of insistence and the CAN of sensation:

I told him not to but he wóuld do it.
I looked out of the window and could see the moon.

The inferential uses of WILL do not seem to be used with past time reference; we would not, therefore, note as examples of them:

The books would fit here.
Dinosaurs would eat anything.

The first is clearly tentative, not past time. The second is a habitual use of *would* that has not yet been discussed.

For the other uses of CAN and MAY the deciding factor seems to be whether there is any possibility of interpretation in terms of subject orientation; if there is, a past time/past tense form even for *might* is possible. Thus there is no *could* of permission any more than there is a *might*. Yet there are past time forms for the generalization use:

A situation like this could/might occur from time to time.

Similarly the general possibility use permits of *could* or *might* provided the activity referred to is habitual:

We could/might then prove that ...

5.3.2 Past time – other forms

Not only do WILL, SHALL, CAN and MAY have no past tense/past time form in some of their uses, but the other four modals MUST, OUGHT, DARE and NEED have no past tense forms at all. There are always ways of referring to past time; some seem to be more closely related grammatically than others.

[i] For the futurity uses of WILL and SHALL other ways of referring to future in the past are available:

He was about to speak.
He was going to speak.
He was speaking the next day.

None of these is the obvious grammatical counterpart.

[ii] We have already noted BE ABLE as a possible suppletive for CAN (5.2.5):

I ran fast and was able to catch the bus.

It could be argued that BE WILLING provides the suppletive for the WILL of willingness (5.2.2):

I asked him and he was willing to come.

The conditions are the same – the non-occurrence of *could* or *would* to refer to a single completed action in the past. There is a similar parallelism where there is reference to volition or ability in the future:

When he's older, he'll be able to lift a hundredweight.
When he's older, he'll be willing to help in the garden.

Similarly there are non-finite forms *to be able*, *to be willing*, *being able*, *being willing* and past perfect forms as in:

He had been able to do it.
He had been willing to do it.

Neither CAN nor WILL can similarly express past perfects. But it does not follow that CAN and BE ABLE, WILL and BE WILLING are the same verbs any more than MUST is the same verb as HAVE (there are similar arguments below). Indeed for WILL, AGREE seems to be closer semantically than BE WILLING, as is shown by:

**He'll come, but he can't.*
**He agrees to come, but he can't.*
He's willing to come, but he can't.

One can be willing to do things that will not take place, but not to agree to do them or to 'will' to do them (in the sense of the modal). (But see also on negation, **5**.3.6.)

[iii] With the discourse oriented modals it is always possible to find a verb that reports the functions expressed by the modal and so to put this into the past tense. Obvious examples are:

You may go. *I permitted you to go.*
You shall have it. *I promised you should have it.*

[iv] For MUST there is the form *had to:*

I must go now.
I had to go then.

This is, however, morphologically and semantically the past tense form of another verb (**5**.2.8, **6**.1.2). It can reasonably be argued that since MUST is, like SHALL and MAY, discourse oriented, it has no past tense/past time form.

[v] The form *daren't* can be used for past time reference:

He wanted to come, but daren't.

This is possibly to be interpreted as **daredn't*, but there is no way of proving such a suggestion.

[vi] For both DARE and NEED the forms of the full verb – *didn't dare*, *didn't need* are available.

[vii] OUGHT, DARE and NEED have forms with the following *have:*

You ought to have come with us yesterday.
I daren't have asked him when we met.
You needn't have said that when he asked.

In all these cases *have* marks past time for the modal not for the following verb – reference is to duty, not having the courage and not needing in the past. These are to be distinguished quite clearly from the *have* forms that occur with the epistemic modals where the full verb, not the modal, is marked for past time (5.1.4, 5.4.3).

5.3.3 Tentative

The use of past tense forms for the tentative use is most characteristic of the modals. We have already noted the much rarer use of non-modal past tense forms (3.2.3). It will be seen that the tentative use of past tense forms of the modals is particularly important for the epistemic modals (5.4.3). There are three kinds of sentences in which the tentative forms are found.

[i] They are used in requests – the tentative form being more polite:

(WILL volition) *Would you pass the salt?*
(CAN permission) *Could I go now?*
(CAN ability) *Could you pass the sugar?*
(MAY permission) *Might I go now?*

[ii] They are found in the uses that make an offer by the speaker:

(WILL volition) *I would do that for you.*
(CAN ability) *I could do that for you.*

It might be argued that these are incomplete unreal conditions (5.5.3) implying '. . . if you asked me'. But they are different from the more obvious incomplete conditionals such as:

(CAN ability) *I could do that* (if I tried).

It could also be argued that the tentative use distinguishes a CAN of willingness from the CAN of ability (5.2.5). Note too that *might* does not occur here (nor the *could* of permission). A request for permission may be tentative, but not the granting of it.

[iii] They occur in the 'general' uses of CAN and MAY, expressing some diffidence in the statement:

(generalization) *A situation like this could/might occur from time to time.*
(general possibility) *We could/might prove that . . .*

The existence of a tentative form is not directly linked to the distinction between subject orientation and discourse orientation, though it is concerned with speaker-hearer relations rather than simple passing of information (it belongs to the 'speech act' rather than the 'proposition').

Tentative forms with *have* (*would have*, *could have*, etc) also occur, to refer to past time, but these are all either unfulfilled conditionals (5.5.3), epistemic (5.5.5) or the forms dealt with below (5.3.4).

5.3.4 *would, should* and *might*

There are some common uses of *would*, *should* and *might* that are not related to the present tense forms *will* and *shall*.

Would is used for simple habitual activity:

He'd go to the park every day.
They would ask all kinds of questions.

In this use it differs little from the non-modal form or *used to:*

He went to the park every day.
He used to go to the park every day.

It is to be distinguished from the characteristic use of WILL, since *will* is not used for simple habitual activity in the present. We can distinguish, then, between:

She'd sit there for hours.
He'd go to the park every day.

The former is related to a present tense form with *will* but not the latter. But there is some similarity between the use of *would* and the general uses of *could* and *might* (5.3.1).

Should is regularly used in ways that are not related to the basic forms of SHALL.

[i] It occurs as an equivalent of OUGHT:

You should do something about that.
He should ask my permission first.

In tag-questions it may in fact be used with *ought to* (and is even the more usual form):

He ought to be here, shouldn't he?

Semantically this is not the tentative form of SHALL, though there is something in common in the notion of 'obligation'. As with OUGHT past time is indicated by *have:*

You should have done something about that.

[ii] It is also found in sentences such as:

It is very odd that he should do that.
It is lucky that the weather should be so fine.
I was sorry that he should be ill just then.

Should is used here for past and present time reference. It can be replaced by a non-modal form with little change of meaning:

It is very odd that he did/does that.
It is lucky that the weather is/was so fine.
I was sorry that he fell ill just then.

In all these sentences there is an expression of emotion, value judgement, etc and *should* occurs in the subordinate clause (which is being evaluated). Not very different is:

Who should I see but Bob!

This is again to be interpreted as either present or past time, and *should* can be replaced by the non-modal:

Who do I see but Bob!
Who did I see but Bob!

The link is semantic – there is surprise or some other kind of emotion.

[iii] It is also used after verbs of requiring, demanding, etc as:

I require that he should go.
I demand that he should be released.

(In formal American English the bare infinitive is used instead – *that he go, that he be released.*)

[iv] Another use of *should* occurs in conditionals (5.5.4).

Might is used for suggestions or requests as in:

You might let me know.

This could possibly be interpreted in terms of the tentative form of the discourse oriented MAY, but the same interpretation does not seem to be available for *might have*:

You might have told me about it.

This is not discourse oriented MAY since discourse oriented modals cannot refer to the past. It is, however, close to *should* and *should have* – with a lesser degree of obligation (and thus to some degree reflects the difference between SHALL and MAY).

5.3.5 Reported speech

We have already seen (5.1.1) that the relationship between *will* and *would*, *shall* and *should*, *can* and *could*, *may* and *might* is clearly established by their function in reported speech. As elsewhere in the language a present tense form is reported by a past tense form with a past tense verb of reporting. We have also seen that the choice of *will* and *shall* depends on the pronoun, not the original form – and the same is true of *would* and *should*:

I shall see him tomorrow.
He said he would see him the next day.
You will see him tomorrow.
He said I should see him the next day.

MUST, OUGHT, DARE and NEED have no past tense forms and in all cases the present tense form may be used with a past tense verb of reporting:

He said he must go.
He said he ought to go.
He said he daren't go.
He said he needn't go.

These could all be interpreted in terms of the continuing validity of the original statement – that the speaker guarantees that it is still true (3.2.2). But this is not necessarily so – they can all be interpreted as if the form of the modal had been past tense, *ie* simple reporting of *must*, *ought*, *daren't* and *needn't*. For *ought* there is no alternative; for *must*, *had to* is available, but it is again (see 5.3.2) doubtful whether this should be related to *must*. For *daren't* and *needn't* the full verb forms can be used:

!He said he had to go.
He said he didn't dare to go.
He said he didn't need to go.

If the original modal is already a past tense form there can be no further variation – *would* is reported by *would* etc:

He would go there every day.
He said he would go there every day.

It will be recalled that with the non-modal forms a past tense may be reported by the past perfect (3.2.2). But there is nothing comparable with the modals. *Would* is not reported by, for instance, *would have*. More strikingly, perhaps, although *ought to have*, *daren't have* and *needn't have* function as past time forms of *ought*, *daren't* and *needn't*, they are not used as the corresponding forms in reported speech:

I ought to go.
He said he ought to go.
! He said he ought to have gone.

The last sentence reports *I ought to have gone* not *I ought to go.*

This is an appropriate point to comment that it might seem that there is a difficult problem arising from the fact that past tense is used for [i] past time, [ii] tentative use, [iii] reported speech, [iv] unreal conditionals (5.5.1, 5.5.3). What happens when there is a combination of any of these? The answer is not as complex as might be supposed since:

[i] Unreal conditions make no distinction of tentative/non-tentative and have their own way of marking past time (5.5.3).
[ii] Past time plus tentative forms are always interpretable as unfulfilled unreal conditions (5.5.3).
[iii] Reported speech normally allows only for the change of the present tense finite form to the corresponding past tense – it does not employ the other forms used for past time and otherwise leaves the form unchanged.

5.3.6 Negation

We have already considered negation with the various modal uses. The problem is whether the negative negates the modal or the full verb. There are five possibilities.

[i] There is no negative form. This seems to be true of the characteristic uses of WILL and CAN; we do not speak of characteristic non-activity. The following sentences, though possible in a different sense, are not the negative forms of the characteristic uses:

! She won't sit there for hours doing nothing.
! She can't be very catty at times.

[ii] There is no distinction between negating the modal and negating the full verb. This is the case with the futurity use of WILL and SHALL (and this, as we have seen, marks them as very like the primary auxiliaries, in a strictly simple phrase). This seems also to be true of the WILL of volition (5.2.2).
[iii] The modal is negated. This is, naturally, the case with the modal that is most like a main verb – CAN in its ability and related uses:

(ability) *He can't lift a hundredweight.*
(sensation) *I can't see the moon.*

[iv] The full verb is negated – obligation, duty, insistence, etc is positively affirmed. This is true of the SHALL of obligation, MUST, OUGHT and the WILL of insistence. Note that it is not restricted to the discourse oriented verbs – it includes one use of WILL and does not include MAY:

(obligation) *You shan't have it next week.*
I mustn't go now.
I oughtn't to go now.
(insistence) *He won't stop acting the fool.*

(The first three might be interpreted as negating the modal, but only if the context makes it clear that they are specific denials of the positive form.)

[v] Either may be negated. This is the case with MAY, perhaps, in all its uses. In the permission use the accent will normally distinguish:

(permission) *You may not go.*
You may nót go.

CAN in the permission sense follows the same pattern. In the generalization use there is ambiguity:

A situation like this mày not occur from time to time.

This could mean either that sometimes it does not occur or that it never (=not-sometimes) occurs (5.2.7). The accent will not always disambiguate, but is more likely to do so in the general possibility use:

We may not now prove . . .
We may nót now prove . . .

In these two uses with CAN the negative would normally negate the modal (it would seem that there is still some connotation here of ability).

We have already noted that *mustn't* negates the full verb and that in order to negate the modal with MUST we can use the negative form of NEED:

I mustn't go now.
I needn't go now.

We may thus contrast *must + not go* (*mustn't*) and *not must + go* (*needn't*). But the relation between NEED and MUST is, perhaps, semantic rather than grammatical. We could equally have offered here (though it is obviously ambiguous):

I may nót go. (=I not-must go)

Similarly there is a positive/negative relationship between:

You may go.
You mustn't go. (=You not-may go)

The semantic point is that no obligation to act equals permission not to act, and no permission to act equals obligation not to act. Hence we have:

Obligation not/no permission – *mustn't* or *may not.*
Permission not/no obligation – *may nót* (or *needn't*).

There is no need to look to other modals for the negative of MAY, but there is for the negative of MUST. Yet it would be no less plausible to say that MUST has no negative form that negates the modal (and that *needn't* merely fills a semantic gap) than to say that it has no past tense form and that *had to* fills that gap.

Needn't also functions as the negative of OUGHT, the orientation contrast with MUST being neutralized – see **5.2.9.**

5.3.7 Passives

Whether a sentence containing a modal can be passivized or not is largely dependent on the distinction between discourse and subject orientation. We should expect to find passivization with the former but not the latter. For with discourse orientation the meaning of the modal relates to the speaker who is exterior to the actors and actions indicated in the sentence, but with subject orientation it is linked to the subject of the sentence – and passivization changes the subject.

This is, in fact, the position with subject oriented WILL and discourse oriented SHALL. With WILL we cannot passivize, with SHALL we can:

John won't meet Mary.
! Mary won't be met by John.
John shall meet Mary.
Mary shall be met by John.

The semantic explanation is obvious. If John agrees to meet Mary, it does not follow that Mary agrees to meet John, but if I guarantee that John will meet Mary, I guarantee that Mary will be met by John.

CAN is, of course, discourse oriented when an alternative to MAY (5.1.3) and then permits passivization:

Parents can visit children at any time.
Children can be visited by parents at any time.

However, with both MAY and CAN it is sometimes necessary to interpret the subject as the person to whom permission is given. Passivization is not then possible:

John may/can meet Mary.
!Mary may/can be met by John.

Giving permission to John to meet Mary is not the same as giving permission to Mary to be met by John.

Subject oriented CAN will not permit passivization in such sentences as:

John can run a mile in four minutes.
**A mile can be run in four minutes by John.*

Passivization is, however, possible if the subject is accented for contrast or emphasis:

Jóhn can do this work.
This work can be done by Jóhn.

Passives are also possible if the agent is unspecified, *ie* in agentless passives or where the agent is 'anyone' (although semantically it is the agent not the subject of the passive sentence that has or does not have ability):

A mile can't be run in four minutes.
A mile can't be run in four minutes by anyone.

This is particularly true of the uses of CAN that are close to those of MAY, where orientation is neutralized:

(generalization) *Difficulties can be encountered from time to time.*
(general possibility) *It can be said that . . .*

In all these examples *can* may be replaced by *may*.

With OUGHT the position is less clear. We appear to have passivization in:

John ought to meet Mary.
Mary ought to be met by John.

The orientation distinction is only partially valid for OUGHT and MUST (5.2.8).

Similarly, with DARE we might not wish to see passivization in:

John daren't neglect this work.
? This work daren't be neglected by John.

But the passive is less unlikely with plural or more general agents:

This work daren't be neglected by students/the government.

There is no problem about the passivization with the WILL and SHALL of futurity. In this respect they function like tense forms (5.2.1). We can also passivize with the WILL of inference; this as we saw is not far semantically from being an epistemic modal (and epistemic modals allow passivization).

5.4 Epistemic modals

The discussion of the epistemic modals has been left to last because they lend themselves to a simple and neat analysis that is quite different from that of the non-epistemic ones. In formal terms they are clearly established by their negative and past tense forms (5.4.2, 5.4.3). Yet there is no absolute dividing line between the two classes. Some of the uses of CAN, MAY and WILL that we have already discussed are not far semantically or syntactically from the uses discussed here, and there are sentences in which it might be impossible to decide in principle whether the modal is epistemic or not.

5.4.1 Basic forms

A simple pattern is presented by the forms of WILL, MAY and MUST:

That'll be the position.
The French will be on holiday today.
He may be working in his study.
He may come to see me tomorrow.
There must be a hundred people there.
He must be a fool to do that.

There is, then, a basic system of three modals and we will base the discussion on three simple sentences:

He will be there.
He may be there.
He must be there.

These indicate three kinds of probability and possibility – WILL probability, MAY possibility and MUST certainty or 'conclusivity' – that he is there. CAN (in the negative form *can't*) and NEED (*needn't*) also fit into the system, but only as negatives (5.4.2).

OUGHT and (more commonly) *should*, however, also function as epistemic modals. They are closely related to MUST but with the meaning 'it is reasonable to conclude' rather than 'the conclusion is'. As with the epistemic modals they allow of the possibility of non-occurrence while MUST does not:

He ought to/should be there, but he isn't.
**He must be there, but he isn't.*

In general the epistemic modals refer, in the present tense, to the probability, certainty, etc, that something *is* now true. For this reason they occur usually only with forms that are either (*a*) progressive, (*b*) habitual or (*c*) forms of verbs of state:

He must be enjoying himself.
He must come every day.
He must live here.

We should not, then, normally interpret as epistemic:

He must come tomorrow.

The only epistemic interpretation of this is that it must be the case that tomorrow is the day that he usually comes (habitual). It would not mean that it is certain that he will come tomorrow.

MAY, however, is an exception to this. It is quite regularly used to refer to a single probable event in the future:

He may come tomorrow.

WILL also may refer to a single event in the future, but it is doubtful whether we can then identify an epistemic use as opposed to simple futurity:

He'll come tomorrow.

We should, perhaps, then allow that only MAY can refer epistemically to single future events. These remarks in no way affect, however, the parallelism with the MUST examples given above – and even the sentences just quoted could be interpreted epistemically to mean that it is possible or probable that tomorrow is the day he usually comes.

Passivization is always possible with epistemic modals because if it is possible, probable, etc that John meets Mary every day it is equally possible, probable, etc that Mary is met by John:

John must meet Mary every day.
Mary must be met by John every day.

But passivization will not distinguish the epistemic modals from the non-epistemic ones since some of the latter (especially the discourse oriented ones) also permit passivization.

5.4.2 Negation

The negative forms *may not*, *will not*, *mustn't* all negate the main verb not the modal, *ie* they do not deny the possibility, probability, certainty, but affirm the possibility, probability, certainty of the negation of the proposition:

He may not be there.	(It is possible he's not there)
He won't be there.	(It is possible he's not there)
He mustn't be there.	(It is certain he's not there)

How then do we negate the modal? With WILL there is no problem. As with the non-epistemic forms negation of the modals and of the verb cannot be distinguished – it is not probable that = it is probable that not. For the other two verbs there is a gap that has to be filled by other modals *can't* and (again) *needn't:*

He can't be there.	(It is not possible that he's there)
He needn't be there.	(It is not certain that he's there)

This would suggest the table:

	Modal negated	Main verb negated
MAY	*can't*	*may not*
MUST	*needn't*	*mustn't*

In practice *needn't* and *mustn't* are not commonly used. For as with the non-epistemic modal *not-may = must-not* and *not-must = may-not*. *Can't* and *may not* thus fill the gaps for MUST as well as for MAY, but in reverse – *may not* negates the modal and *can't* the main verb:

He can't be there.	(It is not possible that he's there)
	(It is certain that he's not there)
He may not be there.	(It is not certain that he's there)
	(It is possible that he's not there)

CAN, moreover, occurs instead of MAY in questions as well as negation:

Can it be true?
What can he be thinking of?

Indeed there is a contrast between CAN and MAY in:

What can that mean?
What may that mean?

The first is an enquiry about possible meanings – the epistemic modal. The second is used, often sarcastically, to ask *What do you mean by that?*

Though a specialized idiomatic use of *may* it is best regarded as an example of discourse oriented non-epistemic MAY.

Oughtn't and *shouldn't* also occur but like *mustn't* negate not the modal but the proposition:

He shouldn't be there. (It's reasonable to conclude that he is not there)

There are not obvious forms available to negate the modal, as distinct from those used to negate MUST (*needn't* and *may not*) – denial of a reasonable conclusion is not distinct from denial of a conclusion.

5.4.3 Past tense

The past tense forms of the modals, *would* and *might* (and negative *couldn't*) are found only with tentative meaning when used epistemically – never for past time:

He would be there.
He might be there.
He couldn't be there.

There is, perhaps, a plausible argument that *ought* and *should* are epistemically tentative forms of MUST, since there clearly is a semantic parallelism – tentative rather than absolute conclusion; the pattern would then be complete.

In general it is only the proposition not the probability, etc of it that can be in past time. Therefore the full verb alone is normally marked for past tense with *have:*

He may have been there.
He'll have been there.
He must have been there.
He can't have been there.

These may, of course, also occur with tentative *might*, *would* and *could*, and also with *ought* and *should.*

If we compare simple statements the modals + *have* seem to be three ways ambiguous. For the proposition in the above sentences may be related to one of three possible statements:

He has been there (since tea time).
He was there (yesterday).
He had been there (since the day before).

For we have:

He must have been there since tea time.

He must have been there yesterday.
He must have been there since the day before.

The *have* forms mark, then, perfect, past and past perfect (with the further possible distinction between past perfect and past past). But it is not that these are essentially ambiguous – it is rather that the distinctions are not made – we should not assume that a distinction made in one place in the language must always be made elsewhere if ambiguity is to be avoided.

It is, however, possible to refer to possibility (and perhaps probability) in the past, *eg:*

Things could be difficult in those days.
Life might be difficult in those days.

But these are better seen as the generalization uses of CAN and MAY ('it was sometimes'). There is one interesting and slightly enigmatic form, *had to:*

It had to be there.

This means 'I knew all along that it was there' and would be said when, for instance, an object had just been discovered in a cupboard and where previously the speaker had said or could have said:

It must be there.

Had to expresses certainty that was justified – where the proposition was shown to be true. There is also the negative counterpart to the *had to* form:

It couldn't be there.

This is, of course, in contrast with the negative counterpart of *must have:*

It can't have been there.

We could argue that with *had to* and *couldn't* we have examples of past tense for past time epistemic modals. There is, perhaps, one alternative – that these are essentially reported speech forms with a past tense verb of reporting *I knew* understood, or alternatively that the past tense (as well as the modality) is epistemic (3.1.7).

5.5 Conditionals

We dealt briefly with conditional sentences in the section on past tense with the primary patterns. But an analysis of conditional sentences deeply involves the modals, and much more must, therefore, be said here.

5.5.1 Tense and modals

The key to understanding conditionals in English lies in understanding the function of first, tense and secondly, the modals.

Let us first consider tense:

If John comes, he usually works in the garden.
If John came, he usually worked in the garden.

Here we have a clear use of tense to mark time. The first sentence contains a present tense verb in both clauses and refers to the present time; the second sentence contains past tense verbs and refers to past time. There is a complete contrast in the function of tense in:

If John comes tomorrow, he will work in the garden.
If John came tomorrow, he would work in the garden.

The formal differences are the same: the first contains present tense forms *comes* and *will*, the second past tense forms *came* and *would*. But there is no difference in the time reference of this pair of sentences – both refer to the future. The difference is in reality: the second with its past tense forms is an 'unreal' conditional, suggesting that the events envisaged are unlikely.

It is possible for a sentence both to be an unreal conditional and to refer to past time. The counterpart to the examples above is:

If John had come, he would have worked in the garden.

Formally, there is nothing new or surprising about a sentence of this kind. In both clauses past tense is marked twice, once for past time, once for unreality. In the *if* clause it is so marked by what is formally a past perfect but here functions as a past past; in the main clause past is marked once by the past tense form *would* and once by *have* (see **3**.3.4).

On the facts so far presented the analysis of conditional sentences is simple. We need distinguish only real and unreal conditionals. Unreal conditionals can be formed from the real conditionals by simply replacing present tense forms by past tense forms (and past tense forms by 'doubly past' forms).

Let us now consider the modals. From what was said in the last section it might be concluded that conditional sentences with past tense forms are ambiguous, since it is not clear whether the past tense is a mark of past time or unreality. In fact such ambiguity is rare for one reason – that unreal conditionals must always contain a modal (past tense) in the main clause. It follows, therefore, that there is no ambiguity in:

If John came, he worked in the garden.

This can only be a real, past tense, conditional. On the other hand, if the main clause contains a modal, ambiguity is possible (but unlikely, since the normal interpretation would be in terms of unreality). There is ambiguity in:

If John came, he would work in the garden.

The most likely interpretation is the unreal one – that in the unlikely event of John coming, he will work in the garden. But it is also possible to interpret the sentence in terms of past time – that if ever John came, he used to work in the garden. Such an interpretation would not be normally envisaged – it would require a special context, in which it was clear that we were talking about past events.

This requirement that an unreal conditional must contain a modal is not the only peculiarity of the modals. Even in real conditionals to refer to future events the modals have a special place in that the main clause will normally contain a modal. In particular WILL and SHALL are regularly used as conditionals to indicate simple futurity even though elsewhere BE GOING would be more usual (see **3.1.6**):

If it rains, the match will be cancelled.
? If it rains, the match is going to be cancelled.

If BE GOING occurs it is in some way 'marked' semantically – it is more than a simple conditional prediction:

If he comes, I'm going to leave.
If he comes, there's going to be trouble.

The first might be taken to indicate a threat, the second an inevitable disaster.

The other modals are also available to refer to the future in the main clause of a conditional sentence:

If you ask him, he'll come.
If we climb down, we can reach it.
If he comes, he shall be rewarded.
If you work hard, you may have a day off.
If they arrive, you must come and meet them.

But they cannot be replaced by near-synonymous forms. For instance, if we replace WILL and CAN by the near-synonymous non-modal forms AGREE and BE ABLE, these must be additionally marked for future time by WILL:

If you ask him, he'll agree to come.
! If you ask him, he agrees to come.

If we climb down, we'll be able to reach it.
! If we climb down, we are able to reach it.

Incidentally, it might also be argued that the non-occurrence of *would* and *could*, in their positive forms, to refer to events in past time (5.3.1) is also related to the conditional nature of WILL and CAN:

**I asked him and he would come.*
I asked him and he agreed to come.
**I ran fast and could catch the bus.*
I ran fast and was able to catch the bus.

For there is no difficulty with:

Why don't you ask him? He would come.
Why not run fast? Then you could catch the bus.

Here there is an implied condition. Where, as in the earlier sentences, there is no possibility of interpretation in terms of an implied condition (for the events have actually taken place) *would* and *should* cannot be used.

5.5.2 Types of conditional

In attempting to distinguish kinds of conditional sentences let us look at present tense real conditionals only. The unreal and past tense forms will be considered in later sections.

[i] The most obvious kind of conditional (perhaps the only 'true' conditional) is the one that predicts that if one event takes place, another will follow:

If it rains, the match will be cancelled.

In such conditionals (which I shall call 'predictive'), reference is to future time indicated in the main clause by a modal (5.5.1) but in the subordinate (*if*) clause by a simple (present tense) form of a verb (not by WILL or SHALL).

[ii] *If* may have a meaning close to *whenever* – to link two habitual actions. This is illustrated by:

If it rains, I go by car.
If they study, they stay in their rooms.

[iii] The condition is a simple implication – the truth of the one clause following from the truth of the other:

If he's here, he's in the garden.
If he acts like that, he's a fool.

This also accounts for the jocular type of sentence:

If he's the Prime Minister, I'm a Dutchman.
If he's Marconi, I'm Einstein.

[iv] The *if* clause may do no more than indicate the conditions under which the main clause has any relevance or news value:

If you're going out, it's raining.
If you want to know, I haven't seen him.

The last type is clearly of a special kind with semantically some kind of ellipsis – *If . . . it is relevant to say that* . . .. But it is not at all clear that the other three types are essentially distinct. Admittedly one predicts, one states regular circumstances and the other states implication. But these could be regarded as mere variations upon the notion of the truth of one statement depending on the truth of another; it could be argued that *if* does no more than state truth relations. However, it is usually possible to distinguish the three types and there is some difference in their function with relation to unreality and past tense. For that reason I shall handle them separately, dealing first with the most 'typical' type, the predictive.

5.5.3 Predictive conditionals

We have already noted that apart from some reservations with BE GOING (5.5.1), a modal must occur in the main clause of:

(1) All unreal conditionals.
(2) Real present 'predictive' conditionals.

The predictive conditionals are in fact essentially 'modal' in that they *must* contain a modal (though the presence of a modal does not, conversely, always indicate a predictive conditional).

There are in fact three possible kinds of predictive modal – real present, unreal present and unreal past:

Real present

If it rains, the match will be cancelled.

Unreal present

If it rained, the match would be cancelled.

Unreal past

If it had rained, the match would have been cancelled.

One might have expected on grounds of pattern to find also real past conditionals, but these cannot occur for an obvious semantic reason. We can predict what will happen (real present), what might happen (unreal present) and what would have happened under different circumstances (unreal past) but not what did actually happen (real past). Thus a sentence such as the following does not predict:

If it rained, the match was cancelled.

This has to be interpreted as one of the other two kinds of conditionals, either as the 'whenever' type or the implication ('it follows that') type. Formally, of course, a form with a past tense modal looks like the past time counterpart of a present real conditional:

If it rained, the match would be cancelled.

But this will never be the case. This would either be unreal present predictive or one of the other types – most likely the 'whenever' kind.

Any of the modals in any of their uses may occur in the main clause of a real present predictive conditional (leaving aside the epistemic modals which raise special problems – 5.5.5). Examples are to be found in 5.5.1. The subject oriented modals WILL and CAN are to be found in their various uses in unreal present and in unreal past conditionals also. Examples (with the present real conditionals given first) are:

WILL	volition	*If you ask them, they'll come.*
CAN	sensation	*If you come here, you can see it.*
	ability	*If you train, you can run three miles.*
		If you asked them, they'd come.
		If you came here, you could see it.
		If you trained, you could run three miles.
		If you had asked them, they'd have come.
		If you had come here, you could have seen it.
		If you had trained, you could have run three miles.

This is true of OUGHT also – with *ought* functioning as a past tense (for unreality):

If he wants to know, he ought to ask me.
If he wanted to know, he ought to ask me.
If he'd wanted to know, he ought to have asked me.

The discourse oriented modals have no unreal forms and do not occur as unreal conditionals, past or present, except, possibly, for discourse oriented CAN:

If you finish early, you can go.
If you finished early, you could go.

Yet MAY is not possible here:

If you finish early, you may go.
**If you finished early, you might go.*

But we cannot be sure that this is an example of discourse oriented CAN – it could be argued that it is subject oriented or that the orientation is neutralized.

For DARE and NEED the forms of the full verb are used:

If he came, you wouldn't need to go.
If he came, you wouldn't dare to go.

A form sometimes used in the *if* clause is *were to* with no difference of meaning except perhaps greater unreality as in:

If you were to go, I should be angry.
(*If you went, I should be angry.*)

This is possible, but rare, with inversion and no *if:*

Were you to go, I should be angry.

Similarly an alternative form of the unreal past conditionals is possible with inversion and no *if:*

Had you asked them, they would have come.

This is quite common – more so than the inverted *were to* forms.

The unreal past conditionals are essentially 'impossible' or 'unfulfilled', and there are a number of forms with no *if* clause that may be explained in terms of implied unfulfilled, unreal conditions – 'if you had asked me', 'if he had wished', 'if things had been different':

WILL	volition	*I would have done that for you.*
CAN	ability	*I could have lifted that.*

We must be careful to note, however, that past tense modal forms may occur in conditionals without indicating either time or unreality in two ways. First, they may merely be tentative forms accounted for quite independently, or the special forms of *would, should* and *might* (5·3·3, 5·3·4). As such they do not affect the status of the real conditional:

If I ask him, he would agree.
If he comes, he should tell me.
If you behave, I might tell you about it.
If you could do that, I shall leave early.
If he would agree, we shall be happy.

Secondly, there is a special use of *should* that occurs in *if* clauses:

If I should see him, I'll tell you.
If you should see him, let me know.

This also occurs with inversion and no *if* to form the conditional:

Should I see him, I'll tell you.
Should you see him, let me know.

This could, because it occurs with pronouns other than *I* and *we*, be related to the SHALL of obligation. But it is not semantically the tentative form of that use. Certainly it is tentative in its meaning – there is an indication of unlikeliness, but it has no present tense counterpart. These too are real conditionals, as the present tense form of the main clause shows – *should* here is not to be explained in terms of an unreal conditional.

5.5.4 Other conditionals

The other types of conditional seem rarely, if ever, to occur as unreal conditionals, but they have more freedom with regard to tense (and phase):

[i] There is no problem with the 'whenever' type. We can freely change tense or phase:

If it rained, I went by car.
If they've studied, they've stayed in their rooms.

There can even be a difference of phase or tense in the two clauses:

If it has rained in the deserts, the flowers blossom.
If they ever won, they had always trained hard.

[ii] With the implication type there is no restriction whatever on any kind of tense or time marking. A statement relating to any time can be made to imply a statement relating to any other time – not merely past and past or present and present:

If he was here, he was in the garden.
If he was here, he's now in the garden.
If he was here, he'll be in the garden soon.
If he's here, he was in the garden.
If he said that, he was a fool.
If he said that, he is a fool.

[iii] With the third type, the 'relevance' type, the *if* clause is likely to be present tense, with no tense/time restrictions in the main clause:

If you want to know, I see/have seen/shall see/saw/had seen him.

We have already noted that modals are not excluded from these types of conditional. They are, indeed, quite normal in the 'whenever' type to refer to past habitual actions – the habitual use of *would* (5.3.4) and the generalization use of *could* or *might* (5.3.1):

If we climbed the hill, we would/could/might see the sunset.

(These could, of course, also be interpreted as unreal present predictive.)

5.5.5 Epistemic modals

The epistemic modals raise a few problems. Semantically they seem closest to the implicational type:

If he's here, he'll be in the garden.
If he said that, he must be a fool.

In particular there is no reference to future events in these examples – only to the present. Equally there are examples of real past:

If he was here, he'll have been in the garden.

On the other hand, we have unreal present and unreal past forms:

If he was here, he'd be in the garden.
If he'd been here, he'd have been in the garden.

This is, of course, characteristic of the predictive type. It seems, then, that the epistemic modals combine the functions of the implicational and predictive conditionals, and thus alone occur in all four theoretically possible types, present real, present unreal, past real and past unreal. Notice, incidentally (see 3.2.3), that in the present unreal forms *were* is possible in place of *was*, but not in the past real:

If he were here, he'd be in the garden.
**If he were here, he'll have been in the garden.*

A rather surprising, and in terms of the overall pattern irregular, form is the use of *may have* for an impossible unfulfilled epistemic condition:

You may have been killed.

This might be uttered to a child who had crossed a road at a dangerous place or time. More 'correct' would be:

You might have been killed.

Finally, let us note that there is striking ambiguity with *could have:*

He could have been there.

This may mean either that he possibly was there or that he was not there but it would have been possible. The second of these is the impossible unfulfilled conditional with tense marked for unreality and past time. The first is a tentative epistemic modal plus reference to past time in the proposition – it is possible (tentatively) that he was. In this case past tense is clearly marked independently in the modal for tentative and in the main verb for past time. With the unfulfilled conditionals past tense is marked twice but not separately – the gloss on *could have been* is not 'would be possible to have been' but 'would have been possible to be'.

5.5.6 WILL again

It was clearly shown in **5.2.1** (and again in **5.5.2**) that WILL and SHALL do not occur in an *if* clause merely to indicate futurity, the simple (present tense) form being used instead. But this is true only where the events in the *if* clause are previous to or contemporary with the events in the main clause. This is, of course, the normal situation since conditionals indicate, in a loose sense, cause and effect, and effects do not precede their causes. But sometimes the condition of an event may be an event subsequent to it or seen as likely to be subsequent to it. Where we have this apparent reversal of time relations *will* may be used in the conditional clause. An example is:

If the play will be cancelled, let's not go.

The suggestion is that we should not go if the play is going to be cancelled subsequent to our going. The cancellation is future to the going and *will* is retained. This sentence is thus quite different from:

If the play is cancelled, let's not go.

Here we have the more normal situation – the going or the decision not to go follows and results from the cancellation of the play.

Sometimes even more is implied in the use of *will* in the conditional clause – that the events described there are a likely result of events mentioned or implied in the main clause. This is illustrated by:

If it'll be of any help, I'll come along.

The 'logic' of this is quite complex. It says, roughly, that I'll come along if it now seems to be the case that by coming along I shall be of some help. It would be possible to say instead:

If it helps, I'll come along.

This is not very different in its implications, but what it says is merely that if my coming along helps, I will come.

A more difficult pair of examples, which nevertheless make the point quite strikingly, is:

If he's left destitute, I'll change my will.
If he'll be left destitute, I'll change my will.

In the first the change of the will follows, and is conditional on, the man being left destitute. In the second the implication is that the man's being left destitute is dependent upon the will or the changing of it. In fact there are two possible interpretations of this example. The first is like that of the *If it'll help . . .* example – I will change my will, if by so doing he will be left destitute. This interpretation is the most obvious from the grammar but contextually a little unlikely (a very spiteful father?). A second possibility sees a rather looser link – I will change my will, if in its present form I shall leave him destitute. In either case the leaving of the man destitute is seen as subsequent to events mentioned in the main clause.

5.5.7 Wishes

In wishes – forms introduced by *eg: I wish, If only* – the position is similar to that in the *if* clause of unreal conditionals. For present time (or future time where the present tense form has future time reference) a past tense form is used; for past time a past perfect or past tense modal plus *have* is used:

I wish I knew.
I wish I was going with you tomorrow.
I wish I could do that.
I wish I had seen him.
I wish I could have gone with you.

But there is one important difference. A simple, non-modal, past tense form is not used to refer to the future, as it is in conditionals. In conditionals we relate:

It'll rain tomorrow.
If it rained tomorrow . . .

Yet we shall not similarly relate:

!I wish it rained tomorrow.

This relates rather to:

It rains tomorrow,

(*ie* tomorrow is the day of the week or year on which it always rains – a fixed pattern, *cf* 3.5.2). The form is, instead:

I wish it would rain tomorrow.

In many cases, however, the occurrence of *would* seems to be an example of the WILL of volition, not plain futurity:

I wish you would make up your mind.
If only he would help!

This could be argued even in the case of *I wish it would rain tomorrow,* since we may attest:

If it'll rain tomorrow . . .

This, of course, must be the WILL of volition since for plain futurity we should find (5.2.2):

If it rains . . .

This is supported by the fact that the following are unlikely:

?I wish I should see him tomorrow.
?I wish I would see him tomorrow.

We have instead:

I wish I was seeing him tomorrow.
I wish I was going to see him tomorrow.

The improbability of *?I wish I would/should* suggests that WILL (and SHALL) do not occur in wishes for simple futurity. Yet this is not indicated, as it is in conditionals, by the simple non-modal form, but by some other form – especially the progressive or BE GOING.

There is one other combination in which past tense forms occur – after *It's time:*

It's time we went.
It's time you could. (In reply to *I can't*)

Notes

1 Palmer and Blandford (1939:131).
2 Boyd and Thorne (1969:58).
3 Ota (1969:2).
4 For a very different approach see Diver (1964).
5 Ehrman (1966:22).
6 *Cf* Huddleston (1971:299).

Chapter 6

Marginal verbs

There are a number of verbal forms that fall only partly within the category of auxiliary (these have already been discussed briefly); there are others that do not strictly belong to the class of auxiliary but have considerable auxiliary-like qualities.

6.1 Auxiliaries as full verbs

Let us consider first BE, HAVE and DO.

6.1.1 BE

There are, it would appear, three other verbs BE, one a full verb, the others problematic.

[i] BE is a full verb in English. We find such sentences as:

He is very sad.
He was in the garden.

In function the verbal forms are exactly paralleled by the forms in the following:

He seems very sad.
He sat in the garden.

Unless we have a completely new definition of 'auxiliary', BE is a full verb in these sentences. It is not followed by any other verb, and has no place at all in the tables that have already been set up. The full verb has the following characteristics of an auxiliary:

(*a*) it has all the finite and non-finite positive forms – *am*, *is*, *are*, *was*, *were*, *been* and *being*, all with the same function with regard to number and person as the auxiliary BE (9.1.1);

b) it has all the weak forms (9.1.3):

I'm sad. [aim sæd]
He's sad. [hiːz sæd]
We were sad. [wiː wə sæd] etc

(*c*) it occurs in negation, inversion, code and emphatic affirmation without DO:

He isn't sad.
Is he sad?
I am sad and so is he.
He ís sad.

Not only do these forms occur without DO, but, with certain exceptions (below), they cannot occur with DO. We shall not find:

**He doesn't be sad.*
**Does he be sad?*
**I am sad and so does he.*
**He dóes be sad.*

It is because of these characteristics of BE, even when a full verb, that H. E. Palmer refers to the 'anomalous finites',[1] which are not to be identified with the auxiliary verbs. The finite forms of BE are anomalous finites' whether they are forms of the full verb or the auxiliary.

[ii] A characteristic of the auxiliaries and of BE as a full verb is that they do not occur with DO. But there are some forms of BE that occur with DO.

(*a*) As we have already seen (3.1.2), there is no imperative form **ben't*; instead *don't be* occurs. *Do be* is also found. But as these are characteristic of the primary auxiliaries, we need take no special note of them when occurring as forms of the full verb:

Do be at home when I call.
Don't be too confident.

(*b*) There is no use of DO with the primary auxiliary, however, that is similar to its occurrence in:

If you don't be quick, you'll miss them.
If he doesn't be a good boy, I shan't give him anything.
Why don't you be careful!

The positive form is even more striking:

If you be quick, you'll see them.

Here *be* occurs as a finite (present tense) form. In fact, we could equally use the 'regular' forms in these sentences:

If you aren't quick . . .
If he isn't a good boy . . .
If you're quick . . .

Moreover, the only positive form with the third person singular is:

If he's a good boy . . .

But there is a difference. *Be* is used to refer only to temporary states, the other forms may refer to permanent states. We may contrast:

If you be quick, you'll catch him.
If you're quick, why do you take such a long time?

There is a very similar use of a verb BE with a finite form *be*, in the sense of 'agree to play the part of':

If you be the queen, I'll be the king.

Again there is a contrast:

If you're the queen, then I'm Julius Caesar!
(= *You're no more the queen than I am Julius Caesar.*)

We must recognize here another verb BE which has *be* as a finite form, as well as *am* and *are*. But there is no similar form to replace *is*, or to replace *was* and *were*. We might expect *[biːz] and *[biːd], and indeed I have attested both in the speech of children.

[iii] Forms of the verb BE are also followed by the *to*-infinitive:

He's to come tomorrow.
You are to be congratulated.
They are to be married next week.
They were to have come today.

BE with *to* has a sense close to that of MUST or OUGHT (first two examples) or of the WILL of futurity (the second two). It is very commonly used for the 'future in the past'. In this usage its forms occur without DO in negation, inversion, etc:

He isn't to do that.
Am I to understand that you are coming?
He's to come and so are you.
They áre to come.

A possible treatment of these forms is in terms of a verb BE that is a modal auxiliary. For it follows the pattern of the modals in not occurring with other modals or being marked for aspect or phase:

**He will be to go.*
**He is being to go.*
**He has been to go.*

It shares with OUGHT alone the characteristic of being followed by the *to*-infinitive. But it differs in one respect from the modals, in that it has the finite forms *am*, *is*, *are*, *was* and *were* (in contrast with *can*, *could*, etc).

Rather different are:

The house is to let.
He is to blame.

For in spite of the active form *to let* and *to blame*, the sense is passive. We may compare (with some difference of meaning, but not of that of active versus passive):

The house is to be let.
He is to be blamed.

These latter sentences do belong to the pattern discussed here. But *to let* and *to blame* must be treated as idioms; we shall not attest similar forms with other verbs:

**The house is to paint.*
**He is to punish.*

6.1.2 HAVE

There are, perhaps, five verbs HAVE, one a full verb, the others problematic.

[i] Like BE, HAVE is a full verb:

He has plenty of money.
He had a fever.

These are completely paralleled by:

He earns plenty of money.
He caught a fever.

But this HAVE has no passive (4.1.2):

**Plenty of money is had by him.*
**A fever was had by him.*

The full verb has the following characteristics of an auxiliary:

(*a*) it has the finite form *has*, which is quite 'irregular' as a form of a full verb (9.1.1);

(*b*) it has weak forms (9.1.3):

He has a nice house. [hiː həz]
They'd nothing to say. [ðeid]
I've a good idea to . . . [aiv]

(*c*) it occurs in negation, inversion, etc:

I haven't anything.
Have you a pencil?
I've a pen and so has he.
He hás some.

Like CONTAIN, POSSESS, HOLD (4.1.2), HAVE in this sense occurs in the passive only where it indicates activity – obtaining rather than mere possession:

Breakfast can be had at ten.

There is one apparent exception:

A good time was had by all.

But this is a fixed phrase, perhaps deliberately unusual. We cannot similarly say:

**A good holiday was had by us.*

As in the case of BE the forms considered here are anomalous finites but not auxiliary verbs.

A common alternative to HAVE is HAVE GOT, morphologically the perfect of GET:

I've got a pound.
I haven't got a pound.
Have you got a pound?
I've got a pound and so has he.

[ii] There are some forms of HAVE which occur with DO even where an anomalous finite would be grammatically possible:

The village shop doesn't have ice-cream.
Did you have a good time?

These forms are not in free variation with the anomalous finites. There is a quite different sentence:

The village shop hasn't ice-cream (or *any ice-cream*).

The first sentence means that the shop does not stock ice-cream, the second that it has none in stock. We can even say:

The shop hasn't any ice-cream, because it doesn't have ice-cream.
The shop hasn't any ice-cream, but it does have it.

But we cannot similarly compare:

Did you have a good time?
**Had you a good time?*

The latter sentence is not possible.

We must, then, recognize another verb HAVE. Perhaps the simplest statement about the difference between the two verbs HAVE is that HAVE with the anomalous finites is used only to refer to actual possession, ownership or characteristics at a given time, while the HAVE whose forms occur with DO is used in all other cases. With this latter verb it may, perhaps, be possible to distinguish two usages, though they are not wholly distinct:

(*a*) The verb is used in the general sense of TAKE, RECEIVE, GET, EXPERIENCE:

Did you have nice weather?
We didn't have a good holiday.
Did you have any trouble getting here?
They had breakfast at ten and so did we.
Did you have a letter from me this morning?
What did she have – a boy or a girl?

(*b*) It is used to refer to habitual 'having', as in:

The village shop doesn't have ice-cream.
Does he have money in his pocket when he goes to school?

The picture is, however, complicated by the fact that even in the sense of 'to have in one's possession', HAVE may occur with DO in certain cases. First, it occurs in the speech of many Americans, and to some degree in my own speech in:

I don't have any money.
Do you have a match?
He has a hat and so do I.
I dó have one.

Secondly, the past tense *did+have* occurs even in standard British speech:

He didn't have any money or *He hadn't any money.*
Did the shop have any ice-cream?
John had a pound and so did Mary or . . . *so had Mary.*

In the inverted form especially, DO is required – sentences such as the following are most improbable:

**Had the shop any ice-cream?*
**Had John a pound?*

[iii] Forms of the verb HAVE are also followed by the *to*-infinitive:

I have to go now.
They had to tell you that.

In this usage HAVE expresses obligation or necessity, and is close in meaning to MUST (but *cf* **5**.2.8).

The forms commonly occur with DO:

I don't have to go now.
Did they have to tell you that?
I had to do it and so did she.
We dó have to see them.

But the anomalous finites are also possible, if less likely:

You haven't to go yet.
Have I to see him?
I have to and so have you.
We háve to go.

This verb occurs with modals and may be marked for aspect and phase:

He will have to go.
He has had to be told.
He is having to think again.

The simplest analysis is to treat HAVE here as a full verb. That some of its forms are anomalous finites is an exceptional feature, but is wholly paralleled by the fact that the other full verb HAVE, as well as BE, follows the pattern of auxiliaries in this respect.

A further point to be noted, which strengthens the case for treating the verb here as a different verb, is that orthographic *have* is frequently phonetically [hæf] with a final voiceless consonant as in:

[ai hæf tə gou nau] *I have to go now.*

The auxiliary and the full verb that was dealt with in the previous section have the form [hæv] but not [hæf] (*cf* 9.5):

[ai hæv teikn it] *I have taken it.*
[ai hæv tu:] *I have two.*

Finally, as with the first verb HAVE a common alternative is HAVE GOT (morphologically the perfect of GET):

I've got to go now.

In rapid colloquial speech this may be [gɔtə]:

[ai gɔtə gou nau].

The past tense *had got* is possible but rarer. We may attest:

I'd got to go.

More common would be:

I had to go.

[iv] HAVE also occurs in such sentences as:

I'm having a new house built.
He has his hair cut once a month.

In these sentences it is a catenative. It does not have an alternative in HAVE GOT:

**He's got his hair cut once a month.*

But GET (not HAVE GOT) is equivalent to HAVE here:

I'm getting a new house built.
He gets his hair cut once a month.

HAVE in this use may be followed by a bare infinitive an *-ing* form, or an *-en* form. Examples are to be found in 7.4.2.

[v] There are two uses of the form *had* in which it occurs with the bare infinitive. These are exemplified by:

I'd better stay at home.
If I'd have known, I wouldn't have gone.

The first of these is quite common (but see **6.2.3**). The strong form of *'d* is *had:*

Had I better stay at home?

If it were not for this the form would fit more easily into the general pattern by interpreting *'d* as the weak form of *would*, since WILL regularly occurs with the bare infinitive (whereas HAVE does not). In this use it follows exactly the pattern of the auxiliaries:

I hadn't better go.
Had I better go?
I'd better go and so had you.
I hád better go.

The second of the usages (*If I'd have known*) is one that will be rejected in a normative grammar and will be interpreted as an error for *If I'd known*. But there can be no doubt that it is attested, and we cannot even exclude:

Had I have known . . .

But the form is quite exceptional. Though it is followed by an infinitive, it is always the infinitive *have*, while the verb that follows i almost always KNOW (*known*). Such sentences as **If I'd have come* . . . are sufficiently rare to be discounted.

6.1.3 DO

There is very little to say about DO apart from the auxiliary.

[i] DO is a full verb in:

He does a lot of work.
I'll do my duty.
He did nothing about it.

Unlike BE and HAVE, there are no anomalous finites of DO as a full verb. We cannot say:

**He doesn't a lot of work.*
**Did he his duty?*

With negation and inversion, that is to say, we require the auxiliary DO:

He doesn't do a lot of work.
Did he do his duty?

Similarly with the emphatic affirmative the auxiliary is required:

He díd do a lot of work.

With 'code' of course it is impossible to tell by the form whether we have the full verb or the auxiliary in:

He does a lot of work and so do I.

The full verb DO has no weak forms, but there is no contrast in this respect between full verb and auxiliary since the weak forms of the auxiliary occur in a position in which the full verb cannot – initially with inversion. Neither of the following is possible:

**He does* [dəz] *a lot of work.*
**He does* [dəz] *come.*

In one respect only does the full verb have a characteristic of an auxiliary – in that its *-s* (in speech) form is irregular:

do [duː] but *does* [dʌz] not *[duːz].

[ii] In 'code' the auxiliary DO functions as what might be called an 'empty'[2] or zero auxiliary – it occurs where an auxiliary is required by the grammatical rule and there is no auxiliary in comparable forms. But it is not possible to interpret the following in this way:

If you want to go you can do so.
They decided not to go. To do so would have made things very difficult.

DO is here a 'pro-form' in the sense that it refers back to, 'stands for', another verb, but a full verb, not an auxiliary. That DO here is not an auxiliary is shown by:

Don't be reading when I come in.
**To be so . . .*
To be doing so . . .

These show that the auxiliaries do not have 'code' function in their *to*-infinitive forms (the question arises only of course for primary auxiliaries – the modals have no infinitives). In *to do so* DO must be an 'empty' full verb, rather than an 'empty' auxiliary.

Similarly DO is used in question forms with the catenatives (7.1.5):

What does he want to do?
What do you like doing?
What do you want them to do?

6.2 Quasi auxiliaries

We now look at a few verbs that have auxiliary-like qualities.

6.2.1 USED

USED is a very marginal member of the primary auxiliaries. In terms of negation, inversion, code and emphatic affirmation its status is very dubious since some forms are much more acceptable than others:

He usedn't to act like that.
? Used he to act like that?
**I used to act like that and so used he.*
He úsed to act like that.

The verb, however, also functions as a full verb with DO:

He didn't use to act like that.
Did he use to act like that?
I used to act like that and so did he.
He díd use to act like that.

Some speakers of English might feel uncomfortable with some of these – that they are slightly substandard. But with code *did* is the only possible form.

The commonest negation form is with *not* [nɔt]:

He used not to act like that.

If we interpret the negative as negating *used* then it is here an auxiliary, but it could be argued that *not* negates the following verb, and that USED is a full verb like PREFER in:

He prefers not to act like that.

The semantics give no answer. It is impossible to distinguish not being in the habit of doing something and being in the habit of not doing something.

The verb looks orthographically like the full verb USE, but it has little in common semantically. Moreover, it is distinct morphologically in that the normal form is [juːst] and not [juːzd], which is the past tense of USE only (we should compare the similar form of *have* [hæf] **6.1.2** and *cf* **9.5**).

6.2.2 BE GOING

Forms of BE GOING are very commonly used for future time reference. Morphologically they share with the auxiliaries the existence of weak forms which vary from [gənə] to [ŋ], with the appropriate form of BE preceding:

I am going to do that.
[aim gənə duː ðæt]
[aiŋ ŋ duː ðæt]

This form is synchronically unrelated to the verb GO. Orthographically we have an identical sentence meaning that I am going somewhere in order to do that. But this cannot have similar weak forms. We cannot, for instance, say:

I'm going to London.
*[aiŋ ŋ lʌndən]

The BE GOING forms are in some sense the 'purest' future forms of English. They simply predict that an action will take place. In most cases there is no demonstrable difference between *will/shall* and BE GOING though many scholars have looked without success for one:[3]

It'll rain this afternoon.
It's going to rain this afternoon.
I shall be better next week.
I am going to be better next week.

Of course WILL, unlike BE GOING, often indicates volition and there is contrast, therefore, in:

He'll come tomorrow.
He's going to come tomorrow.

There are conditions, however, under which WILL and BE GOING would normally be interpreted differently.

First, as we saw in **5.2.1**, BE GOING is not normally used for displaced tense:

The man next to you this evening will be the Mayor.
! The man next to you this evening is going to be the Mayor.

Secondly, WILL but not BE GOING is often interpreted conditionally, in the sense that it indicates events conditional upon certain other events mentioned or implied in the context. This is clear in:

Don't sit on that rock. It'll fall.
Don't sit on that rock. It's going to fall.

The first sentence would always be taken to mean that it will fall if you sit on it; the likely interpretation for the second is that it is going to fall anyway, whether you sit on it or not. *Will/shall* are, of course, commonly used in the main clause of conditionals referring to the future:

If he comes in, I shall leave.

But there is no absolute rule here. The same conditions could be stated by:

If he comes in, I'm going to leave.

Yet, as we have just seen, if the condition is implicit, not explicit, WILL but not BE GOING is to be interpreted conditionally.

Much more subtle is the distinction in:

In an hour, the paint will be dry.
In an hour, the paint's going to be dry.

The first is appropriate where the suggestion is that the paint should be left to dry, but the second might suggest that it should not be left for an hour for then it will be too late (perhaps to retouch it). This again is to be accounted for in terms of implicit condition. The first says 'If you leave it an hour, it will be dry'. The second, however, says 'It will be dry in an hour – and you must take the consequences'.

6.2.3 BETTER, RATHER and LET'S

It was once, half jokingly, suggested that English has three auxiliaries [betə], [ɔːtə] and [gɔtə] (*better*, *ought to* and *got to*). For the 'weakening' of the *to* – see **9.5**. The first is related to *had better* (**6.1.2**) in *eg:*

You hadn't better go.

In the positive form, however, there is often no indication in speech of the *had* form even though it is written:

You'd better go.

But although interpretation in terms of *had better* is the traditional one, it results in a completely idiosyncratic form since HAVE does not otherwise occur with the bare infinitive:

**You had go.*

I have actually heard children say:

[betnt hi]

This is not surprising – *better* sounds like *ought to* and is treated like it. But we can do no more than note that it is a most anomalous verbal form.

Closely associated with *had better* is *would rather*. In normal conversation the distinction of *had* and *would* is lost since both are merely [d]. It could be plausibly argued that these are related in terms of discourse and subject orientation, *had better* indicating what the speaker (or hearer), *would rather* what the subject, regards as desirable. There are no obvious past time forms to support this formally, but it is supported to some degree by the passivization test:

He'd better meet her.
She'd better be met by him.
He'd rather meet her.
! She'd rather be met by him.

Let's is what grammarians would call the 'first person imperative' as in:

Let's go.

It is quite distinct now from the verb LET (=PERMIT) as in:

Let us go.

The *let's* form can have the strong form (*let us*) as well as the weak (*let's*), but the full verb LET can occur only with the 'strong' form. It occurs with the tag *shall we:*

Let's go, shall we?

This relates it to the imperative where the normal tag is *Won't you:*

Go, won't you?

Notes

1 Palmer and Blandford (1939: 122).
2 Twaddell (1965: 148).
3 Most recently Binnick (1972).

Chapter 7

The catenatives

We now turn to look at the catenatives and the 'complex phrase' in which they function. We are concerned with sentences such as:

He kept talking.
I want to go to London.
I saw John come up the street.

In these sentences there are two full verbs, the first a catenative. But there is no limit upon the number of verbs that may co-occur in this way, provided that all except the last are catenatives. Examples of sentences with more than two (the last from a book about Linguistics) are:

I got him to persuade her to ask him to change his mind.
He kept on asking her to help him get it finished.
I don't want to have to be forced to begin to try to make more money.

The term complex phrase is, as we saw in the first chapter, a little misleading in that we must recognize two or more verb phrases, indeed that we have two or more clauses involving subordination. But these complex phrases are grammatical units of a kind that other sequences involving verb forms are not. They are merely one step further in terms of freedom of association from the verb phrases involving first the primary auxiliaries and then the modals. They are quite different, in this way, from sequences such as:

I bought the boat to sail the world.
He walked away thinking about the disaster.

In these we cannot establish any close relationship either semantically or syntactically between *bought* and *to sail*, *walked* and *thinking*. The link is entirely one of the syntax of clauses within the sentences. But there is a much 'tighter' syntactic and semantic relationship between the catenative and its following verb; there is a great deal to be said about the restrictions of occurrence. We cannot, for instance, say:

**He kept to talk.*
**I want going to London.*

These are as ungrammatical as:

**He has talking.*
**He can to go to London.*

It is to emphasize the way that the catenatives share grammatical characteristics with the primary and modal auxiliaries (and in some cases are not clearly distinct from them – see 7.1.2) that the term 'complex phrase' can be justified.

For simplicity we shall deal only with complex phrases involving two verb forms and so talk about the 'main' and the 'subordinate' clause. In longer complex phrases there would be successive 'layers' of subordination, but the grammatical relations between each pair are the same.

7.1 Problems of statement

The first task of the analysis is to establish the basic constructions that are involved, as it was the first task to establish the paradigm of the primary and modal auxiliaries. But there are some difficult theoretical problems involving the relation between the subordinate and the main clauses and between the nominal elements, the noun phrases or NPs, within these clauses. There are also problems about the way in which the catenatives may be classified, about the relevance of the classification to their semantic properties, and about the status of the verbs that seem to belong to more than one class. We shall discuss these problems in some detail before presenting an overall classification in 7.4. There is a further problem, that of distinguishing the complex phrases from apparently related or similar structures. This will be left until the overall classification is completed (7.5).

7.1.1 Basic structures

There are two obvious sets of criteria for the classification of the catenatives in terms of the constructions with which they occur.

First, there are the four types of verb forms with which they may be followed (the four that were first noted in **2.1.1**):

bare infinitive	*He helped wash up.*
to-infinitive	*He wants to go to London.*
-ing form	*He keeps talking about it.*
-en form	*He got shot in the riot.*

For the majority of the catenatives, however, only the second and third are relevant.

Secondly, a noun phrase may or may not occur between the catenative and the following verb. Compared with the sentences above we may note (though not in every case is it possible to keep the same verbs):

bare infinitive	*He helped them wash up.*
to-infinitive	*He wants them to go to London.*
-ing form	*He kept them talking a long time.*
-en form	*He had the rioters shot.*

The precise syntactic status of the noun phrase is a topic for later discussion (**7.2.1**). But we shall be able to refer, quite simply, to complex phrases 'with' or 'without NP'.

7.1.2 Simple and complex phrases

It has already been assumed that catenatives occur in complex rather than simple verb phrases, involving subordination, though it has been stressed that these complex phrases still share some of the characteristics of the simple phrase. As such they are clearly full verbs, not auxiliaries.

One important distinguishing feature is the one just noted – that there can be in the complex, but not in the simple verb phrase, an intervening NP. Yet as we shall see later (**7.2.1**) this NP has a close grammatical relationship with the verb forms around it that actually supports the notion of complex verb phrase.

We must, however, look briefly at the three 'tests' of simple versus complex phrases (see **2.1.4**, **3.1.8**, **5.1.2**).

[i] In terms of negation there can be no doubt that the catenatives occur in complex phrases. Negation may be independently marked with each of the verbs:

He did not agree to do anything.
He agreed not to do anything.
I don't like having a television set.
I like not having a television set.

The bare infinitive and the *-en* form are not often negated, but there is no absolute restriction:

Have you ever known him not come?
I don't like children not taught road safety.

Where there are restrictions they seem to be semantic rather than grammatical:

**He helped not wash up.*
**He failed not to come.*
**She got not hurt in the accident.*
? She saw the children not crossing the road.

We do not 'help', 'fail' or 'get' negative actions or states and are unlikely to see non-events.

[ii] Tense is dealt with in a later section (7.1.3) along with other grammatical categories. We shall see that with some of the verbs it can be freely marked (with *have*):

I prefer to have finished before he comes.
I prefer to finish before he comes.

But there are restrictions.

[iii] Passivization is similarly dealt with in 7.1.3. There are, as we shall see, almost no restrictions at all in the passivization of the subordinate clause, *eg:*

I want them to eat.
I want them to be eaten.

Surprisingly, however, with some verbs the whole sentence may be passivized:

John seems to have seen Mary.
Mary seems to have been seen by John.

These are the 'subject complementation' verbs (7.2.3). In respect of passivization they are more like auxiliaries than main verbs and semantically have some qualities of 'modality' – seeming, happening, etc. Again it is clear that there are no clear-cut divisions between primary auxiliaries, modals and catenatives. There are also some problems involving the intervening NPs and passivization (7.2.1), but since only the complex phrase can have such NPs this does not affect their status.

7.1.3 Aspect, phase, tense and voice

As was seen in **5.1.1** the paradigms of the modal auxiliaries consist of a modal followed by all the possible infinitival forms – eight in all, marking aspect, phase and voice (tense being marked by the auxiliary itself). A similar basic paradigm might seem appropriate for the catenative + verb sequence, *eg:*

(1) *I expect to take.*
(3) *I expect to be taking.*
(5) *I expect to have taken.*
(7) *I expect to have been taking.*
(9) *I expect to be taken.*
(11) *I expect to be being taken.*
(13) *I expect to have been taken.*
(15) *I expect to have been being taken.*

(These are numbered to correspond to the forms of the previous paradigms; the even numbered forms are provided simply by replacing *expect* by *expected.*)

All of these forms are theoretically possible but 11 (and 12), 15 (and 16) are even more unlikely than the corresponding modal forms. There are two other restrictions. First, such a paradigm is possible (even in theory) only with the *to*-infinitive and, secondly, it is not fully possible with all, or even most, of the catenatives. In this respect the catenatives are, surprisingly perhaps, less free in their combinations than the modals. The best way of looking at the problem is in terms of the three grammatical categories marked by the infinitivals and participials – aspect, phase and voice (progressive, perfect and passive respectively). The bare infinitive and the *-en* forms have a very limited, but special, part in this.

Voice is the easiest to deal with. First, the *-en* form is always passive and often is the passive correlate of the bare infinitive:

He saw them eat.
He saw them eaten.
He had them beat the carpet.
He had them beaten.

With other verbs the *-en* form is the passive of the *to*-infinitive, though the passive infinitival is also possible with little difference in meaning:

I want them to beat the carpet.
I want them beaten.
I want them to be beaten.

Apart from these forms the passive is regularly found with both infinitivals and participials. The infinitival forms have been illustrated in the paradigm above; for the participials we may note:

They stopped punishing him.
They stopped being punished.
They stopped them punishing them.
They stopped them being punished.

However, there are some verbs where the passive is unlikely, especially with the *-ing* form, when there is an intervening noun phrase:

They kept them working.
? They kept them being taught.
I want them working.
? I want them being taught.

The restriction is almost certainly semantic. One usually 'keeps' or 'wants' others taking action, not being acted on. Yet we can have a passive with the last sentence with a *to*-infinitive instead of the *-ing* form:

I want them to be taught.

No special discussion about the passive is necessary, except where there is the possibility of the *-en* form.

Aspect is a little more difficult. With some verbs the bare infinitive and the *-ing* form are quite clearly related in terms of aspect:

I saw the boys cross the road.
I saw the boys crossing the road.
He had them beat the carpet.
He had them beating the carpet.

These function like:

The boys crossed the road.
The boys were crossing the road.
They beat the carpet.
They were beating the carpet.

But this contrast is not always possible:

I made him talk to me.
**I made him talking to me.*

It is even lost with the passive of SEE:

They were seen crossing the road.
**They were seen cross the road.*

There are some verbs in which a difference of aspect might be seen in the contrast of *to*-infinitive with *-ing* form:

He started to speak, but was soon interrupted.
He started speaking, and kept on for hours.

But the semantic distinction is less clear here than with SEE. It is even less clear in:

I like swimming.
I like to swim.

Nor can we see a difference in:

I intend going tomorrow.
I intend to go tomorrow.

But a difference in aspect can be marked by using the progressive of the infinitival with LIKE and INTEND:

I like to be swimming.
I intend to be working when he comes.

On the other hand we shall not find:

**He started to be speaking.*

In many cases, however, the *-ing* form appears to be intrinsically progressive, even where there is no contrast with a (non-progressive) infinitive – this explains why there can be no participial forms of the kind **being talking* (see 3.1.2). We should not expect to find:

**He kept being talking.*
**He kept them being talking.*

For the progressive is clearly indicated in:

He kept talking.
He kept them talking.

Yet with some verbs, notably the verbs of attitude (7.4.7) the *-ing* form carries no progressive meaning with it:

I don't like them reading comics.
(*They read comics.*)

We might, then, expect to find:

**I don't like them being reading when he comes.*
(*They are reading now.*)

But this does not occur. The non-occurrence of a progressive marker in addition to the *-ing* form is thus a formal and absolute restriction.

There are no apparent restrictions on the *to*-infinitive forms. The progressive infinitivals are all normal:

I don't like them to read comics.
I don't like them to be reading when he comes.

We shall not talk about the progressive with the *-en* form – this is identical with the passive of the *-ing* form, which has already been considered. There is no need, then, for detailed discussion of aspect in the analysis except where the bare infinitive and the *-ing* form are in contrast as markers of aspect.

Let us now consider phase. HAVE is, of course, a marker of both phase (perfect) and tense (past) with non-finite forms (3.3.4). We find that tense/phase is marked in the subordinate clause, but that there are considerable restrictions. In particular it does not occur with the bare infinitive, though there are no obvious grammatical reasons for this:

**I saw him have crossed the road.*
**I made him have talked to me.*

We have had examples of the perfect infinitivals; for the perfect participials we may note:

I remember going.
I remember having gone.
I remember being beaten.
I remember having been beaten.

But REMEMBER, along with a few other verbs, is idiosyncratic in this respect, since both the perfect and the non-perfect *-ing* forms refer to past time (with no apparent difference of meaning). With many verbs the *have* forms are unlikely either as phase or as tense markers with either participials or infinitivals:

**He decided to have gone.*
**He strives to have finished.*
?I enjoyed having seen him.
**I finished having talked.*
**Can you justify them having done that?*

The dubious examples here are all attitude verbs (7.4.7). There is one set of verbs with which *have* commonly occurs – those of 'reporting' (7.4.3):

I believe John to have gone.
I believe John to have been tricked.

These occur commonly with passivization of the main clause:

John is believed to have gone.
John is believed to have been tricked.

That both past and perfect may be so marked is clear:

John is believed to have gone yesterday.
John is believed to have gone already.
(*John went yesterday.*)
(*John has already gone.*)

7.1.4 Verbal nouns and adjectives

There is a traditional classification of the non-finite forms into 'verbal nouns' and 'verbal adjectives', a result of the view that all words must belong to one of the 'parts of speech'. On this interpretation the bare infinitive, the *to*-infinitive and some of the *-ing* forms (now called 'gerunds') are nouns, while the *-en* forms (the 'past participles') and the remaining *-ing* forms (the 'present participles') are adjectives.

The plausibility of this rests largely on the similarity of their forms to other nouns and adjectives. We may compare pairs such as:

I want to read.
I want a book.
I like reading.
I like books.

It can be argued that *to read* and *reading* have the same function as *a book* and *books* – that they are noun forms, and objects of the sentence. Similarly we may compare:

He keeps reading.
He keeps quiet.
He got hurt.
He got hot.

Reading and *hurt* are, it can be said, exactly like *quiet* and *hot*, adjectives functioning in predicative position. A further argument in favour of this position is the observation that the forms seem to have nominal and adjectival functions in other constructions. The infinitive and gerund may function as the subject of the sentence (though the infinitive is rare in colloquial English) and the participles may act as noun modifiers:

To err is human.
Reading is a pleasant relaxation.

A sleeping child.
A hurt child.

There are, however, great difficulties in accepting this classification.

[i] It breaks down with such sentences as:

I saw them eating.
I saw them eaten.
I saw them eat.

Eating and *eaten* are presumably both adjectival – present and past participles. This is the only possible interpretation for *eaten*; *eating* is by analogy, and by its semantics, most plausibly regarded as also being a participle. But *eat* can only be a noun, an infinitive. Yet the three forms all have exactly the same function in these sentences marking only difference of voice and aspect. The noun/adjective distinction would obscure this identity of function.

[ii] More importantly, perhaps, the distinction runs into great trouble with a problem that worried many of the traditional grammarians, the problem of:

I don't like John coming.
I don't like John's coming.

With the noun/adjective distinction *coming* in the first is an adjective modifying *John*, with a construction like that of *Children singing* in *Children singing are a wonderful sound.* In the second, *coming* is a noun preceded by a possessive to be compared with *John's coming* (or *John's arrival*) in *John's coming* (*arrival*) *surprised us.* The grammarian Henry Sweet[1] suggested that *coming* was a 'half gerund', because he did not feel that *coming* in *I do not like him coming* modifies *him* in the same way as it does in *I saw him coming*. Jespersen,[2] though insisting on the distinction, said 'sometimes it is immaterial whether an *-ing* after a noun or pronoun is to be taken to be a gerund or participle'. But Jespersen also realized that treating the *-ing* form as an adjective where the syntax allowed this would make nonsense of the semantics. It would 'not be applicable to Galsworthy's *I hate people being unhappy* – for it is not the people that I hate, or to Thackeray's *I have not the least objection to the rogue being hung* for he has no objection to the rogue whether hung or not.'

[iii] A fundamental objection is that some of the verbal nouns and adjectives must be allowed to have objects. This establishes them as a

most unusual kind of noun or adjective, so unusual that there seems to be little point in retaining this classification:

I want to read a novel.
I like reading novels.
He keeps reading novels.

This is true even where the relevant clause is not part of a complex phrase:

To read novels is a waste of time.
Reading novels is a waste of time.
Children eating biscuits make a lot of noise.

It will also be necessary to say that the verbal noun or adjective may have a subject:

I want John to read a novel.
I saw the children crossing the street.

7.1.5 Status of the subordinate clause

A more sophisticated view than that proposed in the last subsection sees not the verbal form, but the whole subordinate clause, as nominal, and so as the object of the catenative. We saw in **2.1.4** that even the modals have been thought to have objects – *swim* being the object of *can* in *I can swim*. This was rejected, but is a similar proposal for the catenatives more acceptable? In *I like playing the piano*, *playing the piano* might well be regarded as the object of *like* and in *I want to go to London*, *to go to London* as the object of *want*. If we regard the whole clause as the object of the finite verb, the problem of verbal nouns and adjectives does not arise. The forms function as verbs in the subordinate clause which may have a subject and an object; their non-finiteness marks subordination and we can thus relate:

John reads novels.
I don't like John reading novels.

This treatment of subordinate clauses as themselves composed of clause elements is clearly correct. But it is not so clear that the clauses should be treated as the object of the main verb.

[i] There are a few forms where the *-ing* form, though not itself adjectival, seems to mark an adjectival clause. We must, surely, compare:

He kept talking.
He kept quiet.

We should not, on the other hand, relate them to:

He kept a dog.

But although it would seem plausible to argue that KEEP is followed by an adjectival clause, this will not work for the almost synonymous CONTINUE:

He continued talking.
**He continued quiet.*
He continued the conversation.

The evidence suggests that CONTINUE is followed by a nominal, not an adjectival, clause.

[ii] There are many verbs that do not normally have objects yet are followed by subordinate clauses with *to*-infinitives or *-ing* forms (especially *to*-infinitives):

I hope to see you.
**I hope a fine day.*
He decided to go.
**He decided the plan.*
I intend to come.
I intend coming.
**I intend my arrival.*

The argument that the subordinate clauses are objects rests largely on the fact that they function like other noun objects. Here they occur with verbs that do not take objects. It is true, of course, that some of these verbs occur with prepositions – HOPE FOR, DECIDE ON, that may be followed by noun phrases. But not all of them do; INTEND, for instance, does not. In any case this does not support the argument, for the prepositions show that the verbs are *not* simple transitive verbs.

[iii] The construction that occurs with any particular verb has to a large extent to be stated lexically for each verb (though it will be apparent from later sections that there are some general semantic-syntactic classes). Sometimes there is a choice of structure:

He began talking.
He began to talk.
He continued talking.
He continued to talk.

Sometimes (with no obvious semantic explanation) there is no choice:

He stopped talking.
!He stopped to talk. (a different sense)
He kept talking.
**He kept to talk.*

The verb appears to select the construction, just as a Latin verb selects the case of the noun it governs. We would have, then, a very special kind of syntactical relationship involving objects like that of Latin government. This is perfectly possible, but it would be totally untypical of English grammar, for English does not have anything like Latin government and case.

[iv] An argument that is often put forward to support the view that some verbs have objects and others do not is based upon what is called the 'pseudo-cleft construction'.[3] This construction is exemplified by comparison of:

I offered a prize.
What I offered was a prize.

The interrogative form is, for the purpose intended, just as relevant:

What did I offer?

The point is that these constructions may occur where the verb has an object which is referred to by *what*. If we compare the catenatives we find:

I asked to come early.
What I asked was to come early.
What did I ask?
I advised him to come early.
What I advised him was to come early.
What did I advise him?

But with some this is not possible, or less likely:

I offered to come early.
?What I offered was to come early.
!What did I offer?
I forced him to come early.
**What I forced him was to come early.*
**What did I force him?*

Instead we have sentences with *to do* added:

What I offered to do was to come early.
What did I offer to do?
What I forced him to do was to come early.
What did I force him to do?

This, it is argued, proves that ASK and ADVISE take the subordinate clause as their object (and that these are, therefore, nominal) while OFFER and FORCE do not.

But this test is not a very useful one. First, it is very difficult to draw any clear lines where pseudo-clefting is or is not possible. There is no 'Yes'/'No' division, but a range of acceptability. In the examples above, FORCE is almost certainly impossible without *to do*, but OFFER is more dubious, while with both ASK and ADVISE the occurrence of *to do* would make the sentence appear a little more natural. Secondly, unless the pseudo-cleft test links up with other syntactic features of the catenatives (and it does not) it would seem to prove no more than that some verbs allow pseudo-clefting and others do not! That is to say there is little point in a formal test of a rather specialized kind such as this, that (*a*) has no obvious semantic correlations, (*b*) has no correlation with any major syntactic features.

However, in spite of the arguments presented, it must be admitted that there are some verbs for which analysis in terms of transitive verb plus verbal noun object would seem more appropriate than for the others. These are the 'attitude' verbs (7.4.7), that have already been twice noted. Let us consider DISLIKE. We have all of the following:

I dislike his actions.
I dislike his doing that.
I dislike his having done that.
I dislike him doing that.
I dislike him having done that.

The first sentence obviously has a nominal object, and so too, one can surely argue, have the second and third. The last two verb phrases can still be handled formally in terms of the catenatives (with *-ing* forms and intervening noun phrases), but there are three reasons that make them much more like verbs with object.

[i] The semantic distinction between the forms with *him* and *his* is either non-existent or very small. In fact it seems merely that with common

verbs such as LIKE and HATE, *him* is more likely, whereas with others, *eg* DEPRECATE, DEPLORE, we are more likely to find *his*.

[ii] There are no restrictions at all on phase/tense. There are restrictions on aspect – but these apply equally to the unambiguously nominal form. Both of the following are equally unlikely:

**his having been doing that.*
**him having been doing that.*

[iii] With some verbs the identity relations of the catenatives (7.2.4) do not apply.

But I should not wish to distinguish between catenatives (without object) and other verbs with *-ing* form objects. Rather there is gradience between being more or less 'object-like', beginning with the primary auxiliaries, through the modals to these 'attitude' catenatives.

7.2 Identity relations

This section is concerned with the question of the relationship between subject and object in the subordinate and main clauses and in particular with the status, in these terms, of the intervening NP. In particular we shall be asking whether the subject of the subordinate clause is identical with the object or the subject of the main clause. We shall begin the first section by looking at the 'regular' patterns that account for the vast majority of the catenatives. Following sections will deal with various kinds of other 'identity relations'.

7.2.1 Status of the NP

Let us consider complex phrases where there is or is not an intervening noun phrase:

John wanted to talk.
John kept talking.
John wanted the men to talk.
John kept the men talking.

It is clear intuitively that the subject of *to talk* and *talking* in the first two sentences is *John*, whereas in the second two it is the intervening noun phrase *the men*. This is formally supported by the collocational possibilities of the kind:

The farmer induces his hens to lay more eggs.
The hens lay more eggs.
**The farmer lays more eggs.*

In general, then, we can say that the subject of the subordinate clause is the same as that of the main clause if there is no intervening noun phrase; if there is, this NP indicates the subordinate clause subject. We may formalize the distinction, using round brackets to indicate the unstated subject and indices to indicate 'identity' (with square brackets showing the subordinate clause):

(1) NP_1 V [(NP_1) V]
(2) NP_1 V [NP_2 V]

But this simple picture needs some modification. There are some verbs for which it may be argued that the intervening noun phrase is *both* the object of the verb of the main clause *and* the subject of the subordinate. We need, that is to say, a further formula:

(3) NP_1 V NP_2 [(NP_2) V]

This is needed in order to distinguish between such sentences as:

I wanted the doctor to examine the boy.
I persuaded the doctor to examine the boy.[4]

Here we have three noun phrases, the third being the object of the verb of the subordinate clause. The question at issue is whether the second NP, *the doctor*, is the object of *wanted* and *persuaded* or not, *ie* which of the following formulae is appropriate:

NP_1 V [NP_2 V NP_3]
NP_1 V NP_2 [(NP_2) V NP_3]

There are two arguments that clearly establish the first formula as appropriate for WANT and the second for PERSUADE.

First, if we passivize the main clause we have:

The doctor was persuaded to examine the boy.
**The doctor was wanted to examine the boy.*

The possibility of the first sentence indicates clearly that *the doctor* is the object of *persuaded*, for it is now the subject of the passive; the impossibility of the second shows that it is not the object of *wanted.*

Secondly, there are two possible sentences with the subordinate clause in the passive:

I wanted the boy to be examined by the doctor.
I persuaded the boy to be examined by the doctor.

But they are very different. The first is clearly directly related to the original sentence with passivization of the subordinate clause. The second is not, for there is now a difference of meaning in that it is the boy and not the doctor who is persuaded. Again this is not simply a matter of semantics. There are equally formal restrictions, as shown by:

I wanted John to play the piano.
I wanted the piano to be played by John.
I persuaded John to play the piano.
**I persuaded the piano to be played by John.*

We can account for this contrast by saying that *the doctor*, in the original sentence, is not the object of *wanted*. It is, however, the object of *persuaded*, but there is a condition with such sentences – that the object of the main clause must be identical with the subject of the subordinate. The issues become clear if we spell out the formulae with words:

I wanted [*the doctor to examine the boy*].
I persuaded the doctor [*the doctor to examine the boy*].

We can now passivize the subordinate clause of the first to produce the required sentence. But if we passivize the subordinate clause of the second, we get:

I persuaded the doctor [*the boy to be examined by the doctor*].

The object of the main clause is now no longer the subject of the subordinate. For this reason we cannot simply passivize the subordinate clause. To produce the required sentences we must also substitute *the boy* for *the doctor* in the main clause:

I persuaded the boy [*the boy to be examined by the doctor*].

This argument no less than the first shows that *the doctor* is the object of *persuaded* but not of *wanted*. It also establishes the identity of the object of the main clause and the subject of the subordinate.

We have, then, three basic constructions that will account for the majority of the catenatives:

(1) NP_1 V [(NP_1) V]
(2) NP_1 V [NP_2 V]
(3) NP_1 V NP_2 [(NP_2) V]

These are, of course, formulae of the 'abstract' kind since the bracketed NPs do not actually occur. They are, that is to say, 'deep structure' rather than 'surface structure' representations.[5]

We might expect that most verbs function either like WANT, in occurring with the first two constructions, or like PERSUADE, occurring with the last. This turns out not to be true of a whole class of verbs exemplified by LONG, that occur only with the first:

I long to come.
**I long John to come.*

Most of these occur instead with *for* (7.3.2):

I long for John to come.

But there are also a number of other verbs that either do not accord clearly with the WANT/PERSUADE distinction (7.2.2) or fit into quite different patterns (7.2.3, 7.2.4).

7.2.2 Problematic constructions

In the last subsection a very clear distinction was made between verbs like WANT and verbs like PERSUADE in terms of the intervening NP, the former occurring only with construction 2 (as well as 1) and the latter only with construction 3. Semantically and syntactically this NP is the object of verbs such as PERSUADE, but not of verbs like WANT. The picture is complicated by the fact that there are a number of verbs that fit into both patterns and that in some cases it seems difficult, if not impossible, to establish which construction is being employed in any given sentence.

Let us begin by looking at ORDER.[6] This would seem at first sight to be like PERSUADE:

I ordered the chauffeur to fetch the car.
The chauffeur was ordered to fetch the car.

Main clause passivization clearly establishes *the chauffeur* as the object of *ordered*, and we could substitute PERSUADE, but not WANT, in these two sentences. Yet we also find that ORDER seems to function like WANT:

I ordered the chauffeur to fetch the car.
I ordered the car to be fetched by the chauffeur.

Here the passivization of the subordinate clause suggests that *the chauffeur* is not the object of *ordered*, and WANT could be substituted for ORDER in both sentences.

Semantically, too, ORDER seems to function in two ways. Either orders are given to someone to do something or they are given that certain things shall be done. These two meanings accord well with the two possible constructions. We could argue that there are two verbs ORDER, one like WANT the other like PERSUADE, with structures such as:

I ordered [the chauffeur to fetch the car].
I ordered the chauffeur [the chauffeur to fetch the car].

Yet it seems rather to be the case that ORDER is not unambiguously either of the one type or the other. For it is not possible to establish which of the two constructions is an appropriate analysis for a sentence like:

I ordered the chauffeur to fetch the car.

In order to establish whether ORDER is like WANT or PERSUADE we should need to appeal to the meaning – to whether orders were given to the chauffeur or not. Unfortunately it is not clear what is meant by 'giving orders to the chauffeur'. Does this mean only to him personally? Or can they be given via someone else? How, in other words, do we differentiate between giving orders to someone and giving orders that someone should do something? The semantic distinction is very far from clear, yet the syntax depends upon making that distinction. It is not then a matter of ORDER belonging to two verb classes, but that the distinction between these two classes is not valid for ORDER. There is just one point, however, that makes ORDER rather more like PERSUADE than WANT. It does not occur with construction 1:

**I ordered to fetch the car.*

There is a slightly different problem with EXPECT, though it leads to similar conclusions. It appears at first sight to be of the same type as WANT (even occurring with construction 1):

I expect to examine John.
I expect the doctor to examine John.
I expect John to be examined by the doctor.

Yet we also have passivization of the main clause, which suggests rather that the verb is like PERSUADE:

The doctor was expected to examine John.

There is a semantic explanation available again. We may either expect someone to do something (expect it of him that he will do it) or expect that someone will do something. With the former meaning EXPECT is syntactically and semantically like PERSUADE, with the latter like WANT.

Yet this does not fully account for the behaviour of EXPECT. Passivization of the main clause is possible, as in the sentence illustrated, even where there is no expectation directed at someone; it is not necessarily true that we are talking about expecting (*ie* requiring) the doctor to take action. This point is confirmed by the behaviour of BELIEVE and other verbs of 'reporting' (7.4.3) where the main clause can be passivized normally:

The doctor is believed to have examined John.

There is no question here of believing the doctor, only of believing that he examined John.

Semantically BELIEVE is not, then, like ORDER. We can account for the passivization of the main clause with ORDER in terms of the semantics, so that ORDER may partake of both constructions. But BELIEVE, semantically at least, occurs only with construction 2, where the NP is not the object of the verb of the main clause. Yet the main clause may be passivized. One way of accounting for this is the device known as 'subject raising',[7] where the subject of a subordinate clause is 'raised' to a higher or main clause. On this interpretation *the doctor* would be the subject of the subordinate clause in deep structure, but would then be 'raised' to be the object of the main clause. It would then become its subject when the sentence is passivized. But though this would account for BELIEVE it would still leave unsolved the problem of all the intermediate verbs. We should hardly wish to say that with EXPECT sometimes the NP is the object of the main clause and so permits normal passivization, but that sometimes it is the subject of the subordinate clause so that passivization is possible only after 'subject raising'. Other verbs are no less problematic, *eg* INTEND and MEAN, where passivization is possible but rarer:

It was intended to be seen.
?John was intended to be examined by the doctor.
John was meant to come at four.
? The doctor was meant to examine John.

There is a great deal of indeterminacy here; the best we can do is to state the facts – that there are verbs that may occur with either construction, *ie* may or may not have the NP as the object of the main clause, though often with no clear distinction between the two, and that there are others such as BELIEVE that permit main clause passivization, even though there is semantically no case for suggesting that they occur with construction 3 – with the NP as the object of the main clause.

7.2.3 Subject complementation[8]

A different problem is provided by sentences (which we have already briefly considered in 7.2.1) such as:

John seems to have seen Mary.
Mary seems to have been seen by John.

Here we have passivization of the whole sentence – as if it were a single clause (*ie* with a simple verb phrase) with *John* as the subject and *Mary* as the object. It was precisely passivization of this kind that was used as evidence in the arguments about the status of the modals. We could, of course, simply say that verbs such as SEEM (others are HAPPEN and TEND) function as auxiliaries rather than as main verbs. But there is another possible solution, again using the concept of subject raising. We might have thought of analysing the sentence as:

NP_1 V [(NP_1) V NP_2]
John seems [John to have seen Mary].

But this would not account for the passivization of the whole sentence. An alternative solution is that the subordinate clause is in deep structure the subject (not the object) of the main clause, *ie:*

[NP_1 V NP_2] V
[John to have seen Mary] seems.

John is then raised to subject position in the main clause to become the subject of *seems* to give the required sentence. For the passive sentence, the subordinate sentence is first passivized:

[NP_2 V_{pass} *by* NP_1] V
[Mary to have been seen by John] seems.

The subject of the subordinate clause is now *Mary* and it is this that is raised to the subject position in the main clause to become the subject of *seems*. This ingenious solution treats SEEM, etc, as 'subject complementation' verbs – and this is the heading under which they will be treated (7.4.9), though for obvious reasons I do not wish to talk about 'object complementation'. One possible objection to the analysis is that by analogy we ought to handle the passive BELIEVE examples in a similar way, *ie:*

The doctor is believed to have examined the boy.
[NP_1 V NP_2] V
[The doctor to have examined the boy] is believed.

On this solution we first passivize the main clause to produce the above structure and only subsequently raise the subject of the subordinate clause to be the subject of the main clause. But this is more complex than the solution earlier suggested – that there is first subject raising to raise the subject to be the object of the main clause and then passivization. This is far more plausible because it simply says that BELIEVE is treated like PERSUADE for the purpose of the passivization of the main clause, *ie* that *the doctor* is treated as if it were the object of *believed* as it is the object of *persuaded*. The new analysis would totally obscure this simple fact.

There are a few verbs that seem to follow the pattern of SEEM as well as that of the more usual pattern of the other catenatives, *eg* BEGIN in:[9]

John began to read a book.
The rain began to destroy the flowers.

For the first sentence cannot be passivized but the second can:

**The book began to be read by John.*
The flowers began to be destroyed by the rain.

This is a further argument against the subject complementation analysis of SEEM, for we should now have two totally different underlying structures for BEGIN; the distinction would depend on whether the subject of the active sentence is in some way responsible for the activity – not at all unlike the situation with WILL (5.1.2). The differences between the proposed structures are far greater than those proposed for ORDER – and the analysis less plausible.[10]

7.2.4 Other identity relations

There is a different problem with:

I promised John to go.

For this is not:

NP_1 V NP_2 [(NP_2) V]

This would imply that the meaning was that I promised John that he would go. It is rather:

NP_1 V NP_2 [(NP_1) V]

This shows that the meaning is that I promised John that I should go.

The verb PROMISE is unique in this respect. It alone produces a structure that looks superficially exactly like that of PERSUADE, etc, but is quite different in its identity relations. There are, however, other verbs with prepositions that are similar:

I agreed with John to go.
I undertook with John to go.
I offered to John to go.

PROMISE seems to be alone in a set of verbs referring to agreement in not requiring a preposition of this kind. All of them occur without an NP:

I agreed to go.
I undertook to go.
I offered to go.

Where there is an NP, indicating with whom the agreement is made, all the other verbs require a preposition. PROMISE does not; and thus it produces a structure that is superficially like that of PERSUADE, etc, but is quite different in terms of identity relations.

Another modification to our proposed structures is required by:

The boy needs to wash.
The clothes need washing.

These are not like:

The boy began to wash.
The boy began washing.

With NEED, *to wash* appears to be active, but *washing* appears to be passive. Alternatively and preferably, we may say that with *need washing* the subject of the main clause is the object of the subordinate clause, the subject being unstated (and indicated in our formula by $\triangle$). We have then for our first two sentences:

NP_1 V [NP_1 V]
NP_1 V [$\triangle$V NP_1]

There are only a very few verbs of this kind. The fact that the main clause subject and the subordinate clause object are identical is marked by the *-ing* form.

Finally, there is an apparent problem with:

I don't advise doing that.
I don't recommend going there.

Here the subject of the subordinate clause is semantically not *I* but *we* or *you* or even 'anyone'. But here again we are concerned with verbs of 'attitude' – precisely those that are least like true catenatives. This is yet another indication of their marginal status, though it is difficult to draw a clear line between those verbs that qualify as catenatives and those that do not.

7.3 Classification of the catenatives

It would be possible to classify the catenatives simply in terms of the constructions and non-finite forms with which they occur – those occurring with the first only or with the first and second, those with the *to*-infinite or the *-ing* form, and so on. Alternatively we could list for each separate form and construction the catenatives that occur with them. Neither approach would be very illuminating. A particular difficulty is that there are many borderline cases.

In fact, the verbs will be handled in eight subsections under eight headings, all except one having semantic connotations. Under each heading there will be subclasses that are identified by a typical member of the class. For example, we shall have in 7.4.3, the verbs of 'reporting' with subclasses BELIEVE, ADMIT and DENY. But the verbs are so varied that *any* classification is bound to be arbitrary and over-simplified.

7.3.1 Semantics and structure

Although the headings are semantic, the basis of the verb classes is a formal one, except that where there are a few verbs that are formally exceptional in terms of the semantic class to which they belong, they will not normally be handled in a separate section, but discussed together with the verbs that they resemble semantically.

One major semantic/formal class is that of the 'futurity' verbs. These all refer to actions contemplated for the future – planned, foreseen, ordered, etc. Formally they are distinguished by the possibility of the occurrence of adverbials of future time in the subordinate clause:

I hope to come tomorrow.
I want John to come tomorrow.
I persuaded John to come tomorrow.
I promised John to come tomorrow.

These exemplify the three basic constructions that were proposed in 7.2.1 plus the more unusual construction associated with PROMISE (7.2.4):

NP_1 V [(NP_1) V]
NP_1 V [NP_2 V]
NP_1 V NP_2 [(NP_2) V]
NP_1 V NP_2 [(NP_1) V]

Semantically this is easily explained. For, first, one can plan for the performing of an action by oneself or by someone else – NP_1 or NP_2 in the subordinate clause. Secondly, one can involve someone else in the planning - NP_2 in the main clause (or not – no NP_2 in the main clause). Hence the four possibilities. The last construction is, of course, unique to PROMISE. The third, the only other one that involves NP_2 in the main clause is required for only two other sets of verbs – those of 'process' and the 'causatives' (7.4.2, 7.4.5). For although passivization of the main clause is also possible with verbs of 'reporting', some other solution, *eg* subject raising, is more appropriate.

Other semantic/formal classes are the verbs of 'reporting', which have an alternative *that* construction, and which permit passivization of both main and subordinate clause (7.2.2), and the verbs of 'perception', which mark aspect by the contrast of bare infinitive and *-ing* form (7.1.3). The verbs of 'attitude' are those that have most object-like constructions with the alternative of a possessive instead of simple NP (7.1.5). The verbs of 'process' are formally more heterogeneous but account for the *-ing* forms that do not belong to the other classes, while those of 'effort and achievement' account for *to*-infinitive forms not handled elsewhere. There is a smaller set of very common verbs that have been labelled 'causative'. The 'subject complementation' verbs and those of 'needing' are syntactically of classes of their own (7.2.3, 7.2.4).

Within each class it is sometimes possible to see further semantic/formal subclasses. For the verbs of futurity, for instance, we may suggest:

[i] verbs of persuading, inducing, etc, that occur only with the NP_1 V NP_2 [(NP_2) V] construction – where some person is always persuaded, induced, etc to act (*eg* PERSUADE).

[ii] verbs of ordering, compelling, etc, that occur with both the NP_1 V NP_2 [(NP_2) V] and the NP_1 V [NP_2 V] constructions – someone may be ordered, etc or the action may be ordered without reference to the recipient of the order (*eg* ORDER).

[iii] verbs of asking, etc that occur with the NP_1 V NP_2 [(NP_2) V] and the NP_1 V [(NP_1) V] constructions – we may ask someone to do something or ask that we may do it (*eg* ASK).

But this is not an exhaustive list. There are other verbs typified by DECIDE, MEAN, EXPECT and INTEND that are formally, but not in any obvious way semantically, different. We shall not, for this reason, look here for semantic subclasses.

7.3.2 Prepositions in the structure

There are some apparent gaps (in both semantic and syntactic terms) in the constructions that may occur, which may nevertheless be filled if certain prepositions are introduced. These are of two kinds.

First, the subordinate clause may be preceded by *for*. There are many 'futurity' verbs that occur with the NP_1 V [(NP_1) V] construction, but rather surprisingly not with NP_1 V [NP_2 V]. Indeed, the number that occur with these two alone is very small. We may contrast:

I want to come.
I want John to come.
I long to come.
**I long John to come.*
I long for John to come.

WANT, but not LONG, enters into both constructions; LONG requires *for* for the second.

Secondly, with a few verbs the intervening NP must be preceded by a preposition, even though an NP_1 V [(NP_1) V] construction also occurs:

I undertook to come.
I undertook with John to come.

Most of these are the verbs like PROMISE in which the NP subject of the subordinate clause is identical with the subject of the main clause, *ie* NP_1 V NP_2 [(NP_1) V]. (PROMISE is the only verb of this type that does not require a preposition before the NP – see **7.2.4** and **7.4.1**, [vii].) But some verbs are idiosyncratic. For PLEAD we find:

I pleaded to come.
I pleaded with John to come.
I pleaded with John to be allowed to come.

These are:

NP_1 V [(NP_1) V]
NP_1 V NP_2 [(NP_2) V]
NP_1 V NP_2 [(NP_1) V]

As far as I am aware, no verb without a preposition occurs with these three constructions. (The third construction seems only to occur, too, with a passive verb in the subordinate clause.)

There are many verbs that always occur with a preposition. These are very like the catenatives, but will not be discussed further in this book, *eg:*

I reacted against going there.
I insisted upon going there.
He persisted in going there.

There are also verbs that require prepositions when followed not by subordinate clauses but by NPs with nouns:

He hoped for a victory.
He escaped from prison.
He decided on the proposal.

These, however, occur as catenatives without prepositions:

He hoped to win.
He escaped jailing.
He decided to go.

The occurrence of the preposition in these cases is, thus, irrelevant to the analysis of the catenatives.

7.3.3 Homonyms

The classification of the catenatives specifically takes into account the fact that one verb may occur with more than one construction or with more than one non-finite form. But we are left with some verbs that have to be listed in two sections or subsections. By treating them in separate places we are essentially regarding them as not one verb but two, as homonyms. There can be no clear principle for the decision, but there are some obvious guidelines.

First, we shall not consider the fact that a verb occurs both with and without NP but with predictable identity relations as evidence of homonymity. Nor is the fact that it occurs with different non-finite forms that either mark aspect or have little or no semantic difference. (There is some arbitrariness – SEE clearly marks aspect with the bare infinitive and *-ing* form, but the position with START, LIKE and INTEND is less clear – 7.1.3.)

Nor shall we see homonymity with verbs such as BEGIN and ORDER, even though these verbs have different constructions clearly established by the passivization tests (7.2.2). For not only can we account for this in semantic terms, but, more importantly, it is not always possible to draw a clear line between the two semantic/syntactic types. If the language fails to make a clear distinction, we ought not, surely, to try to do so!

But there are some problem cases. There are some further distinctions to make with SEE. In addition to the (perception) meaning 'observe', it has the (reporting) meaning 'see that', especially in the passive. Consider:

He was seen walking away.
He was seen to walk away.
He was seen to be walking away.

The first has the perception meaning, but the other two the reporting 'see that' meaning. Notice that *He was seen to walk away* is not the non-progressive correlate of *He was seen walking away* – in the passive the perception SEE does not mark aspect as it does in the active (see 7.1.3, 7.4.4).

There is yet another SEE, meaning 'imagine', as in:

I can't see him ever owning a house.

This is different again since there is no possibility of marking aspect with this SEE:

**I can't see him ever own a house.*

The *-ing* form is not here an indication of the progressive. This is conclusively proved by the fact that it occurs as in this example with a 'non-progressive' verb, OWN (3.7.2).

How many SEE verbs are there? We find that almost all the verbs of perception may also function as verbs of reporting:

I heard him coming.
I heard him to be very foolish.
I found him working in the garden.
He was found to have been stabbed.

We shall, surely, not want to distinguish pairs of homonyms for every one of these verbs – but rather state, as a generalization, that they have this double function. This does not, however, account for the 'imagine' SEE. This simply has to be treated as an isolated case; it is semantically and syntactically different, and so a different verb.

The status of FEEL is a little more doubtful. Semantically it might seem that there is FEEL_1 (=have tactile sensations) and FEEL_2 (=believe instinctively). But formally we have merely a verb of perception with the function of a verb of reporting as well, just like SEE, etc. The semantic difference between perception and reporting seems greater, but formally there is no case for distinguishing two verbs here.

A more extreme example is TRY. This verb is unique in having the meaning 'attempt to do something' with the *to*-infinitive and 'test the usefulness of' with the *-ing* form. Since we cannot make any kind of general statement about these alternatives it would seem sensible to identify two verbs TRY_1 and TRY_2.

More difficult is REMEMBER. With the *-ing* form it means 'to remember that one performed' the action; with the *to*-infinitive it means 'to remember and therefore to perform' the action, as in:

I remembered doing it.
I remembered to do it.

There is no obvious general statement that can be made about the *to*-infinitive and *-ing* form carrying such a distinction in meaning (unlike, for instance, the distinctions with SEE). But the pattern is also found with the 'opposite' verb FORGET. It also applies to REGRET in:

I regret to tell you.
I regret telling you.

HATE also functions in this way, but, strangely enough, LIKE does not. The semantic-syntactic patterns are found, separately, with other verbs – HASTEN with *to*-infinitive, MISS with *-ing* forms, but this does not explain why one verb should fall into both types, or whether it is in fact not one verb but two.

A verb that seems to have several homonyms is GET:

I got to see that I was wrong.
I got them to see that they were wrong.
I got working hard at the project.
I got them working hard at the project.
I got hurt in the crash.

The first has the meaning 'eventually saw' and is like COME in *came to see*. The second means 'caused them to see' and belongs to PERSUADE. The third and fourth are examples of a process verb like KEEP. The fifth is the alternative passive marker dealt with in 4.1.4.

Whether we recognize homonymity or not is ultimately a purely practical matter. Here it simply depends on whether we wish to handle a few fairly idiosyncratic verbs in one section or subsection or not. It depends thus on the overall analysis rather than on any specific relationship between possible semantic or syntactic characteristics of a verb.

Where a verb has to be handled in more than one place we shall use subscript numerals, *eg* SEE_1, SEE_2, to identify and distinguish them. The verbs so handled are CHANCE (7.4.7, 7.4.9), FANCY (7.4.1, 7.4.4, 7.4.7), FORGET (7.4.3, 7.4.6), GET (7.4.1, 7.4.5, 7.4.6 and Chapter 4), IMAGINE (7.4.3, 7.4.4), REGRET (7.4.6, 7.4.7), REMEMBER (7.4.3, 7.4.6), SEE (twice in 7.4.4), TRY (7.4.5, 7.4.6) and WANT (7.4.1, 7.4.8).

7.4 Catenative classes

We now look at the possible classes of catenatives individually.[11] As we have seen, each class and subclass can be formally distinguished. But the classes have considerable semantic homogeneity and may thus be given semantic labels. The subclasses are identified by a typical member of the subclass. But we must again stress that *any* classification is bound to be arbitrary and an over-simplification.

7.4.1 Futurity

The first class of verbs refers semantically to plans, etc for the future and is formally distinguished by the possibility of adverbials of future time in the subordinate clause. With the exception of one subclass these verbs occur only with the *to*-infinitive (and so may mark both aspect and voice). Except for this the subclassification (eight subclasses in all) is in terms of the constructions with which they occur. These will, for convenience, be identified in this section by numbers:

(1) NP_1 V [(NP_1) V]
(2) NP_1 V [NP_2 V]
(3) NP_1 V NP_2 [(NP_2) V]
(4) NP_1 V NP_2 [NP_1 V]

Examples with passivization of the main and subordinate clauses will distinguish 2 and 3. 4 is of course rare – with PROMISE only.

[i] WISH. There are a few verbs, WISH and DESIRE, that occur with 1 and 2 only:

I wish to meet Mary.
I wish John to meet Mary.
I wish Mary to be met by John.
**John is wished to meet Mary.*

Phase/tense may be marked in the subordinate clause:

I wish to have finished before she comes.
I wish John to have finished before she comes.

WANT is like WISH but occurs also with 2 and the *-ing* form, to indicate the distinction of aspect. In this it is unique among this class of verbs:

I want them to work when I leave.
I want them working while I am there.

Semantically these are verbs of 'wishing', but there are semantically similar (but syntactically different) verbs in the next group, *eg* LONG, YEARN. We ought, perhaps, also to include here LIKE in *would like, should like* with the meaning 'wish':

I should like to meet Mary.

With this meaning the *-ing* form does not occur. Formally, however, the distinction cannot be drawn since LIKE occurs as an attitude verb (7.4.7) with *to*-infinitive. But the semantics place *should/would like* here.

[ii] DECIDE. There are many verbs that occur only with construction 1:

He decided to come tomorrow.
**He decided John to come tomorrow.*

Semantically all the verbs in this group refer to plans, hopes, wishes, etc for future activity by the subject of the main clause. A list is ACHE, AIM, ASPIRE, CHOOSE, CONDESCEND, DECIDE, DECLINE, DETERMINE, ELECT, FEAR, HESITATE, HOPE, LONG, LOOK, LUST, PLOT, PREPARE, REFUSE, SCORN, SWEAR, YEARN. Phase/tense may be marked with some of these verbs. It seems to be very unlikely with those verbs that refer to specific acts of planning, etc, but much more likely with those of more general attitude:

I aim to have finished it by tomorrow.
I hope to have finished it by tomorrow.
?I decline to have finished it by tomorrow.
?I choose to have finished it by tomorrow.

If we ignore the forms with prepositions (7.2.4, 7.3.2) we should add here AGREE, ARRANGE, OFFER, PLEAD and UNDERTAKE. But if the prepositions were considered these would belong with PROMISE (below [vii]) except for PLEAD which is idiosyncratic (see 7.3.2).

HAVE also might be included here – see **6.1.2** [iii].

Two verbs that fit into the same formal pattern, but differ semantically, are STAND (= 'be likely to') and (CAN'T) AFFORD:

I stand to lose a lot of money.

Although none of these verbs occur with construction 2, it is possible with most of them to refer to future activity by others by introducing *for*:

**I hope John to come.*
I hope for John to come.
**I long John to come.*
I long for John to come.

With a few verbs it is less likely that there will be reference to the activity of others, *eg* HESITATE and, perhaps, SCORN. With these there is no place for a *for* construction.

PLAN and PROPOSE are like DECIDE in referring to future plans by the subject, but, except for INTEND, which appears in [v], they are alone among the futurity verbs in occurring with the *-ing* form as well as the *to*-infinitive:

I plan going there tomorrow.
I plan to go there tomorrow.

There is little or no difference in meaning.

[iii] PERSUADE. There is a large class of verbs that occurs only with construction 3:

I persuaded John to meet Mary.
!I persuaded Mary to be met by John.
John was persuaded to meet Mary.

All these verbs refer, semantically, to inducing someone to act. Obvious members are ACCUSTOM, ADVISE, APPOINT, ASSIST, BRING (often with *self*), CHALLENGE, COAX, COERCE, COMMISSION, DIRECT, DRIVE, ENTICE, ENTREAT, FORCE, GET_1, INVITE, LEAD, LEAVE, MOTION, OBLIGE, PRESS, REMIND, REQUEST, TEACH, TELL, TEMPT, TROUBLE, URGE, WARN, WORRY and GIVE (in GIVE . . . TO UNDERSTAND only).

[iv] ORDER. Next we have those verbs that occur with constructions 2 and 3 and seem to be simultaneously members of both the WANT and PERSUADE class:

I ordered the chauffeur to fetch the car.
The chauffeur was ordered to fetch the car.
I ordered the car to be fetched by the chauffeur.

The problem of these has already been discussed in detail (7.2.2). Phase is not normally marked. Members of the class include ALLOW, CAUSE, COMMAND, ENABLE, FORBID, ORDER, PERMIT – all verbs of 'making' or 'letting' someone perform an action.

[v] EXPECT. There are a few verbs that occur with constructions 2 and 3 like ORDER, but also with 1:

I expect to meet Mary.
I expect John to meet Mary.
I expect Mary to be met by John.
John is expected to meet Mary.

Other verbs are INTEND and MEAN, though INTEND is rare with main clause passivization. Phase may be marked normally:

I expect to have seen Mary by tomorrow.

FANCY$_1$, belongs here semantically but does not occur with construction 1.

[vi] ASK. Several verbs of asking occur with constructions 1 and 3:

I asked to meet Mary.
I asked John to meet Mary.
!I asked Mary to be met by John.
John was asked to meet Mary.

Semantically this pairing of constructions is a little odd. The pairing of 1 and 2 is obvious enough – one can plan for an action by oneself or by someone else. But 3 also involves someone else in the planning – it is here John who is asked, whereas 1 does not. Yet it is clear that semantically even with 1 we ask someone else that we may act. We seem almost to have the further construction:

NP_1 V (NP_2) [(NP_1) V]

But this is unnecessary. The person involved is not mentioned, and ASK here functions exactly like AIM, CHOOSE, etc in construction 1. As with these verbs, moreover, we can refer to the activity of others without involving them in the decision (*ie* semantically construction 2) by introducing *for:*

I asked for John to meet Mary.
I asked for Mary to be met by John.

Verbs in this group are ASK, BEG, PRAY, REQUIRE and possibly DARE (it belongs formally, but it may not be semantically appropriate).

[vii] PROMISE. This verb is unique in that it occurs with construction 4 as well as 1:

I promised to meet Mary.
I promised John to meet Mary.
**John was promised to meet Mary.*
!I promised Mary to be met by John.

There are similar verbs occurring with prepositions – AGREE, ARRANGE, OFFER, UNDERTAKE (see [ii] above and 7.2.4).

7.4.2 Causatives

This is the best place to handle four very common verbs that are quite idiosyncratic – HAVE, HELP, LET and MAKE. They have semantically much in common and are all 'futurity' verbs (HELP perhaps less obviously so).

[i] HELP occurs with construction 1 and bare infinitive and with construction 3 with both bare infinitive and *to*-infinitive:

You can help push the car.
He helped them build the house.
He helped them to build the house.

With main clause passivization only the *to*-infinitive is possible:

They were helped to build their house.

[ii] MAKE occurs with construction 3 and bare infinitive, but with *to*-infinitive when the main clause is passivized:

He made the boy finish his work.
The boy was made to finish his work.

[iii] LET occurs with NP and bare infinitive alone:

I'll let them stay a while.

Semantically this would seem to be construction 3, but main clause passivization is not normal:

**They were let* (*to*) *stay a while.*

[iv] HAVE occurs with NP and bare infinitive, the *-ing* form and the *-en* form. Main clause passivization is not possible:

He had them come early.
He had them all singing.
He had all the prisoners punished.

(HAVE is further discussed in **6.1.2.**)

7.4.3 Reporting

There is a group of verbs of 'reporting', 'saying', 'believing', etc that can be formally distinguished by the fact that there is an alternative construction with *that:*

I believe John to be clever.
I believe that John is clever.

Moreover all of these verbs occur with NP and *to*-infinitive and most of them with both main clause and subordinate clause passivization (for the problematic status of the constructions see 7.2.2).

With the *to*-infinitive there are two common characteristics:

(*a*) Main clause passivization is not merely possible, but is almost the norm:

John is believed to be clever.

With SAY it is obligatory:

John is said to be clever.
**I say John to be clever.*

(*b*) Phase/tense may be marked with HAVE, but the most common pattern is for the subordinate clause verb either to be perfect/past with HAVE (usually past) or progressive, or to consist of the copula:

John is assumed to have gone.
He was thought to be working at the time.
John is considered to be clever.

With the *have* forms in particular, main clause passivization is likely. Other verbal forms are much less likely – the *that* construction being preferred:

**I believe Mary to arrive tomorrow.*
? Mary is believed to arrive tomorrow.
I believe that Mary arrives tomorrow.

[i] ALLEGE. Many of these verbs occur only with NP and the *to*-infinitive:

The boy was alleged to have taken the car.

Verbs of this type include ACCEPT, AFFIRM, ALLEGE, ANNOUNCE, ARGUE, ASSERT, CERTIFY, CLAIM, CONJECTURE, ESTIMATE, KNOW, PROVE, READ, RECKON, REPORT, REPRESENT, RUMOUR, SAY, STATE, SURMISE, SUSPECT, TAKE, THINK, UNDERSTAND and also almost all of the verbs of perception (7.4.4).

[ii] CONSIDER. Some verbs occur not only with NP and the *to*-infinitive but also with NP and the *-en* form, usually but not exclusively with the reflexive *-self* as the NP:

They considered him to be a rogue.
They considered themselves beaten.
The chairman considered the meeting closed.

It is not possible to draw a clear line between this group and the preceding one, but obvious members are BELIEVE, CONSIDER, DECLARE, DISCOVER, IMAGINE$_1$, SUPPOSE. With main clause passivization SUPPOSE is semantically like EXPECT (7.4.1):

He is supposed to come tomorrow.

The perception verbs also occur with NP and *-en* form, but in that construction are clearly perception rather than reporting verbs – see 7.4.4.

[iii] ADMIT. There are a few verbs that occur without NP and with the *-ing* form as well as with NP and the *to*-infinitive (and so with the identity relations of constructions 1 and 2):

I admit being a fool.
I admit John to be a fool.
John is admitted to be a fool.

With the first construction phase/tense may be marked with or without HAVE:

I admit seeing John.
I admit having seen John.

Verbs of this type are ADMIT, ACKNOWLEDGE, CONFESS, DENY. But ADMIT and CONFESS often occur with the preposition *to* when followed by the *-ing* form:

I admit to being a fool.

DENY is rare with NP and the *to*-infinitive.

[iv] REMEMBER$_1$. REMEMBER occurs both with and without NP and the *-ing* form as well as with NP and the *to*-infinitive but differs from the verbs in the other groups in that main clause passivization is not possible:

I remember coming to see you.
I remember my father going to London.
I remember my father to have been kind.

Besides REMEMBER, the other verbs are RECOLLECT and FORGET (all 'memory' verbs), but FORGET is rare:

?*I forget coming to see you.*
?*I forget my father going to London.*
**I forget my father to have been kind.*

FORGET seems to require negation (*ie*=REMEMBER):

I shall never forget coming to see you.
I shall never forget my father going to London.
I shall never forget my father to have been kind.

7.4.4 Perception

There is a formally quite distinct set of verbs, all of 'perception', that occur with NP and bare infinitive, *-ing* form and *-en* form, marking thereby both aspect and voice. These form the 'basic' set [i] below, but there are some others that seem also to belong here:

[i] SEE_1. The full range of patterns is illustrated by SEE:

I saw the children eat their lunch.
I saw the children eating their lunch.
I saw the children beaten by their rivals.

Aspect in the passive may, further, be marked by the participial:

I saw the children being beaten by their rivals.

Main clause passivization is possible, but there is then in the subordinate clause only contrast of voice, active and passive – none of aspect:

The children were seen eating their lunch.
The children were seen being beaten by their rivals.

It may have been expected that the sentences above exemplified the progressive forms, the non-progressive ones being:

The children were seen to eat their lunch.
**The children were seen beaten.*
or *The children were seen to be beaten.*

But this is not so. One of these forms (asterisked) does not occur. The other two are to be interpreted not as perception but as reporting verbs. For almost all the verbs of perception function also as verbs of reporting:

He saw the children to be eating their lunch.
The children were seen to be eating their lunch.
He saw that the children were eating their lunch.

The *to*-infinitive forms illustrated above can all be formally handled in terms of reporting; semantically they will always be so interpreted. The verbs that belong to this group are BEHOLD (archaic), FEEL, FIND, HEAR, NOTICE, OBSERVE, PERCEIVE, SEE_1, SMELL and WATCH, but with the exception of HEAR and SEE there are some restrictions and probabilities:

(*a*) Only FEEL, HEAR, SEE, SMELL and WATCH occur regularly with the bare infinitive (SMELL only with BURN).

(*b*) Only HEAR, SEE and WATCH regularly occur with the *-en* form unless the NP is a reflexive *-self* form (SMELL does not occur at all), *eg:*

She felt herself overcome by the fumes.

As we have observed almost all these verbs are also 'reporting' verbs – SMELL and WATCH are exceptions:

?I heard him to be famous.
I noticed them to have come early.
**I smelled the meat to have burnt.*
**I watched them to have come into the house.*

[ii] IMAGINE. There are some verbs that occur only with the *-ing* form and make no aspect distinction. This point is clearly shown by the occurrence of the *-ing* form with non-progressive verbs:

I can't imagine him knowing all that.

The verbs of this type are semantically of two kinds, 'imagining' – CONCEIVE, ENVISAGE, $FANCY_2$ (only in the imperative, *eg Fancy him knowing that*), $IMAGINE_2$, SEE_2 (see 7.3.3) and 'portraying' – DEPICT, DESCRIBE, PORTRAY. All of these verbs function also as verbs of reporting.

[iii] KNOW. KNOW belongs here as well as with the reporting verbs in that it occurs with the bare infinitive with NP and with the *to*-infinitive when the main clause is passivized. It is in this respect like a perception verb, although it does not occur with *-ing* or *-en* forms:

Have you ever known them come on time?
They have been known to get very angry.

The KNOW of reporting also occurs, of course, with main clause passivization and *to*-infinitive, but normally only with HAVE (phase/tense) or BE:

They were known to be foolish.
They are known to have been there.

We could recognize two verbs KNOW$_1$ and KNOW$_2$, but it seems that we have here a verb of reporting functioning (partly) as a verb of perception – the reverse of our usual pattern, but accounted for in the same way.

7.4.5 Process

We now consider a number of verb-types that are not semantically a very obvious group, though the description 'process' is applicable to many of them. Formally, however, they are grouped together in that all occur with the *-ing* form (but are clearly not either 'sensation' or 'attitude' verbs – either formally or semantically).

[i] KEEP. A few verbs occur with or without NP and with *-ing* form, and permit main clause passivization:

He kept talking.
He kept them talking.
They were kept talking.

Only GET$_2$, KEEP and STOP belong to this group. KEEP also occurs with *-en* forms:

He kept his mouth shut.

But this is not a catenative construction – the *-en* form is purely adjectival as in:

He kept his mouth open.

[ii] START. Another group has the same pattern as KEEP except that without NP it also occurs with *to*-infinitive and seems, by this, to mark aspect (see **7.1.3**):

He started to talk (but was interrupted).
He started talking (and carried on for an hour).
He started them talking.
They were started talking.

BEGIN and START are the only members of this group. BEGIN is unlikely to occur with main clause passivization:

**They were begun talking.*

[iii] FINISH. There are a number of verbs of two semantic kinds, of 'ending and avoiding' and of 'effort', that occur only without NP and with the *-ing* form:

He finished talking at four.
You should try working a bit harder.

Verbs of these types are AVOID, COMPLETE, DELAY, ESCAPE, EVADE, FINISH, POSTPONE, QUIT, and SHUN; ATTEMPT, PRACTISE and TRY_1. GO belongs formally here too:

He went fishing.

[iv] CEASE. CEASE is like FINISH but also occurs with the *to*-infinitive:

He ceased to worry me, when he became older.
He ceased worrying me, when he became older.

There is again the semantics of aspect in this distinction.

[v] LEAVE. A few verbs occur with NP and the *-ing* form and with the possibility of main clause passivization:

He left them standing in the street.
They were left standing in the street.

The verbs are CATCH, LEAVE, SEND and SET. SEND usually occurs with verbs implying motion – SEND PACKING, SEND FLYING, etc. CATCH rarely occurs with bare infinitive:

? You won't catch him do it twice.

This would place it among the sensation verbs, rather than here.

[vi] PREVENT. This verb occurs with NP and *-ing* form only. With main clause passivization a preposition, *from*, is required:

He prevented the men leaving.
The men were prevented from leaving.

Besides PREVENT, HINDER functions in this way. FORBID rarely occurs with NP and *-ing* form – its normal place is with the verbs like PERSUADE (7.4.1).

7.4.6 Effort and achievement

We have again a set of verbs that are semantically of several kinds. Formally they all occur with *to*-infinitive, but are not futurity verbs.

All the verbs in this section occur only without NP and with the *to*-infinitive:

He managed to come.
You should try to work a bit harder.
I remember to visit him.
He failed to see the truth.

These are all verbs of effort such as TRY_2 (compare, of course, TRY_1 – 7.3.3, 7.4.5) or else verbs that merely state the circumstances under which the activities indicated by the subordinate clause verb were carried out. Thus *I remembered to see him* means 'I saw him – I remembered'. Some of these verbs are negative in their semantics, *eg* NEGLECT, FAIL. The verbs that belong here are ATTEMPT_2, COME, ENDEAVOUR, FAIL, FORGET_2, GET_3, HASTEN, MANAGE, NEGLECT, OMIT, PROCEED, REGRET_1, REMEMBER_2, SERVE, STRIVE, STRUGGLE, TRY_2.

Semantically and in terms of the *to*-infinitive construction the verbs of subject complementation belong here too. But they have such idiosyncratic characteristics that they require a separate section (7.4.9).

7.4.7 Attitude

As we noted earlier, verbs of attitude are at one extreme end of the catenatives – with most object-like subordinate clauses. This is shown by two facts:

(*a*) there is never main clause passivization involving the intervening NP;
(*b*) the intervening NP may be replaced usually by a possessive – *him* by *his*, etc:

I can't contemplate John coming tomorrow.
I can't contemplate John's coming tomorrow.
**John can't be contemplated coming tomorrow.*

With all these verbs phase/tense can be marked with HAVE to mean 'the fact that . . . has/did . . .' etc. But the HAVE forms are less common and with some verbs most unlikely – our attitudes are usually towards activities irrespective of time.

[i] LIKE. The more common verbs of this type occur with or without NP and with either the *to*-infinitive or with the *-ing* form.

I like to go to the theatre.
I like going to the theatre.
I like the children going to the theatre.
I like the children to go to the theatre.

With these verbs the possessive form is most unlikely. (For any semantic contrast see 7.1.3):

**I like his going to the theatre.*

Verbs of this type are ABHOR, (CAN'T) BEAR, HATE, LIKE, LOVE, PREFER. There are other verbs that would normally not occur with the *to*-infinitive except in unfulfilled conditions:

I couldn't stand to wait for three hours.
?I can't stand to wait for three hours.

I can't stand waiting for three hours.
I should dislike the children to gamble.
?I dislike the children to gamble.
I should dislike the children to gamble.

The *to*-infinitive, that is to say, has a conditional meaning. The verbs of this type include DISLIKE, LOATHE, (CAN'T) STAND.

HATE with the *to*-infinitive belongs more with REMEMBER (7.4.6) and is close semantically to REGRET (and similarly DREAD), *eg:*

I regret to say that . . .
I hate to tell you this.

In these the meaning is 'I say with regret', 'I tell you, though I hate to do so'. It is a little surprising, perhaps, that LIKE does not function in the same way – though there are other semantically similar forms, *eg* 'I'm glad to say . . .', 'I'm happy to tell you . . .'.

[ii] MISS. Other verbs occur without or with intervening NP but only with the *-ing* form:

I miss going to the theatre.
I miss them coming to see me every week.

The possessive is possible with the latter construction. Verbs of this type are CHANCE_1, CONSIDER, CONTEMPLATE, COUNTENANCE, DETEST, DISCUSS, ENJOY, (DON'T) FANCY_3, JUSTIFY, (DON'T) MIND, MISS, REGRET_2, (DON'T) RELISH, RESENT, RISK, WELCOME. Many of these will normally occur with a negative – CAN'T CONTEMPLATE, DON'T WELCOME, etc. There are many others with prepositions – COUNT ON, DELIGHT IN, THINK ABOUT, etc.

[iii] DEPLORE. The least catenative-like of all are the verbs that occur only with NP and the *-ing* form. These are commonly found with the possessive; some may occur also with no NP but without subject identity (7.2.4):

I deplore them doing that.
I deplore their doing that.
I don't advocate you going there tomorrow.
I don't advocate your going there tomorrow.
I don't advocate going there tomorrow.

Verbs of this type are ADVOCATE, ANTICIPATE, DEPLORE, DEPRECATE. There are a few others with prepositions – APPROVE OF, DISAPPROVE OF.

7.4.8 Needing

We saw in 7.2.4 the active/passive contrast between *to*-infinitive and *-ing* form with NEED:

The boy needs to wash.
The clothes need washing.

Alternatively, and perhaps preferably, we should say that with the *to*-infinitive there is identity between the subject of the main clause and the subject of the subordinate, but with the *-ing* form between the subject of the main clause and the object of the subordinate. The verbs of this type are DESERVE, NEED and WANT_2. WANT_1 belongs with the futurity verbs. Hence the first but not the second sentence is ambiguous:

The man wants to watch. ('desires' or 'needs')
The man wants watching. ('needs' only)

7.4.9 Subject complementation

Verbs such as SEEM and HAPPEN are, as we have seen, in some respects like the 'achievement' verbs of 7.4.6. But they are different from all other catenatives in that they permit the passivization of the whole sentence:

John seems to like Mary.
Mary seems to be liked by John.
The boy happened to meet her in the street.
She happened to be met in the street by the boy.

In this respect these complex phrases are, of course, very like the simple phrases. In particular they are like the modals – especially the epistemic modals. A particularly striking point is that, like the epistemic modals, SEEM and HAPPEN often occur in the present with a *have* form of the following verb.

He happens to have been there.
He seems to have seen her.

These can be paraphrased 'It happens that he was there', 'It seems that he was there'. There is reference to a past event, but to present 'happening' or 'seeming', where the remarks relate to present circumstances, *eg* in a context where it is denied or questioned whether he was there. On the other hand if we are merely relating past events the catenative itself will be in the past tense:

He happened to be there.
He seemed to be there.

SEEM has a further peculiarity that we have sentences containing CAN'T SEEM in, *eg:*

I can't seem to do it.

This means 'It seems that I can't do it'. Semantically *can't* belongs with the subordinate clause with the equivalence of:

I seem not to be able to do it.

The obvious verbs in this class are APPEAR, CHANCE$_2$, HAPPEN, SEEM, TEND, though TEND will not usually occur with the present tense + *have* construction mentioned above. In terms of sentence passivization alone other verbs, especially those of process such as BEGIN might also be included. The dividing line is by no means clear.

7.5 Related and contrasting structures

There are some sequences that are superficially exactly like catenative constructions, but are not to be treated as complex phrases at all:

I ran to catch the train.
The car hit the boy running across the street.
We eat our meat cooked.

These are to be contrasted with:

I want to catch the train.
The man saw the boy running across the street.
We had our meat cooked.

No contrast with bare infinitive is possible since this does not occur except in the complex phrase.

7.5.1 With *to*-infinitive

There are a few problematic structures with *to*-infinitive.

[i] It is clear enough that we want to exclude all 'infinitives of purpose':

I ran to catch the train.
I caught the train to go to London.

The occurrence of the *to*-infinitive is totally independent of the preceding verb and it always expresses purpose. The whole clause can, moreover, be transposed to initial position, though sometimes rather unnaturally:

To catch the train, I ran.
To go to London, I caught the train.

We may even contrast infinitives of purpose and catenative forms with the same words (the written language indicates the distinction with a comma, speech by timing):

I promise to make you happy.
I promise, to make you happy.
I told him to keep him quiet.
I told him, to keep him quiet.

(Notice that with the complex phrase the two *him* forms cannot refer to the same person, but they do with the infinitive of purpose.)

But there is a problem with WAIT. It is by no means clear whether there is a clear distinction between:

I'm waiting to hear your answer.
I'm waiting, to hear your answer.

WAIT seems to be a catenative of the futurity type but it is, obviously, not entirely distinguished from WAIT with an infinitive of purpose.

[ii] We shall also exclude 'infinitives of result':

I ran all the way to find that he had gone.

But it is not clear whether this is the best interpretation of:

He woke to find he was alone.
He lived to be ninety.

It would be possible to handle WAKE and LIVE here as catenatives of the 'achievement' kind.

iii] With verbs of emotion the *to*-infinitive occurs:

He rejoiced to hear the news.
I grieve to tell you this.

There is the nursery rhyme too:

The little dog laughed to see such fun.

Clearly these verbs are very like REGRET, etc among the achievement verbs of 7.4.6. But they are also very like constructions with adjectives:

He was happy to hear the news.
I am sorry to tell you this.

Once again we are clearly in a borderline area. We could put all verbs of emotion into the achievement class – but it would not be easy to define them. In the appropriate contexts we might need to include not only GRIEVE, LAUGH, REJOICE, but also SMILE, YELL, ROAR, WHISTLE, etc.

7.5.2 With *-ing* form

We shall not want to include such sentences as:

He arrived puffing and panting.

This is no more an example of a complex phrase than:

He arrived hot and miserable.

But there is a problem with:

She sat talking.
We stood talking.

SIT and STAND are semantically not far from KEEP and could be treated as catenatives of the 'process' type (formally with FINISH).

Notes

1 Sweet (1903:121).
2 Jespersen (Vol. v) (1940:144).
3 See especially Quirk and Greenbaum (1973: 416–17).
4 *Cf* Chomsky (1965:22).
5 Precisely what is deep structure is today a matter of great controversy. It is enough for our purposes that the constructions are clearly not 'surface structures'.
6 Huddleston (1969:245–6).
7 Kiparsky and Kiparsky (1970:357).
8 Rosenbaum (1967:71).
9 Huddleston (1969:261).
10 For discussion of the problems in this section, see Palmer (1973).
11 An excellent source of information about the syntax of individual catenatives is Van Ek (1966).

Chapter 8

Compound verbs

Any dictionary of English must account for a very large number of what we may call 'compound verbs' – verb + particle combinations of the kind GIVE IN, LOOK AFTER, CARRY ON, PUT UP WITH, as illustrated by:

The enemy finally gave in.
He looked after his aged father.
She carried on the family tradition.
I can't put up with that noise.

These are extremely common, especially in spoken English. Some of their more obvious characteristics are:

[i] There is probably a limited number of particles that can rightly be included in the combinations. Some of the more obvious are DOWN, IN, OFF, ON, OUT, UP, and although there may be no obvious limit to the verbs, some, such as PUT, TAKE, GET, MAKE, combine most freely.

[ii] The combinations are not all freely formed; there are severe collocational restrictions. This is very clearly seen if we substitute the particles in the examples given above for what would seem to be their opposites. In all four cases we should end up with very different, and in varying degrees, much less likely, sentences. With two of them we should have sequences of verb and particle that can hardly be interpreted as combinations at all; for although we can *look after* someone, we cannot similarly *look before* him, and although we can *put up with* something, we cannot *put down with* it (or *put up without* or *put down without*) it. GIVE OUT and CARRY OFF, however, are quite obviously similar combinations, but with meanings that are not the

opposites of GIVE IN and CARRY ON. Both are transparent, *ie* have 'literal' meanings deducible from the meanings of the verb and particle separately, and also have (respectively) the meanings 'run short' and 'win' (*eg* a prize).

[iii] All of them can be replaced, with little change of meaning, by single word verbs, GIVE IN by YIELD, LOOK AFTER by TEND, CARRY ON by CONTINUE, PUT UP WITH by TOLERATE. In all cases the single word is less colloquial; TEND in particular belongs to a literary style.

[iv] All of them (except, naturally, the sentence with the intransitive GIVE IN) have passive forms:

His father was looked after by the nurse.
The family tradition was carried on by the son.
She's a person who simply can't be put up with.

8.1 Grammar and lexicon

In the main, the characteristics considered in the last section are indications of the idiomatic nature of the verb+particle combinations. Yet idiomaticity is essentially a lexical feature, something to be dealt with in the lexicon or dictionary rather than the grammar. If this was all that had to be discussed, there would be no place for these forms in this book. But, as we shall see, there are syntactic features that mark off some of these combinations as close-knit grammatical units.

The grammatically defined combinations that we shall be discussing will be referred to as 'compound verbs' or as 'prepositional verbs' and 'phrasal verbs'[1] – depending on whether the particle is identified as a preposition or as an adverb. This is a departure from the usage in the previous edition of this book where these terms were used only for the idiomatic combinations, the non-idiomatic ones being referred to simply as 'verb+preposition' and 'verb+adverb'. A clear contrast was drawn there of:

GIVE IN with COME IN	*The enemy gave in.*
	The guests came in.
TAKE TO with GO TO	*I didn't take to him.*
	I didn't go to London.
MAKE UP with BRING UP	*She made up the whole story.*
	She brought up a book (to a child in bed).
PUT DOWN in two different meanings	*The ruler put the rebellion down.*
	The teacher put the book down.

There are two reasons for the decision to widen the terms to include the non-idiomatic forms as well as the idiomatic ones. First, it is very difficult to draw a clear line between what is an idiom and what is not and the notion of idiom is not itself a grammatical one. It would not be easy to decide which, if any, of the following combinations with PUT were idiomatic:

Put about a rumour.
Put back the clocks.
Put down a rebellion.
Put up a candidate.
Put in an application.
Put out a pamphlet.
Put over an idea.
Put off a meeting.

Secondly, as I have already commented, there are syntactic reasons for establishing these classes. They are to be distinguished from much 'looser' sequences of verb and preposition or adverb. We can contrast, for instance:

He ate in the garden.
He went in the garden.
He pulled the rope upwards.
He pulled the rope up.

The second of each of these pairs illustrates a compound verb – GO IN and PULL UP. The first of each pair does not – we have no compound verb EAT IN or PULL UPWARDS. This is intuitively obvious, but can be supported by formal criteria.

8.2 Preposition and adverb

The term 'particle' has been used in order not to distinguish, as yet, between preposition and adverb. For although it is possible to decide in almost any sentence whether a particle is an adverb or a preposition, a striking characteristic of many, but not all, of the particles is that they can function as either. Examples are IN and UP in:

John sat in the chair.
John came in.
He climbed up the tree.
She got up early.

It is important, however, to see the ways in which they are closely related and the ways in which they contrast.

8.2.1 Prepositional-adverbs

It might be plausible to argue that English does not, in fact, have two word classes adverb and preposition, but a single class 'particle' or, perhaps, 'prepositional-adverb'. For there is considerable similarity in their function. Often the adverb can be replaced, with little or no change of meaning, by the preposition plus a noun phrase:

He got across.
He got across the river.
He came down.
He came down the hill.

Indeed, if the relevant noun phrase had already been mentioned, it would be semantically redundant and therefore normally omitted:

He walked to the hill and ran up (the hill).
He ran to the fence and crawled under (the fence).

Even when it has not already been mentioned, the relevant noun phrase can be deduced:

She took the sheets off (the bed).
He put his clothes on (himself).

Such examples as these are, however, at one extreme. It would be less easy to supply the 'missing' noun phrase in:

The canvassers handed out leaflets.
The secretary gave in her notice.
They set up a temporary office.

Nevertheless, there is even here some indication of motion in relation to some object. The leaflets are handed out from the point at which the canvassers are standing, the secretary gives her notice into the central office, the temporary office is upon some site or other. In other words, the possible object of a prepositional phrase may be, in varying degrees, unspecified.

This will not be the case, of course, with purely idiomatic combinations. It would be difficult to see what kind of direction could be implied by the particles in:

The enemy gave in.	('surrendered')
The contestant gave up.	('retired')
The old car gave out.	('stopped working')

Or we can compare:

She took the washing in.
She took the homeless children in.
She takes in washing.
The conjuror took the whole audience in.

In the first *in* clearly means into the home; in the second its meaning is a little vaguer – it is more 'into her home' with all that home implies; in the third the meaning is largely idiomatic though there is some direction; in the fourth the meaning is wholly idiomatic and no direction can be inferred.

Nevertheless even with an idiom a prepositional phrase may occasionally replace the adverb:

He hung about.
He hung about the house.

Here in spite of the idiomatic use of HANG there is for both adverb and preposition a fairly literal sense of ABOUT.

8.2.2 Formal contrasts

In spite of the similarity of the function of adverb and preposition, in any one sentence they can, and must, be formally distinguished. An often quoted pair of sentences is:

He ran up a hill.
He ran up a bill.

The second of these differs from the first in being idiomatic; indeed it is very restricted in this use, referring only to increasingly incurring debt. Moreover, for reasons that will become apparent later the definite article *the* is preferable here. A better pair of examples is, then:

He ran up the hill.
He ran up the flag.

It would usually be said that in the first of these *up* is a preposition and in the second an adverb. There are three fairly obvious grammatical differences:

[i] The adverb, but not the preposition, may occur after the noun phrase:

He ran the flag up.
**He ran the hill up.*

[ii] Where there is a pronoun object the adverb occurs only after the pronoun (and the preposition before). The only possibilities, then, are:

He ran it up. (the flag)
He ran up it. (the hill)

However, this is not an absolute distinction since, if there is considerable emphasis on the pronoun and it is accented, the adverb may precede:

Fancy taking on hér.
You'll never take in mé.
We could put up hím.

This we shall see to be a natural consequence of the function of phrasal verbs (**8**.3.2). In general, however, the pronoun test, where the pronoun is unaccented, is a useful one.

[iii] If the particle occurs in final position in the sentence, the adverb will normally be accented, the preposition not:

That's the flag he ran úp.
That's the hill he rán up.

The question of accent is, however, complicated by two things. First, we must ignore contrastive accent as in:

This is the hill he ran úp, not the hill he ran dówn.

Secondly, we have to distinguish, as we shall see later (**8**.4.1), between two kinds of preposition. One will normally be always unaccented; the other, the preposition of our 'prepositional verb', of which RUN UP is an example, may be either accented or unaccented.

These differences can be further illustrated by comparing IN and OVER as prepositions and adverbs in FLY IN and LOOK OVER. If we are talking about a passenger flying in a plane, IN is a preposition; if we are talking about a pilot, IN is, or may be, an adverb. If we are talking about a spectator looking over my shoulder, OVER is a preposition; if we are talking about a doctor (examining it), OVER is an adverb. Hence:

[i] *The passenger flew in the plane.*
The pilot flew in the plane.
! The passenger flew the plane in.
The pilot flew the plane in.

[ii] *The passenger flew in it.*
The pilot flew it in.

[iii] *This is the plane the passenger fléw in.*
This is the plane the pilot flew ín.

[i] *The spectator looked over my shoulder.*
The doctor looked over my shoulder.
! The spectator looked my shoulder over.
The doctor looked my shoulder over.

[ii] *The spectator looked over it.*
The doctor looked it over.

[iii] *This is the shoulder the spectator lóoked over.*
This is the shoulder the doctor looked óver.

Another possible difference is that with the adverb, but not the preposition, the sentence can be passivized:

The flag was run up.
**The hill was run up.*

But this is not an absolute restriction. It is difficult to construct a really satisfactory example with FLY IN:

This plane's been flown ín recently. (adverb)
? This plane's been flówn in recently. (preposition)

It is easier with LOOK OVER:

My shoulder was looked over by the doctor. (adverb)
I don't like my shoulder being looked over at football matches. (preposition)

A further suggestion that has been made is that an 'action nominal' (*the . . .ing of the . . .*) is possible only with the adverb. But this is not true of our first example:

The running up of the flag was spectacular.
The running up of the hill was the hardest part of the exercise.

It certainly seems to be true of FLY IN, but not so clearly of LOOK OVER:

? The looking over of my shoulder by the spectator annoyed me.

8.2.3 Semantic problems

The simple adverb-preposition relationship that was noted in **8.2.1** does not hold, semantically, for some non-idiomatic forms. For consider the difference between the following pairs:

She washed out the stain.
She washed out the clothes.
She wiped out the dirt.
She wiped out the sink.

In the first of each pair we have the normal relationship – the adverb can be replaced by a preposition plus noun phrase:

She washed the stain out of the clothes.
She wiped the dirt out of the sink.

In the second of each pair, however, the noun phrase that follows the preposition in this extended version (*the clothes, the sink*) actually occurs. *Prima facie* it might seem that *out* is here a preposition (*out* (*of*) *the clothes, out* (*of*) *the sink*) and that it is the object of the verb (*the stain, the dirt*) that has been omitted. But this is clearly wrong – *out* even here is an adverb as shown by the pronoun test. For both members of each pair we have:

She washed it out.
She wiped it out.

We have a similar pair in:

She tidied up the room.
She tidied up the mess.

There is a difference, in that in neither case can the adverb be replaced by a preposition plus a noun phrase. But the semantic relation of *room* and *mess* is like that of *clothes* and *stain, sink* and *dirt.*

Clearly such verbs as these are counter-examples to what was said in **8.2.1.** The verb plus adverb combination, even when fairly transparent, has to be treated as a single semantic unit in relation to the object, etc indicated by the noun phrase. As such they belong together with other, single word, verbs of the language that have varying semantic relationships to their grammatical objects, *eg:*

They presented the prize to John.
They presented John with the prize.

We can present a prize or present a person; equally we can wash out stains or wash out clothes.

8.2.4 'Postpositions'

It has been argued that sometimes prepositions may follow rather than precede the noun phrase (and so are 'postpositions'). For these the test of order obviously fails. Examples are:

He has travelled the world over.
I pass their arguments by.
They ran him over.
Will you look it over for me?

The reason for thinking that these are prepositions rather than adverbs is the fact that they may, with little or no change of meaning, precede the noun phrase in sentences where they are much more plausibly to be regarded as prepositions:

He has travelled over the world.
I pass by their arguments.
They ran over him.
Will you look over it for me?

In the first set of sentences, it is suggested, the preposition has been postposed. But this argument is not at all convincing. For with the first sentence the preposition can be omitted:

He has travelled the world.

Although this is not possible with the second, the verb PASS is often used without a particle in a very similar (but literal) sense:

I passed the old buildings.

This suggests that the particle is not a preposition, but an adverb, for adverbs, but not prepositions, are freely omitted.

Implicit in the argument, no doubt, is the fact that the particles appear to be semantically prepositional – 'over the world', 'by their arguments'; but semantic relationships of this kind are not a good guide, as the examples of **8.2.3** show.

Admittedly, even if these particles are adverbs in final position they are prepositions in non-final position (as the pronoun test will show). In this sense they are unusual, since the adverbs usually occur also before the noun phrase and are there in contrast with prepositions. But this shows only the marginal nature of these verbs. RUN OVER in particular, seems to be in the process of becoming a phrasal verb, but does not yet fully contrast with the homonymous prepositional verb. But nothing, I would argue, is gained by talking about 'postpositions' – these are merely the adverbial particles of 'marginal' phrasal verbs.

8.3 Phrasal verbs

The essential characteristic of compound verbs is, of course, that they consist of two elements, a verb and a particle. Phrasal verbs have the further characteristic that the particle may take one of two positions, both before and after the object noun phrase. We must first define the phrasal verb more accurately and then see what the greater syntactic flexibility implies.

8.3.1 Formal characteristics

We have already seen that with compound verbs the difference between prepositions and adverbs (and so between prepositional and phrasal verbs) can be formally established by the fact that the preposition will always precede the noun phrase whereas the adverb may follow it.

This test does not, however, distinguish the phrasal verb from sequence of verb plus adverb. It is usually suggested that the occurrence of the particle before the noun phrase is sufficient for this distinction since 'ordinary' adverbs do not occur in that position. To consider a pair of examples we considered earlier we find:

He pulled the rope up.
He pulled the rope upwards.

But we shall find only one of the following:

He pulled up the rope.
**He pulled upwards the rope.*

By this test PULL UP, but not PULL UPWARDS, is a phrasal verb.

For this test to work, however, we must further define the object noun phrase as a 'simple definite noun phrase', *ie* either a proper noun or a noun phrase consisting of a common noun with no modifiers. For it would be perfectly possible to say:

He pulled upwards the largest of the two ropes.

The presence of *upwards* before the noun phrase does not establish PULL UPWARDS as a phrasal verb. Similarly we have:

He pulled down the blinds.
**He pulled downwards the blinds.*
He pulled downwards all the blinds there were.

Similarly ORDER ABOUT is not a phrasal verb since we cannot say:

**He ordered about the men.*

This is not disproved by:

He ordered about the men who were standing there.

The test to distinguish between phrasal verb and verb plus adverb is that the particles of the phrasal verb may precede the object noun phrase, when that phrase is a 'simple definite noun phrase' as we have defined it.

8.3.2 Accent and position

There is a difference of meaning between:

Shall we sell it or throw it awáy?
Shall we sell it or thrów it away?

In the first there is a simple choice between selling and throwing away; in the second it is already assumed that we shall be getting rid of the object in question and the choice is between doing so with or without financial reward. This second meaning is made possible by the fact that the phrasal verb THROW AWAY consists of two words, and that it is possible to separate, for purposes of contrast, the concepts of getting rid of and of making no financial gain. By putting *away* in unaccented final position we make it semantically 'redundant' – already known from the context. Since both SELL and THROW AWAY contain the notion of getting rid of, but differ in the question of gain, by making *away* semantically redundant we indicate overtly that the choice does not include getting rid of, but only of doing so with or without financial gain.

If a single verb, *eg* DISCARD, had been used this contrast would not have been possible; we could not have singled out the concept of making no gain. We have the possibility only of:

Shall we sell it or discárd it?

This would be equivalent to the first sentence above. Similarly we cannot make the contrast if the other verb does not contain the notion of getting rid of. Thus with KEEP we have only one possible sentence:

Shall we keep it or throw it awáy?
**Shall we keep it or thrów it away?*

There is more to it than this, however. There are four different meanings in the four sentences:

This student wants to give linguístics up.
This student wants to give úp linguistics.
This student wants to give linguistics úp.
This student wants to give up linguístics.

Unaccented final position indicates, as we have just seen, semantic redundancy. (In the case of the phrasal verb, if the particle is final and both particle and verb are unaccented, the whole phrasal verb is semantically redundant.) In the first two sentences, therefore, *give up* and *linguistics* are, respectively, semantically redundant. The first sentence would be likely in a context in which there had already been discussion of students giving up a subject, perhaps a meeting at which permission was given for such a change. The second would occur in a discussion that was centred around linguistics, and it was being stated, perhaps with some incredulity, that there was a student who wished to give it up. Accented final position indicates relative semantic importance but does not imply semantic redundancy of previous unaccented words. The third and fourth sentences, therefore, would both be possible in contexts where neither 'giving up' nor 'linguistics' was redundant – the choice between them would depend on whether giving up or linguistics was the more important, the more newsworthy, item.

Naturally the same four contrasts would not be possible if instead of GIVE UP we used a single-word verb such as DROP. For although the difference of accent is still possible, there can be no variation of the word order – *drop* can only precede *linguistics*. We thus have two possibilities only. The first makes *linguistics* redundant and so has a meaning like that of our second sentence above, but the second fails to distinguish between the other three meanings:

This student wants to dróp linguistics.
This student wants to drop linguístics.

8.3.3 Intransitive forms

The definite noun phrase test works only, of course, for transitive phrasal verbs, *ie* those with object nouns. But there are many verb plus particle combinations that are intransitive, yet seem to belong to the class of phrasal verbs. Consider, for instance, the verbs in:

The plane flew in.
The enemy finally gave in.
Term breaks up next Wednesday.
She broke down when she heard the news.

There is no doubt that the particle is an adverb, not a preposition, but can we establish that these are phrasal verbs rather than mere sequences of verb and adverb? Since we have no decisive formal test it may be argued that (*a*) we cannot identify such forms as phrasal verbs and (*b*) there is no advantage to be gained in so doing.

There are, however, both syntactic and semantic reasons for associating these forms with the transitive phrasal verbs. Syntactically these forms can be related to their transitive counterparts in three ways.

[i] Some of them can be regarded as identical with transitive forms, but

with the object 'deleted' or 'understood'. The relationship is, that is to say, like that of *He was eating* and *He was eating his lunch:*

They carried on.
They carried on the business.
He turned over.
He turned over the page.

[ii] Some of them are related to transitive phrasal verbs in terms of the transitivity relation of the familiar type exemplified by such verbs as BREAK in *It broke* and *He broke it* (4.2.1), one being semantically active, the other passive:

The house blew up.
They blew up the house.
The chimney-pot blew down.
The wind blew the chimney-pot down.

[iii] An extension of the relationship considered in [ii] involves the use of different lexemes, but with, otherwise, the same syntactic and semantic relationships:

He brought about his own downfall.
His downfall came about.
He brought in his friend.
His friend came in.

To state in detail the semantic reasons for treating these forms as phrasal verbs would be to anticipate the discussion in later sections. It is enough to point out that the statements about semantics in the following section apply equally to both the transitive and the intransitive forms.

It is also relevant and important to note now that the semantic analysis of the prepositional verbs in **8.4.3** is largely dependent upon the analysis of these intransitive phrasal verbs (but there is no question-begging – the points could equally be made, though with less convenient exemplification, with transitive forms).

8.3.4 Semantics

If, to begin with, we restrict our attention to the phrasal verbs with a literal meaning, we find that in all cases there is a verb of motion. The particle indicates the direction of the motion. There is a further semantic feature of the phrasal verb as a whole – that of occupying a final resultant position. Consider once again:

He ran the flag up.
The pilot flew the plane in.

The operations were completed – the flag was up (up the pole), and the plane was in (in the airport). This accounts for the difference between:

He pulled up the rope.
**He pulled upwards the rope.*

To pull up means to pull to a final up position; to pull upwards does not. Hence the first, but not the second, is semantically (as well as formally) a phrasal verb.

With PULL UPWARDS final position is absent. On the other hand, with LEAVE UP there is no motion. Hence this too would not be a phrasal verb:

Leave the flag up.
**Leave up the flag.*

(LEAVE OUT and LEAVE IN are, however, phrasal verbs by the formal test; the reason may be that they function as the negatives of the phrasal verbs TAKE OUT and TAKE IN – and so function, by analogy, like them.)

There are many phrasal verbs which do not have the literal locational meaning, but nevertheless share with the literal ones the notion of final result – a meaning not at all unlike the meaning of the perfect in English and therefore appropriately referred to as 'aspect'. The possible variations depend upon the particle. For UP some of the possibilities are shown by:

The work piled up.
Has he turned up yet?
The ice broke up.
We can't just give up.
They speeded up.

The first indicates simple direction and result (even though in a non-concrete sense). The second extends the directional use of UP to indicate proximity to the speaker (just as students, especially at Oxford or Cambridge, COME UP and GO DOWN). In the third, we have perfectivity – in the sense of the resultant condition. The fourth is perfective in the sense of completion and the fifth in a further extension of meaning – high intensity. Similar statements, a little less complex usually, can be made for the other particles.

8.3.5 Idioms

We have already noted (**8.1**) how difficult it is to distinguish between literal and idiomatic phrasal verbs. In the previous section it was suggested that there is a range of meanings from the most literal (locational) to the most abstract (aspectual), associated with most of the particles. But the term 'idiomatic' is not a very clear one. With the phrasal verbs there seem to be three ways in which it may be used.

First, it is clear that there is some collocational restriction upon the combinations. It is possible to think up explanations for some of these restrictions, but not possible to give any general rules concerning them. Thus we find the possible and impossible pairs:

I helped him out.
**I aided him out.*
He yielded up all his property.
**He abandoned up all his property.*
Can you fit out this expedition?
**Can you equip out this expedition?*

Secondly, we could use 'idiomatic' to refer to all the combinations that are not literal in the sense of being locational. But these non-literal combinations are still very largely (though in varying degrees) transparent, *ie* their meaning can be inferred from the meaning of the parts. A native speaker of English would have no difficulty in understanding or forming new combinations using the adverb in one of its aspectual senses even with a new verb. If, for instance, there were a verb *ACIDIZE meaning 'to burn with acid', there would be no problem with:

**He acidized out a hole.*
**He acidized up the body.*

The third possible use of 'idiomatic' would be simply for those combinations that are totally opaque (non-transparent) – whose meanings cannot be inferred from the meanings of the individual words (though there is no absolute cut-off point between these and the last type). We have already noted examples with GIVE IN, GIVE OUT, BREAK UP, BREAK DOWN. Some verbs have various degrees of idiomaticity. One can make up a bed, a fire, a face or a story. Only with the last of these does MAKE UP with the meaning of 'invent' seem to be a complete idiom. With TAKE IN there are four possibilities, as we have already seen (**8.2.1**).

Being idiomatic in the last two senses of the term is wholly a semantic, not a syntactic, matter. (Whether it is so in the first sense is debatable.) Yet it has an effect on the syntax. In general the more closely related semantically are the verb and adverb, the less likely they are to be separated. This may be illustrated in three different syntactic patterns.

[i] The inverted structure with the adverb in initial position is likely only where there is no idiomatic use:

Down he sat.
In he went.
**Down he broke.*
**In he gave.*

[ii] An ordinary adverb may much more easily separate the elements of the phrasal verb if it is not idiomatic:

The money he gave happily away.
**The subject he brought angrily up.*
The troops marched briskly in.
**The troops fell briskly in.*

[iii] With transitive phrasal verbs there is a greater likelihood of the particle preceding the noun phrase if idiomatic, and of following it, if not:

They covered up the crime.
They covered the body up.

There are some idiomatic forms that permit no separation at all (or very rarely):

He put up a good fight.
**He put a good fight up.*
They found out the truth.
? They found the truth out.

8.4 Prepositional verbs

It is not enough to distinguish between preposition and adverb and to recognize phrasal verbs. For, to refer back to our FLY IN examples, there is a further possibility that is different from either:

The sparrow flew in the stationary plane.

This sentence is to be taken in the sense that the sparrow flew into (*ie* through the open doors of) the plane. *Into* might seem preferable here in view of the ambiguity but *in* could be used and there would be no ambiguity in:

He went in the house.

We will, therefore, use this sentence to illustrate clearly the possible contrasts. Here IN is a preposition in view of:

The pilot flew it in.
The passenger flew in it.
The sparrow flew in it.

But the function of the preposition is different. With *the passenger* the sentence is not unlike:

The passenger slept in the plane.

The prepositional phrase merely indicates where he was at the time of flying or sleeping (or perhaps in the case of flying the means by which it was achieved). With our new example (*the sparrow*), the preposition is closely associated with the verb as well as the noun phrase, indicating motion and, as we shall shortly see, the same kind of locational characteristics as the adverb of the phrasal verb. In my revised terminology these verb and preposition combinations are to be distinguished as 'prepositional verbs', the others being simply referred to as verb + preposition.

Similar contrasts can be found with the three-way ambiguous:

He ran down the road.

With the pronoun we have:

He ran it down. (disparaged it)
He ran down it. (did his running there)
He ran down it. (descended it)

The first is a phrasal verb, the second a verb and preposition, the third a prepositional verb.

8.4.1 Formal characteristics

Formal tests of the prepositional verb to distinguish it from verb + preposition are not as many as those for distinguishing the phrasal verb from verb + adverb. The only precise one is related to the accent of the particle in final position (and this modifies the statement made in **8.2.3**). With a prepositional verb the final particle may be either accented or unaccented with little difference in meaning. Hence we have three possibilities:

This is the plane he flew ín. (phrasal verb)
This is the plane he fléw in. (verb and preposition)
This is the plane he flew ín. }
This is the plane he fléw in. } (prepositional verb)

We obviously cannot identify a prepositional verb in any given sentence by this test, since its alternative possibilities are, separately, identical with the possibilities for phrasal verb and verb + preposition. But the fact that the prepositional verb may occur with either is its distinguishing criterion.

Another possible test is that with a prepositional verb an adverb may come between the preposition and the noun, illustrating the closeness of the verb and the preposition. Hence we may have:

He ran, pell mell, up the first hill he saw.
He ran up, pell mell, the first hill he saw.

This is not possible with a verb and preposition such as TOWARDS:

He ran, pell mell, towards the first hill he saw.
**He ran towards, pell mell, the first hill he saw.*

But the test is not a clear one. There are other factors involved, including the length of the noun phrase – or possibly the question of it being a simple definite noun phrase. For we should not expect:

? He ran up, pell mell, the hill.

8.4.2 Transitive forms

For the purposes of contrast we have been considering only prepositional verbs without objects since these have to be distinguished from phrasal verbs with objects. But there are many verbs that seem equally prepositional that may yet have objects:

He ran the flag up the pole.
He drove the car down the road.

An example with *in* is more difficult to attest. We might suggest:

He flew the plane in the airport.

Here, however, *into* is certainly to be preferred – this sentence would almost certainly be interpreted to mean that the airport was the place in which he did his flying, not into which he flew.

The formal contrast of accent is again available, though it is difficult to find satisfactory identical sentences:

This is the place he taught the chíldren in. (verb and preposition)
This is the place he drove the shéep in. }
This is the place he drove the sheep ín. } (prepositional verb)

8.4.3 Semantics

It is, above all, the semantics of the prepositional verbs that make it worthwhile treating them as a special class. All the prepositional verbs that we have been considering have two characteristics. First, the verb is a verb of motion and secondly, the preposition has a meaning similar to that of the adverb of the phrasal verbs – motion plus terminus. Obvious examples are:

He walked across the bridge.
He ran up the hill.

In these there is the motion-act of walking or running in relation to the bridge or the hill, and the terminus position, across the bridge, up the hill.

It has been argued that the preposition in such cases is essentially an 'adprep', since it functions both as an adverb and as a preposition. Syntactically it is to be compared with compound prepositions:

He walked across the road.
He walked across, across the road.
He walked over, across the road.

There is thus 'fusion' of elements; there are three possibilities as exemplified by the following suggested derivations:

He ran down – along the road → *He ran down along the road.*
He walked in – to the house → *He walked into the house.*
He walked in – in the house → *He walked in the house.*

In the first there is no fusion at all, in the second there is fusion, and in the third there is complete fusion, or rather overlap.

The semantic point is clear. The preposition (adprep) has exactly the same semantic function as the adverb – motion plus terminus.

8.4.4 Idioms

The prepositional verbs that we have been discussing are both semantically transparent and syntactically fairly free. There are a number of other combinations that are both syntactically and semantically more restricted. We may distinguish a number of different types.

[i] There are some combinations that have both a literal meaning and a non-literal one, *eg:*

He came across the road.
He came across the missing papers.
He ran into the house.
He ran into an old friend.

[ii] There are some combinations where the non-literal meaning is a fairly obvious extension of the literal one:

You can't see through the glass.
You can't see through his deception.
They went into the house.
They went into the affair.

There are borderline cases between [i] and [ii]. I am not at all sure how transparent are:

He came into a fortune.
He came by a fortune.

[iii] There are some combinations with several meanings in varying degrees of transparency:

The thieves broke into the shop.
The children broke into a rash.
The athlete broke into a trot.

[iv] There are some combinations which, in their literal meanings, would not qualify as prepositional verbs at all:

I'm looking for my glasses.
He looked after his aged father.
She went for the man in a fit of temper.
I can do without all the worry.
I didn't take to that young man.

[v] These are some combinations where the verb does not normally occur with any other than one preposition. These are, admittedly, more collocationally restricted than idiomatic:

I can cope with that rogue.
You can rely on me.
She dotes on her husband.

Of these COPE may occur with no preposition, but not the others (perhaps DOTE marginally):

I can cope all right.
**You can rely.*
?She is one to dote.

There are no very clear formal tests that set these apart from the other prepositional verbs, though in general the combination functions more like a single unit. Two possible but not very rigorous tests are separation and passivization.

The test of separation may be applied by using a relative clause. This works fairly well for the [i] examples:

The road across which he came.
**The missing papers across which he came.*
The house into which he ran.
**The old friend into whom he ran.*

But this formation is today a rather unnatural one. Attempts to produce it are liable to result in oddities such as the (actually attested):

*. . . *with whom we could not do without.*

With [ii] it seems only that the less literal forms are a little less natural.

The glass through which they could see.
? The deception through which they could see.
The house into which they went.
? The affair into which they went.

This may, perhaps, distinguish COME INTO from COME BY (the latter as more idiomatic):

The fortune into which he came.
**The fortune by which he came.*

With [iii] only BREAK INTO in its first sense seems to allow separation:

The shop into which they broke.
**The rash into which the children broke.*
**The trot into which the athlete broke.*

This is, of course, the most transparent of them; it suggests breaking a door or window to get in. Similarly with [iv] only the fairly transparent LOOK FOR seems to permit separation:

The glasses for which I was looking.
**The aged father after whom he was looking.*
? The man for whom she went in a fit of temper.
**All the worry without which I can do.*
**The young man to whom I didn't take.*

All the [v] examples allow separation, but they do not, perhaps, strictly belong here at all. The separation test does, then, to some degree indicate those combinations that are less idiomatic.

The passivization test produces rather different results. With [i] the literal forms seem to have no passives:

**The road was come across.*
**The house was run into.*

One of the non-literal forms is marginal, the other most unlikely:

? The missing papers were soon come across.
**The old friend was run into.*

With [ii] only one seems not to passivize:

The glass can be seen through.
The deception can be seen through.
**The house was gone into.*
The affair was gone into.

There is a contrast between:

**A fortune is not easily come into.*
A fortune is not easily come by.

With [iii] only one passivizes:

The shop was broken into.
**A rash was broken into.*
**A trot was broken into.*

With [iv] only the two LOOK examples passivize easily:

My glasses are being looked for.
His aged father was looked after.
**He was gone for.*
? All this worry can be done without.
**The young man wasn't taken to.*

Moreover, there are sequences of verb and preposition that are not prepositional verbs, yet have passives:

She slept in the bed.
The bed was slept in.
They sat on the chair.
The chair was sat on.

More marginal, but possible, examples are:

? This office has never been worked in.
? The hill was run down by everyone.

Passivization then seems to have only partly to do with idiomaticity. Another factor is that we passivize when the relevant noun phrase is naturally seen as undergoing the action – shops get broken into, but we do not usually want to talk about rashes or trots in the same way. Beds are slept in, chairs sat on, but houses not usually thought of as run into or gone into.

None of the transitive prepositional verbs seem to be idiomatic, though like other verbs of the language they may occur together with particular noun phrases such as:

He put his cards on the table.

8.5 Related constructions

There is no clearly defined class of phrasal or prepositional verbs, though I have attempted in the previous section to isolate some characteristics to establish the classes. There are other combinations – verbs and particles that are not by our criteria phrasal verbs and verbs plus elements other than particles – that otherwise satisfy the criteria.

8.5.1 Verb and particle constructions

We ought to have a place for the combination of verb and two particles, one adverbial the other prepositional as in:

I can't put up with that woman.
He did away with his wife.

The term 'phrasal prepositional verb' may be appropriate for these.

There are again degrees of idiomaticity. Only the verb and adverb are idiomatic in:

You can always put up with Mrs Brown when you come to Bristol.

There may, of course, be no idiomaticity at all:

She walked up with her brother to visit me.

An interesting pair where only the latter is at all idiomatic (but still reasonably transparent) is:

He got away with her purse.
He can get away with anything.

Other idiomatic constructions involving another word between verb and particle (a noun apparently except in the case of *rid*) are illustrated by:

He took care of the matter.
The men set fire to the house.
He got rid of his old car.

All have passives:

The matter was taken care of.
The house was set fire to.
The car was got rid of.

Some prepositional verbs collocate with particular noun phrases in particular idiomatic meanings:

He came off his high horse.
She went for him in a big way.
She went for him hammer and tongs.

By our tests there are no phrasal verbs in (8.3.1):

They brought the man to.
He ordered the men about.

For we cannot say:

**They brought to the man.*
**He ordered about the men.*

Yet these are idiomatic. This shows only that syntactic and semantic criteria do not coincide.

8.5.2 Verbs plus other elements

The combination of verb plus adjective functions exactly like a phrasal verb in:

I cut open the melon.
He made clear his intentions.
They cut short the interview.

This is clear from the position of the adjective – before the object noun phrase (though it may also occur after it). But whether the adjective may occur here or not depends upon the semantics of both verb and adjective. Thus we find:

They packed tight the wadding.
**They packed loose the wadding.*

Yet the reason for the acceptability of the first, but not of the second, is clearly related to the semantics of the particles of the phrasal verb – resultant condition, and more specifically, completeness. For one aims usually to pack tight. Packing loose is to fail to complete the task. But there is a whole area of syntax and semantics that cannot be discussed here.

Two other similar types are verb plus infinitive and verb plus preposition and noun phrase:

He let slip the opportunity.
It brings to light the facts.

Note

The complete rewriting of this chapter owes a great deal to *The Phrasal Verb in English* by Dwight Bolinger (Cambridge: Harvard University Press, 1971). Many of the ideas and examples are taken from this book, but the overall classification and the terminology is not. But the problem of compound verbs is a vast one and this chapter cannot possibly do justice to the subject, or to Bolinger's brilliant attempt to clarify and illustrate.

Chapter 9

Morphology

We shall look first at the morphology of the auxiliaries and then of the full verbs.

9.1 The auxiliaries

The auxiliary verbs differ morphologically from the other verbs in several ways. First, none of them have a present third person singular form that differs from other present forms only by having a final *-s* [s] , [z] or [iz] (9.2.2). Most of them have no distinct third person form (*I can, he can*) at all, while the forms *is*, *has* and *does* [dʌz] cannot (in spoken form) be interpreted phonologically as *am* (or *are*), *have* and *do* [duː] respectively, plus *-s*. The verb BE has other idiosyncratic forms too. Secondly, most of them have negative forms; there is indeed a good case for talking about 'a negative conjugation', since negation is essentially morphological; though *not* occurs commonly in writing, the form [nɔt] rarely follows an auxiliary form in speech. Thirdly, most of the auxiliary verbs have 'weak' forms, as well as 'strong' forms, the former occurring only when unstressed.

9.1.1 Irregular forms

Apart from the negative and weak forms the auxiliary verbs have a number of forms that do not follow the pattern of the full verbs and are in this sense 'irregular'.

[i] The verb BE has five wholly irregular finite forms.

(*a*) In the present tense there is a distinct form, *am* [æm], for the first person singular; for all other verbs the form is identical with the plural form.

(*b*) The third person singular and plural form of the present tense are wholly idiosyncratic – *is* [iz] and *are* [ɑː].

(*c*) There are two past tense forms *was* [wɔz] (in my own speech [wʌz]) and *were* [wəː]; these are again idiosyncratic in form. Moreover, no other verb has distinct past tense forms for singular and plural; a further peculiarity is that the first person singular form is identical with the third singular (*was*) – in all other paradigms, apart from the present tense of BE, the first person singular form is identical with the plural forms and it is the third person singular that stands alone – *I love*, *they love*, but *he loves*.

[ii] The third person singular present tense form of HAVE is *has* [hæz], not **haves* (the past tense form *had* too is irregular, but so too are many such forms of full verbs).

[iii] The third person singular present tense form of DO is *does* [dʌz] not *[duːz], in spite of *do* [duː]. Even as a full verb DO has the irregular form (see **6.1.3** and **9.4**).

[iv] Apart from BE, HAVE and DO, none of the auxiliaries has a distinct form for the third person singular of the present – no form in *-s*. (*Dares* and *needs* are not to be regarded as forms of the auxiliary, see **2.2.7**.)

9.1.2 Negative forms

The auxiliaries have negative forms ending in orthographic *n't*, phonetically [nt], but the relations between the positive and the negative forms are of several kinds:

[i] The negative form differs only in the addition of [nt] in the case of *is*, *are*, *was*, *were*, *has*, *have*, *had*, *does*, *did*, *would*, *should*, *could*, *might*, *ought*, *dare* and *need*.

[ii] The negative form lacks the final consonant of the positive form in the case of *must* [mʌst] [mʌsnt]. This is also true of the quasi-auxiliary USED (**6.2.1**), which will be included in the discussion in this chapter [juːst] [juːsnt].

[iii] The negative form has a different vowel from that of the positive form in the case of *do* [duː] [dount].

[iv] The negative form has a different vowel from that of the positive form and lacks the final consonant in the case of *will* [wil] [wount], *shall* [ʃæl] [ʃɑːnt], *can* [kæn] [kɑːnt]. With these three the differences are paralleled by differences in the orthography too – *won't*, *shan't* and *can't* (not **cann't*).

[v] *Am* has no negative form in statements; the negative form of a sentence containing *am* contains the form *not* [nɔt]:

I'm going. [aim gouiŋ] *I'm not going.* [aim nɔt gouiŋ]

In questions with inversion, however, there is a negative form [ɑːnt]:

Am I? [æm ai] [ɑːnt ai]

The only possible orthographic form of this is *Aren't I?*, but in a formal style this is avoided presumably because it is felt to be the negative of *are* and not of *am*; *Am I not?* is used in its place. But the form is no stranger than *can't*, *won't* or *shan't* either in transcription or in orthography. Similarly, as was noted in **2.2.2**, there is, for many speakers, no negative form corresponding to *may* (**mayn't*) and *usedn't* is uncommon. There is no negative form corresponding to *be*, though by analogy with the imperative form *don't*, one might expect **ben't* (see **3.1.2**).

Finally we may note one further feature – that in the case at least of orthographic *can't*, *won't*, *shan't* and *don't* the final nasal and stop may be homorganic with the following consonant – these forms that is to say have final nasality and non-nasal 'obstruence' (a plosive, an affricate or a fricative), but the place of the articulation is wholly determined by the initial consonant of the following word. This may be shown by using transcriptions such as [kɑːmp], [kɑːŋk]:

[ai kɑːmp biː ðɛə] *I can't be there.*
[ʃi wouŋk kɛə] *She won't care.*
[ai ʃɑːmp pei] *I shan't pay.*
[wi douŋk gou ðɛə] *We don't go there.*

In many cases, however, there is nothing to justify the writing of non-nasal obstruents – one at the end of the auxiliary and the other at the beginning of the following verb. There is simply homorganic nasality and obstruence as a feature of the whole complex. This is true of alveolar articulation as well as bilabial and velar:

[ai doun θiŋk sou] *I don't think so.*
[ai kɑːm bi ðɛə] *I can't be there.*
[ʃi wouŋ kɛə] *She won't care.*

9.1.3 Weak forms

Most of the auxiliaries have forms that occur only in unstressed positions. These are the so-called 'weak' forms. Some of these are non-syllabic;

the others are syllabic but contain vowels of the kind that are associated with absence of stress in English – most commonly [ə], or a syllabic consonant:

[ail kʌm]	*I'll come.*	*Cf* [ai wil kʌm]
[dʒɔn kən kʌm]	*John can come.*	*Cf* [dʒɔn kæn kʌm]

It must not, however, be supposed that strong forms may not occur in unstressed position. Indeed strong forms often occur initially, even without stress (though this raises fundamental problems regarding the nature of stress – it could be argued that the occurrence of a strong form in an environment where a weak form is possible is itself an exponent of stress):

[hæv juː siːn him]	*Have you seen him?*
[kæn ai kʌm]	*Can I come?*

Moreover, in clause-final position, when the verb is acting in 'code' function, the weak form does not occur at all; though the form is unstressed the form is always the strong one:

He's working harder than I am.	[ai æm]
She can't do it but he can.	[hiː kæn]

The weak forms are difficult to describe because 'weakness' is not, so to speak, a 'yes or no' characteristic but a 'more or less' one. There are, that is to say, many degrees, and a whole gradation of forms. For instance, there are a number of forms corresponding to orthographic *we are* that differ phonetically between [wiː ɑː] and [wə]. Only some of the gradation may be represented phonetically – [wiː ə*] [wiə*] [wi*] and [wə*]. Even when it is important to contrast two forms phonetically, it is not certain that the contrast will always be observable. For instance we would usually distinguish the vowel sequences of orthographic *key will* and *he will:*

He'll be waiting.	[hiːl] or [hil]
The key'll be waiting.	[kiːəl] or [kiəl]

But it would be rash to maintain that the difference is always maintained. The statements that follow are thus only approximations. Not only is the number of distinctions that are made based on an arbitrary (though now traditional) choice, but it is not supposed that distinctions that are shown are always clear.

One important classification of the forms, however, is into those that are syllabic and those that are not. The forms are set out, and this distinction made in the following table. The asterisk indicates that there is a 'linking r' before vowels:

ORTHOGRAPHIC	STRONG	WEAK SYLLABIC	WEAK NON-SYLLABIC
am	æm	əm	m
is	iz		z, s
are	ɑː*	ə*	*
was	wɔz	wəz	wz
were	wəː*	wə*	w*
have	hæv	həv, əv	v
has	hæz	həz, əz	z, s
had	hæd	həd, əd	d
shall	ʃæl	ʃəl, ʃl̩	ʃl
should	ʃud	ʃəd	ʃd
will	wil	əl, l̩	l
would	wud	wəd, əd	d
can	kæn	kən, kn̩, kŋ	kn
could	kud	kəd	kd
must	mʌst	məst, məs	ms
do	duː	du, də	d
does	dʌz	dəz	dz
did	did		dd, d
be	biː	bi	
been	biːn	bin	

The basic problem is simply to state the conditions under which the non-syllabic form occurs. This depends on no less than five factors:

(*a*) position of the form in the sentence;
(*b*) the verbal form itself (they do not all function in the same way);
(*c*) whether the preceding word is (a form of) a noun or a pronoun;
(*d*) whether the preceding form ends in a consonant or a vowel;
(*e*) if the preceding form (noun forms only) ends in a consonant, the place of articulation of that consonant.

The types of weak form that occur medially in the clause are different from those that occur initially. The two types are therefore dealt with separately.

In terms of the patterns of weak forms in medial position the auxiliaries fall into three main classes.

[i] The forms corresponding to orthographic *is* and *has* may be non-syllabic, except where the final element of the preceding word is a sibilant or palatal consonant. Where this condition does not apply the

auxiliary form is 'fused' with the preceding noun or pronoun form, the whole piece having the phonological characteristics of a single word. Phonetically the form may be voiceless or voiced – [s] or [z]:

[ðə kæts kʌmiŋ] *The cat's coming.*
[ðə dɔgz kʌmiŋ] *The dog's coming.*

But the absence or presence of voice is shared by both the sibilant and the final element of the preceding noun or pronoun form. The auxiliary is phonetically identical with the *-s* of plurality and the possessive *-'s* (these occur with nouns only). In all cases the final element is a sibilant accompanied by voice or voicelessness, but this final voice or voicelessness is essentially a characteristic of the noun in all its forms:

[dɔgz]	*dog's* (*dog is, dog has*)	*dogs*	*dog's, dogs'*
[kæts]	*cat's* (*cat is, cat has*)	*cats*	*cat's, cats'*
[biːz]	*bee's* (*bee is, bee has*)	*bees*	*bee's, bees'*

With pronouns we have only:

[hiːz] *he's* (*he is, he has*)
[ʃiːz] *she's* (*she is, she has*)
[its] *it's* (*it is, it has*)

The element with which the auxiliary is 'fused' is not necessarily the head of the noun phrase:

The girl with the ticket is waiting for you. ([tikits])

If the noun ends in a sibilant or a palatal the auxiliary must have a syllabic form. With *is* this can only be [iz], while with *has* it is commonly [əz], *eg:*

[tʃəːtʃ iz] *church is*
[tʃəːtʃ əz] *church has*
[fens iz] *fence is*
[fens əz] *fence has*

Yet it is misleading to write the forms in phonetic script as two words. For the pattern is the same as that of the forms with *s* plural and *'s* possessive except that the *has* form has a central vowel (and this is not important since the vowel qualities of both forms show considerable variation). We may add to the table above if we omit the space between the noun and auxiliary forms:

[hɔːsiz]	*horse's* (*horse is*)	*horses*	*horse's, horses'*
[hɔːsəz]	*horse's* (*horse has*)		

[ii] The forms corresponding to orthographic *am*, *are*, *will*, *would*, *have* and *had* have a similar feature when preceded by pronoun forms ending in a vowel. The pronoun and verb forms again have the phonological characteristics of one word. They are best set out paradigmatically; indeed there is a strong case for treating them as if they were comparable to the paradigms of 'inflected' languages. For completeness the table that follows includes *he* and *she* with *is* and *has*, which were dealt with under [i]:

am/(*is*)/*are*	*had* or *would*	*will*	*have*/(*has*)
aim	aid	ail	aiv
(hiːz)	hiːd	hiːl	(hiːz)
(ʃiːz)	ʃiːd	ʃiːl	(ʃiːz)
wiə*, wi*, wə*	wiːd	wiːl	wiːv
juə*, jɔː*, jə*	juːd	juːl	juːv
ðeiə*, ðεə*, ðə*	ðeid	ðeil	ðeiv

Two points are to be noted: first, the degrees of 'weakness' (not all of them shown) that may be indicated for some of the forms, and secondly the vowels of [jɔː*] and [ðεə*].

This feature of 'fusion' is restricted to pronouns plus finite form. It is not, therefore, characteristic of all sequences of pronoun form plus *have*, etc. We shall not have [aiv], for instance, in:

Should I have gone. ([ai əv])

Here *have* is an infinitive and not the finite form with *I* as the subject. The auxiliary forms now being considered are normally syllabic when preceded by forms of nouns or the pronoun form *it*, the 'weakest' forms being [ə*], [l̩], [əv] and [əd], though *would* is usually [wəd] and so distinct from *had*. In spite of [mænz] (*man is*, *man has*) we do not find [*mænd] (*man had*, *man would*), but only [mæn əd] or [mæn wəd]. Similarly a contrast can be made with *she* and the diminutive of Sheila which I shall write *Shei*:

[ʃiː əl bi kʌmiŋ]	*Shei'll be coming.*
[ʃiːl bi kʌmiŋ]	*She'll be coming.*
[ʃiː wəd bi kʌmiŋ]	*Shei'd be coming.*
[ʃiːd bi kʌmiŋ]	*She'd be coming.*

But there is no difference between *She's* and *Shei's* (except in the different feature that the former may be unstressed).

[iii] Nothing yet has been said about the forms with two consonants – those of *can*, *could*, *shall*, *should* and *must*. After a final consonant

these must be syllabic. But we might recognize non-syllabic forms after a vowel – especially when following pronoun forms (thus patterning with the forms considered under [ii]); a set of contrasts between *Shei* and *she* can again be made. But we are again faced here with the problem of degrees of weakness. For we might write [kd] in:

[ai kd ɑːsk] *I could ask.*

But this would not imply that the [k] was unreleased. It would be different from the unreleased [k] of:

[laik dɑːts] *Like darts.*

The release of the [k] may here then be treated as a mark of a syllable – and in that case the problem is not one of syllabic versus non-syllabic forms, but of degrees of syllabicity. A further point to be noted is that *can* may occur as [kŋ]. Yet since there is homorganic nasality, there is no release of the [k] before the [ŋ]. But if [ŋ] is not syllabic it will occur in phonologically impossible positions (syllable initially and in the middle of a cluster of consonants):

[ai kŋ ɑːsk im] *I can ask him.*
[juː kŋ teik wʌn] *You can take one.*

There are two other points to be noted. First, among the syllabic forms of *can* we may note [kəm] and [kəŋ] with nasality that is homorganic with the following consonant:

[ai kəm pei] *I can pay.*
[ai kəŋ gou] *I can go.*

But statements of this kind ought not to be considered as special statements about certain of the forms; they are rather indications of the limits of phonetic transcription. There are similar features with all the forms, but they are more difficult to show. Secondly, nothing has been yet said about the non-finite forms *be, been* and *being*. In unstressed position *be* and *been* have weak forms. It is usually stated that *being* has no weak form, and it is always written [biːiŋ]. But this is misleading; we are justified at times in writing [biːŋ] and even perhaps [biŋ].

Let us now consider weak forms initially. With the exception of forms of DO, syllabic forms are much more common at the beginning of a sentence:

[kən ai kʌm] *Can I come?* (not *knai)
[wəd juː gou] *Would you go?* (not *djuː)

The forms of HAVE are those with initial [h]:

[həv juː siːn im] *Have you seen him?*
[həz iː gɔn] *Has he gone?*

A non-syllabic form of *do* is common, often linked phonologically to the following consonant:

[dwiː nou ðəm] *Do we know them?*
[dʒə wɔnt tu] *Do you want to?* (Palatal affricate)
[dðei sei sou] *Do they say so?* (Interdental [d])

A similar feature may be noted for *does* especially when followed by *she:*

[dzʃi wɔnt tu] *Does she want to?*

Did may be represented by an initial voiced alveolar stop alone; its duration may often, but not always, justify the transcription [dd]:

[dd ai sei sou] *Did I say so?*
[dai sei sou]

There can be no confusion with *Do I* which must always have rounding – a rounded vowel or [w] – [du ai], [dwai]. But there is the possibility of ambiguity in:

[dðei sei sou] *Do they say so?* or *Did they say so?*

The forms of *can* that have homorganic nasality with the following consonant occur initially too:

[kəm bɔb kʌm] *Can Bob come?*
[kəŋ keit kʌm] *Can Kate come?*

9.2 Full verbs: *-ing* and *-s* forms

We may dispose quickly of the morphology of the *-ing* form. In all cases it differs from the simple form only by the addition of [iŋ]:

cut [kʌt] *cutting* [kʌtiŋ]

In rapid conversation style the final nasal is often alveolar [n] instead of velar [ŋ]. Forms with the alveolar nasal are often regarded as substandard but they certainly occur in my speech and in that of others.

The *-s* form differs from the simple form by the addition of an alveolar fricative (a sibilant). Phonetically there are three possibilities:

[i] a voiceless sibilant [s] where the final element of the simple form is voiceless and is not sibilant or palatal,

[ii] a voiced sibilant [z] where the final element of the simple form is voiced and is not sibilant or palatal,
[iii] a voiced sibilant [z] preceded by the vowel [i] where the final element of the simple form is sibilant or palatal.

These features are entirely determined by phonetic characteristics; their differences are grammatical. The phonological exponent of the *-s* form is simply 'sibilance', and the English orthography, which does not make a distinction but merely writes a final *-s*, is grammatically more appropriate than phonetic notation which writes each of the three phonetically different forms in three different ways. We have then:

[i]	*hate* [heit]	*hates* [heits]
[ii]	*love* [lʌv]	*loves* [lʌvz]
	stay [stei]	*stays* [steiz]
[iii]	*miss* [mis]	*misses* [misiz]

For BE, HAVE and DO see **9.4**. Apart from these there is only one verb in English that is irregular in respect of its *-s* form – SAY, whose *-s* form, though spelt *says*, is [sez] not [*seiz].

9.3 Full verbs: past tense and *-en* forms

For most of the verbs the past tense and *-en* forms are identical; even when they differ they are often related by a simple phonological feature. It is clearly convenient to handle them together.

There is one 'regular' or 'productive' formation that would apply to any word newly introduced into English; this is the 'regular *-ed* formation' of *lick/licked*, *like/liked*, *sin/sinned* (**9.3.1**). The other formations might seem to be all irregular, but this is not in fact justified. Many of them belong to what I shall call the 'secondary *-ed* formation', which differs from the regular one in having three simple phonological rules (**9.3.2**). A third small class can be dealt with in terms of a specific kind of vowel change (**9.3.3**), while a fourth has the suffix *-en* for its *-en* forms (**9.3.4**). Between them there are four classes accounting for the vast majority of the verbs. There are a few that are wholly idiosyncratic (**9.3.5**).

9.3.1 Regular *-ed* formation

For most verbs the past tense and *-en* forms are formed by the addition of an alveolar plosive. This has, *mutatis mutandis*, the same kind of characteristics as the alveolar sibilant of the *-s* forms. The alveolar plosive will be:

[i] voiceless [t] when the final element of the simple form is a voiceless consonant that is not an alveolar plosive, *eg:*

like [laik] *liked* [laikt]

[ii] voiced [d] when the final element of the simple form is a voiced consonant that is not an alveolar plosive or is a vowel, *eg:*

love [lʌv] *loved* [lʌvd]
stay [stei] *stayed* [steid]

[iii] a voiced consonant [d] preceded by the vowel [i] when the final element of the simple form is an alveolar plosive [t] or [d], *eg:*

hate [heit] *hated* [heitid]

What we find with both the *-s* form and the *-ed* form is that we have:

(*a*) Assimilation in terms of voicing such that the suffix is voiceless after a voiceless consonant and voiced after a voiced one;

(*b*) A special kind of dissimilation that prevents the immediate co-occurrence of two consonants of the same type of articulation – the sibilant does not immediately follow a sibilant or palatal, or the alveolar plosive another alveolar plosive. They are always separated by a vowel [i] – and the suffix is voiced since the vowel is voiced.

9.3.2 Secondary *-ed* formation

There are many other verbs whose formation can be handled in terms of the addition of an alveolar plosive provided three phonological features are noted leading to three phonological rules that are not applicable to the regular formation.

(*a*) With a number of verbs that end in a lateral [l] or an alveolar nasal [n], the suffixed alveolar plosive may be voiced as in the regular formation (since laterals and nasals are voiced) or voiceless *eg: burn/burnt* [bəːnt]. This feature we shall call 'devoicing'. (It would be possible to argue that the suffix was in its basic form the voiceless plosive [t], which is voiced through 'assimilation' in the regular formation only, but this would complicate the analysis of forms such as BUILD and FLEE – see below.)

(*b*) The pattern *keep/kept* [kiːp]/[kept] suggests that there is a 'vowel shortening rule' whereby the 'long' vowel [iː] is replaced by the 'short' vowel [e] when the suffix is added. This is plausible in the light of the identical vocalic pattern of such pairs as *serene* [səriːn] and *serenity* [səreniti], and, with different vowels [ei]/[æ], *profane* and *profanity*, or [ai]/[i], *revise* and *revision.* It is worth noting that the orthography indicates the relationship while the phonetic transcription does not. There is only one small class of verbs, all with the same vowels as KEEP, that exhibit this feature alone, but there are other verbs whose formation is to be accounted for by this feature plus some other (see in particular the next paragraph). We shall refer to the feature as 'vowel shortening'. (A more general phonological rule would make vowel shortening operate not when a suffix is added, but simply before the sequence of two consonants; but this would not permit a similar analysis for FLEE and SHOE – see below.)

(*c*) There are about twenty verbs in English that appear to have no past tense/-en form suffix at all, *eg* HIT. But all of these end in an alveolar plosive – either [d] or [t]. Since English phonology does not permit within the word either the sequence [dt] or [tt] (or, indeed, any similar combination of consonants) we may argue that the suffix is dropped or deleted in this context. This is preferable to simply saying that these verbs have 'zero' past tense/*-en* form suffix for two reasons. First, it gives an explanation for the forms themselves; they are not just irregular – their final consonants are significant. Secondly, it helps to generalize the formation of such forms as *bleed/bled.* Here we have vowel shortening again, but it was suggested that vowel shortening takes place when a suffix is added. Since this verb too ends in an alveolar plosive we can argue that the suffix is added but then deleted. We shall call this feature 'consonant reduction'.

We can now handle a number of verbs in six classes, each involving either one or two of these phonological features.

[i] Devoicing alone is found in:

smell [smel] *smelt* or *smelled* [smelt]

The verbs that belong to this class (all ending in an alveolar nasal or a lateral) are BURN, LEARN, SMELL, SPELL, SPILL, SPOIL and the now slightly archaic DWELL. In the orthography the ending is either *-t* or *-ed.*

[ii] Vowel shortening alone is found in:

keep [kiːp] *kept* [kept]

All the verbs in this class have the same vowels and final consonant – CREEP, KEEP, LEAP, SLEEP, SWEEP, WEEP. We need not handle these in terms of our devoicing feature – the voicelessness of the suffix is in accordance with the regular pattern. We should also notice here:

flee [fliː] *fled* [fled]

FLEE is the only verb of this type. Notice that, if we include it here, vowel shortening takes place when the suffix is added, but not before two consonants. There is no devoicing – the alveolar plosive is voiced in accordance with the regular pattern.

[iii] Consonant reduction alone is found in:

hit [hit] *hit* [hit]

The verbs that belong here (all with final alveolar plosive) are BET, BURST, CAST, COST, CUT, HIT, HURT, LET, PUT, QUIT, RID, SET, SHED, SHUT, SLIT, SPLIT, SPREAD, THRUST, UPSET. WET functions either like these or in the regular formation.

[iv] Devoicing and vowel shortening together are found in:

mean [miːn] *meant* [ment]

All the verbs of this class have the vowel [iː] and [e] and, with one exception, end in an alveolar nasal or lateral (and thus combine the characteristics of the verbs of [i] and [ii]) – DEAL, FEEL, KNEEL, LEAN, MEAN. The only exception is DREAM; it, too, ends in a nasal, but in a bilabial, not an alveolar, one.

[v] Devoicing and consonant reduction together are found in:

bend [bend] *bent* [bent]

The verbs that belong to this class end in an alveolar nasal or lateral plus alveolar plosive (and thus combine the characteristics of the verbs in [i] and [iii]) – BEND, BUILD, LEND, REND (now rather archaic) SEND and SPEND. GIRD might be added, but it does not have the same final consonants, and is now obsolete.

[vi] Vowel shortening and consonant reduction together are found in:

bleed [bliːd] *bled* [bled]

The verbs that belong to this class all end in an alveolar plosive and have the vowels [iː]/[e] (and so combine the characteristics of the verbs of [ii] and [iii]) – BLEED, BREED, FEED, LEAD, MEET, READ, SPEED. With a different pair of vowels we have:

light [lait] *lit* [lit]

The only verbs in this group are LIGHT and SLIDE.

There are a few other verbs that are best dealt with in this section. Vowel shortening involving different vowels (plus consonant reduction in the first example) is to be seen in:

shoot [ʃuːt] *shot* [ʃɔt]
shoe [ʃuː] *shod* [ʃɔd]

This is a less common vowel pattern but found in, *eg: lose/loss.* Otherwise these verbs are like BLEED and FLEE. SHOOT and SHOE are the only examples. Finally we have both types of vowel shortening again exemplified in:

leave [liːv] *left* [left]
lose [luːz] *lost* [lost]

The idiosyncratic feature of these is the devoicing of the final consonant [v] → [f] and [z] → [s], LEAVE and LOSE are the only examples.

Overall there is a remarkable regularity. Even these last few examples, though apparently totally irregular at first sight, are evidence of the existence of the patterns.

9.3.3 Back vowel formation

We have dealt with vowel shortening. There is another kind of vowel change that involves a change from a front vowel in the simple form to a corresponding back vowel in one or both of the other forms.

[i] The most striking pattern is that of:

drink [driŋk] drank [dræŋk] drunk [drʌŋk]

We have here what one might call the 'vowel-triangular formation'. There are three vowels all short and all at the extremes of the vowel diagram – front close, open and back close. At a purely phonetic level we would have expected the triangle to be that of [i], [æ] and [u], not [i], [æ] and [ʌ]. But there is a simple explanation – [u] does not occur in English before a nasal. We can argue, in fact, that [ʌ] and [u] are closely related and differ only in the absence or presence of 'rounding' and that 'rounding' does not occur before [ŋ]. Hence in this environment [u] is replaced by [ʌ], and the triangle thus is upheld. The verbs that belong to this class are BEGIN, DRINK, RING, SHRINK, SING, SINK, SPRING, STINK, SWIM.

[ii] The same pattern but without a separate [æ] form for past tense is found with:

win [win] *won* [wʌn]

Verbs in this class are CLING, DIG, FLING, SLING, SLINK, SPIN, STICK, STING, STRING, SWING, WIN and WRING. The same comment about the final nasal applies to all of these except DIG and STICK. But it is also true that [u] does not occur before [g]; it occurs, however, before [k] (*eg: rook*) – STICK is, therefore, exceptional.

[iii] A straightforward change is found in:

get [get] *got* [gɔt]

The two vowels are counterparts phonetically (both half open); GET is alone in this class.

[iv] A change involving only the last element of a diphthong is found in:

find [faind] *found* [faund]

Verbs in this class are BIND, FIND, GRIND, WIND.

[v] Less clear-cut cases are:

shine [ʃain] *shone* [ʃɔn]
SHINE
fight [fait] *fought* [fɔːt]
FIGHT
strike [straik] *struck* [strʌk]
STRIKE
stride [straid] *strode* [stroud]
ABIDE (archaic), STRIDE

The simple form has a front diphthong, the other a variety of back vowels. STRIDE is idiosyncratic in that it has no *-en* form – *strode* is past tense only. ABIDE has regular *-ed* forms also.

[vi] Back vowel formation cannot, however, account for all vowel changes. One can do little more than list the following:

sit [sit] *sat* [sæt]
SIT, SPIT
hang [hæŋ] *hung* [hʌŋ]
HANG
hold [hould] *held* [held]
HOLD

Some have in addition the suffix of the regular formation:

sell [sel] *sold* [sould]
SELL
hear [hiə] *heard* [həːd]
HEAR
say [sei] *said* [sed]
SAY

[vii] Even more idiosyncratic are the verbs that have a vowel change form for the past tense but an *-en* form that is identical with the simple form:

come [kʌm] *came* [keim] *come* [kʌm]
BECOME, COME
run [rʌn] *ran* [ræn] *run* [rʌn]
RUN

9.3.4 *-en* suffix

There are some verbs that actually have orthographic *-en* or *-n*, phonetic [n] as the *-en* suffix! Apart from this they belong with many of the verbs we have been considering.

[i] Within the regular *-ed* formation is:

sew [sou] *sewed* [soud] *sown* [soun]
SEW, SHOW, SOW and the now archaic HEW.

[ii] In the secondary *-ed* formation with consonant reduction is:

beat [biːt] *beat* [biːt] *beaten* [biːtn]
BEAT

[iii] In the secondary *-ed* formation with consonant reduction and vowel shortening (the latter applying to the *-en* form as well as to the past tense) is:

bite [bait] *bit* [bit] *bitten* [bitn]
BITE, HIDE

[iv] With a variety of vowel changes (none strictly in the back vowel formation) are:

see [siː] *saw* [sɔː] *seen* [siːn]
SEE
eat [iːt] *ate* [et] *eaten* [iːtn]
EAT
forbid [fəbid] *forbade* [fəbeid] *forbidden* [fəbidn]
BID, FORBID, FORGIVE, GIVE
take [teik] *took* [tuk] *taken* [teikn]
FORSAKE, SHAKE, TAKE
fall [fɔːl] *fell* [fel] *fallen* [fɔːln]
FALL
draw [drɔː] *drew* [druː] *drawn* [drɔːn]
DRAW

grow [grou] *grew* [gruː] *grown* [groun]
BLOW, GROW, KNOW, THROW
slay [slei] *slew* [sluː] *slain* [slein]
SLAY

[v] With vowel change (past tense) and vowel shortening when the *-en* suffix is added we find:

ride [raid] *rode* [roud] *ridden* [ridn]

ARISE, DRIVE, RIDE, RISE, SMITE (now archaic), WRITE

[vi] There are some verbs that form the past tense by vowel change, but the *-en* form by the addition of the *-en* suffix to the past tense form, not as in the preceding examples to the simple form. The vowel changes are varied, but the first two below are clear examples of back vowel formation:

forget [fəget] *forgot* [fəgɔt] *forgotten* [fəgɔtn]
BEGET (archaic), FORGET, TREAD
break [breik] *broke* [brouk] *broken* [broukn]
BREAK, WAKE
steal [stiːl] *stole* [stoul] *stolen* [stouln]
CLEAVE, FREEZE, SPEAK, STEAL, WEAVE
bear [bɛə] *bore* [bɔː] *borne* [bɔːn]
BEAR, SWEAR, TEAR, WEAR
lie [lai] *lay* [lei] *lain* [lein]
LIE [=lie down]
choose [tʃuːz] *chose* [tʃouz] *chosen* [tʃouzn]
CHOOSE

[vii] Only one verb has different vowels in all three forms:

fly [flai] *flew* [fluː] *flown* [floun]
FLY

[viii] A particularly idiosyncratic verb has a regular past tense form but an *-en* form with vowel change:

swell [swel] *swelled* [sweld] *swollen* [swouln]
SWELL

9.3.5 Idiosyncratic forms

There are only a few verbs that have peculiarities that we have not discussed. Yet even these have some 'shape'.

[i] MAKE would be regular if we could account for the loss of final [k]:

make [meik] *made* [meid]

[ii] STAND, UNDERSTAND and WITHSTAND would belong with the vowel change verbs if the loss of the nasal consonant could be accounted for:

stand [stænd] *stood* [stud]

[iii] Six verbs – BUY, BRING, THINK, TEACH, SEEK, CATCH (with archaic BESEECH like TEACH) all differ in the simple forms but have similar past tense/*-en* forms:

buy [bai] *bought* [bɔːt]
bring [briŋ] *brought* [brɔːt]
think [θiŋk] *thought* [θɔːt]
teach [tiːtʃ] *taught* [tɔːt]
seek [siːk] *sought* [sɔːt]
catch [kætʃ] *caught* [kɔːt]

[iv] GO alone has a suppletive past tense form (with a vowel-change *-en* suffix *-en* form):

go [gou] *went* [went] *gone* [gɔn]

9.4 BE HAVE and DO

The full verb BE has exactly the same forms as the auxiliary, including negative and weak forms (**6.1.1**). It is completely irregular except for its *-ing* form *being* and the past participle *been*, which belongs to the *-en* formation.

The full verb HAVE also has the same forms as the auxiliary (**6.1.2**); it also has an *-en* form *had* that the auxiliary lacks. The formation is like that of MAKE in that it would be regular if the loss of the final consonant could be accounted for. (This is true of the *-s* as well as the past tense form.)

DO, however, is different. It shares with the auxiliary only the *-s* form and the past tense form. It has no negative or weak forms, but has an *-ing* form that the auxiliary lacks. Its *-s* form *does* [dʌz], its past tense *did* [did] and its *-en* form *done* [dʌn] are all quite irregular.

9.5 Forms with *to*

We have already noted some phonological features associated with the *to* of the *to*-infinitive following an auxiliary or a 'marginal' verb:

[i] With OUGHT there is 'loss' of a consonant in that there is not in normal conversation a 'geminate' [t] ([ɔːt tə]) as might be expected, but a single consonant [ɔːtə] – see **5.1.1.**

[ii] With HAVE the final consonant is devoiced before *to* [hæftə] – **6.1.2.**

[iii] With USED there is both devoicing and 'loss' of a consonant [juːstə] – **6.2.1.**

These are, no doubt, indications of the close relationship between *to* and the preceding word – it is treated phonologically as if it were part of that word. There are a few, at least two, other forms which exhibit the same close relationship – *'ve got* and *want*:

I've got to go [aiv gɔtə gou]
I want to go [ai wantə gou]

References

AUSTIN, J.L. (1962) *How to do things with words*. London: O.U.P.

BINNICK, R.I. (1972) '*Will* and *be going to*'. Papers from the Seventh Regional Meeting Chicago Linguistics Society 40–52.

BOLINGER, D.L. (1971) *The phrasal verb in English*. Cambridge, Mass: Harvard University Press.

BOYD, J.C. and THORNE, J.P. (1969) 'The semantics of modal verbs'. *Journal of Linguistics* 5, 57–74.

CHOMSKY, N. (1957) *Syntactic structures*. The Hague: Mouton.

CHOMSKY, N. (1965) *Aspects of the theory of syntax*. Cambridge, Mass: M.I.T. Press.

CRYSTAL, D. (1966) 'Specification and English tenses'. *Journal of Linguistics* 2, 1–34.

CRYSTAL, D. (1969) *Prosodic systems and intonation in English*. Cambridge: The University Press.

DIVER, W. (1963) 'The chronological system of the English verb'. *Word* 19, 141–81.

DIVER, W. (1964) 'The modal system of the English verb'. *Word* 20, 322–52.

EHRMAN, M. (1966) *The meaning of the modals in present-day American English*. The Hague: Mouton.

FILLMORE, C.J. (1968) 'The case for case' in Bach, E. and Harms, R.T. (eds) *Universals in linguistic theory*. New York: Holt, Rinehart & Winston.

FIRBAS, J. (1964) 'On defining the theme in functional sentence analysis'. *Travaux linguistiques de Prague* 1, 267–80.

FIRTH, J.R. (1968) *Selected papers of J.R. Firth 1952–59* (ed Palmer, F.R.) London: Longman.

HALLIDAY, M.A.K. (1967) 'Notes on transitivity and theme in English 1'. *Journal of Linguistics* 3, 37–81.

HALLIDAY, M.A.K. (1968) 'Notes on transitivity and theme in English 3'. *Journal of Linguistics* 4, 179–216.

HATCHER, A.G. (1951) 'The progressive forms in English: a new approach'. *Language* 27, 254–80.

HOCKETT, C.F. (1958) *A course in modern linguistics*. New York: Macmillan.

HILL, A.A. (1958) *Introduction to linguistic structures: from sound to sentence in English*. New York: Harcourt, Brace.

HUDDLESTON, R.D. (1969) 'Predicate complement constructions in English'. *Lingua* 23, 241–73.

HUDDLESTON, R.D. (1971) *The sentence in written English*. Cambridge: The University Press.

JESPERSEN, O. (1909–49) *A modern English grammar* I–VII. Heidelberg: Karl Winter, and Copenhagen: Einar Munksgaard.

JONES, D. (1956) *An outline of English phonetics*. Cambridge: Heffer.

JOOS, M. (1964) *The English verb: form and meaning*. Madison: The University of Wisconsin Press.

KIPARSKY, R. and KIPARSKY, C. (1970) 'Fact' in Bierwisch, M. and Heidolph, K. (eds). *Progress in linguistics*. The Hague: Mouton.

LAKOFF, R. (1970) 'Tense and its relation to participants'. *Language* 46, 838–49.

LYONS, J. (1968) *Introduction to theoretical linguistics*. Cambridge: The University Press.

NESFIELD, J.C. (1898) *Manual of English grammar and composition*. London: Macmillan.

OTA, A. (1969) 'Modals and some semi-auxiliaries'. Unpublished.

PALMER, F.R. (1964) 'Grammatical categories and their phonetic exponents'. *Proceedings of the Ninth International Congress of Linguists*. The Hague: Mouton. 338–45.

PALMER, F.R. (1967) 'The semantics of the English verb'. *Lingua* 18, 179–95.

PALMER, F.R. (1971) *Grammar*. Harmondsworth: Penguin.

PALMER, F.R. (1973) 'Noun phrase and sentence: a problem in semantics/syntax'. *Transactions of the Philological Society* 20–43.

PALMER, H.E. and BLANDFORD, F.G. (1939) *A grammar of spoken English on a strictly phonetic basis* (2nd edition). Cambridge: Heffer. (The 3rd edition (1969) has been completely revised and rewritten by Roger Kingdon.)

QUIRK, R. and GREENBAUM, S. (1973) *A university grammar of English.* London: Longman.

ROBINS, R.H. (1959) 'Some considerations of the status of grammar in linguistics'. *Archivum Linguisticum* 11, 91–114.

ROSENBAUM, P.S. (1967) *The grammar of English predicate construction.* Cambridge, Mass: M.I.T. Press.

ROSS, J.R. (1969) 'Auxiliaries as main verbs'. *Journal of Philosophical Linguistics* 1, 71–162.

SVARTVIK, J. (1966) *On voice in the English verb.* The Hague: Mouton.

SWEET, H. (1903) *A new English grammar* III. Oxford: Clarendon.

TWADDELL, W.F. (1965) *The English verb auxiliaries* (2nd edition). Providence: Brown University Press.

VAN EK, J.A. (1966) *Four complementary structures of predication in contemporary British English.* Groningen: Wolters.

VENDRYES, J. (1921) *Le langage.* Paris: La renaissance du livre.

ZANDVOORT, R.W. (1957) *A handbook of English grammar.* London: Longman.

Books dealing with the English verb not mentioned in the references:

ALLEN, R.L. (1966) *The verb system of present-day American English.* The Hague: Mouton.

CHRISTOPHERSEN, P. and SANDVED, A.O. (1969) *An advanced English grammar.* London: Macmillan.

GLEASON, H.A. (1965) *Linguistics and English grammar.* New York: Holt, Rinehart & Winston.

KRUISINGA, E. (1931–2) *A handbook of present-day English.* Groningen: Noordhoff.

OTA, A. (1963) *Tense and aspect in present-day American English.* Tokyo: Kenkyusha.

POUTSMA, H. (1926–29) *A grammar of late modern English.* Groningen: Noordhoff.

QUIRK, R., GREENBAUM, S., LEECH, G. and SVARTVIK, J. (1972) *A grammar of contemporary English.* London: Longman.

SCHEURWEGHS, G. (1959) *Present-day English syntax: a survey of sentence patterns.* London: Longman.

STRANG, B.M.H. (1968) *Modern English structure.* London: Edward Arnold.

VISSER, F.T. (1969–70) *An historical syntax of the English language* I–III. Leiden: Brill.

Verb index

The phrasal verbs, etc, of Chapter 8 are not listed under the heading of the verb only, but a few combinations that are not single verbs are listed.

ABHOR, 206
ABIDE, 251
ABLE (BE), 109, 116, 122, 125–6, 141
ACCEPT, 200
ACCUSTOM, 197
ACHE, 73, 196
ACKNOWLEDGE, 201
ADMIT, 201
ADVISE, 179, 197
ADVOCATE, 207
AFFIRM, 200
AFFORD, 196
AGREE, 126, 141, 196, 198
AIM, 196
ALLEGE, 200
ALLOW, 197
ANNOUNCE, 200
ANTICIPATE, 207
APPEAR, 209
APPOINT, 197
APPROVE, 207
ARGUE, 200
ARISE, 253
ARRANGE, 196, 198
ASK, 179, 198
ASPIRE, 196
ASSERT, 200
ASSIST, 197
ATTEMPT, 205–6
AVOID, 205

BE, 18–26, 30–1, 40, 78, 89, 152–5, 237–243, 254
BEAR, 206, 253
BEAT, 252
BECOME, 252
BEG, 198
BEGET, 253
BEGIN, 66, 187, 204, 209, 250
BEHOLD, 203
BELIEVE, 71, 185–7, 201
BELONG, 73
BEND, 249
BESEECH, 254
BET, 249
BETTER, 164–5
BID, 252
BIND, 251
BITE, 252
BLEED, 249
BLOW, 224, 253
BREAK, 90, 223, 225–7, 231–3, 253
BREED, 249
BRING, 84, 197, 213, 224, 227, 235–6, 254
BUILD, 249
BURN, 203, 248
BURST, 249
BUY, 254

CAN, 19–25, 94–151 (*esp* 115–20), 209, 238–41, 243–5

CARRY, 212–3, 224
CAST, 249
CATCH, 205, 254
CAUSE, 197
CEASE, 205
CERTIFY, 200
CHALLENGE, 197
CHANCE, 207, 209
CHOOSE, 196, 253
CLAIM, 200
CLEAVE, 253
CLING, 251
COAX, 197
COERCE, 197
COME, 206, 213, 224–5, 230–3, 235, 252
COMMAND, 197
COMMISSION, 197
COMPLETE, 205
CONCEIVE, 203
CONDESCEND, 196
CONFESS, 201
CONJECTURE, 200
CONSIDER, 201, 207
CONSIST, 73
CONTAIN, 73, 85
CONTEMPLATE, 207
CONTINUE, 177, 213
COPE, 231
COST, 86, 249
COUNT, 207
COUNTENANCE, 207
COVER, 227
CREEP, 248
CUT, 92, 235, 249

DARE, 19, 26–8, 94–151 (*esp* 122–3), 198, 238
DEAL, 249
DECIDE, 177, 196
DECLARE, 201
DECLINE, 196
DELAY, 205
DELIGHT, 207
DENY, 201
DEPEND, 73
DEPICT, 203
DEPLORE, 180, 207
DEPRECATE, 180, 207
DESCRIBE, 203
DESERVE, 73, 208
DESIRE, 195
DETERMINE, 196
DETEST, 207
DIG, 251
DIRECT, 197
DISAPPROVE, 207
DISCOVER, 201
DISCUSS, 207
DISLIKE, 179, 207
DO, 18–28, 31, 153, 155, 157–8, 160–2, 231–4, 237–8, 241, 245, 254
DOTE, 231
DRAW, 252
DREAD, 207
DREAM, 249
DRINK, 250
DRIVE, 197, 229, 253
DROP, 223
DWELL, 248

EAT, 252
ELECT, 196
ENABLE, 197
END, 66
ENDEAVOUR, 206
ENJOY, 207
ENTICE, 197
ENTREAT, 197
ENVISAGE, 203
EQUAL, 85
ESCAPE, 205
ESTIMATE, 200
EVADE, 205
EXPECT, 184–5

FAIL, 206
FALL, 227, 252
FANCY, 194, 198, 203, 207
FEAR, 196
FEED, 249
FEEL, 71, 73, 75, 193, 203, 249
FIGHT, 251
FINISH, 66, 204–5
FIND, 203, 227, 251
FIT, 226
FLEE, 248–9
FLING, 251
FLY, 205, 217–18, 223, 227–9, 253
FORBID, 197, 205, 252
FORCE, 179, 197
FORGET, 71, 194, 201–2, 206, 253
FORGIVE, 252

FORSAKE, 252
FREEZE, 253

GET, 89–90, 156, 159, 194, 197, 204, 206, 212, 234, 251, 255
– RID OF, 234–5
GIRD, 249
GIVE, 84, 197, 212–13, 222–3, 225–6, 252
GO, 205, 213–14, 225, 227, 231–3, 235, 254
GOING (BE), 37, 39, 115, 141, 149, 163–4
GRIEVE, 211
GRIND, 251
GROW, 253

HANG, 216, 251
HAPPEN, 208–9
HASTEN, 194, 206
HATE, 180, 194, 206–7
HAVE, 18–26, 31–2, 41–2, 54–5, 85, 122, 126, 155–60, 165, 173, 199, 237–8, 240–3, 245, 254–5
HEAR, 71, 75–6, 203, 251
HELP, 199, 226
HEAT, 91
HESITATE, 196–7
HEW, 252
HIDE, 252
HINDER, 205
HIT, 248–9
HOLD, 251
HOPE, 71, 177, 196
HURT, 249

IMAGINE, 71, 201, 203
INSIST, 191
INTEND, 172, 177, 185, 197–8
INVITE, 197
ITCH, 73

JUSTIFY, 207

KEEP, 177, 204, 247–8
KNEEL, 249
KNOW, 200, 203, 253

LACK, 85
LAUGH, 211
LEAD, 197, 249
LEAN, 249
LEAP, 248
LEARN, 248
LEAVE, 84, 197, 205, 225, 250
LEND, 249
LET, 199, 236, 249
LET'S, 164–5
LIE, 253
LIGHT, 249
LIKE, 172, 180, 194–6
LISTEN TO, 75
LIVE, 206, 210
LOATHE, 207
LONG, 183, 191, 195–6
LOOK, 75, 196, 212–13, 217–20, 231–3
LOSE, 250
LOVE, 206
LUST, 196

MAKE, 199, 212–13, 226, 235, 254
MANAGE, 206
MARCH, 92, 227
MARRY, 85
MATTER, 73
MAY, 19–25, 94–151 (*esp* 118–20), 238, 241
MEAN, 185, 198, 249
MEASURE, 86
MEET, 249
MIND, 207
MISS, 207
MOTION, 197
MUST, 19–25, 94–151 (*esp* 120–2), 154, 238, 241

NEED, 19, 26–8, 94–151 (*esp* 122–3), 188, 208, 238
NEGLECT, 206
NOTICE, 203

OBLIGE, 197
OBSERVE, 203
OFFER, 179, 196, 198
OMIT, 206
OPEN, 90–3
ORDER, 183–4, 197, 221, 235
OUGHT, 19–25, 94–151 (*esp* 120–2), 154–5, 238, 255
OWN, 73

PACK, 205, 235
PASS, 219–20
PERCEIVE, 203
PERMIT, 197
PERSIST, 191
PERSUADE, 181–2, 197
PILE, 225
PLAN, 71, 197
PLEAD, 191, 196
PLEASE, 73
PLOT, 196
PORTRAY, 203
POSTPONE, 205
PRACTISE, 205
PRAY, 196
PREFER, 206
PREPARE, 196
PRESENT, 219
PRESS, 197
PREVENT, 205
PROCEED, 206
PROMISE, 187–8, 191, 198
PROPOSE, 197
PROVE, 200
PULL, 214, 221, 225
PUT, 212–14, 227, 234, 249

QUIT, 205, 249

RATHER (WOULD), 164–5
REACT, 191
READ, 200, 249
RECOLLECT, 201
RECKON, 200
REFUSE, 110–11, 196
REGRET, 194, 206–7
REJOICE, 210
RELISH, 207
RELY, 231
REMEMBER, 76–7, 173, 193–4, 201–2, 206–7
REMIND, 197
REND, 249
REPORT, 200
REPRESENT, 200
REQUEST, 197
REQUIRE, 198
RESEMBLE, 85
RESENT, 207
RID, 249
RIDE, 253
RING, 90, 250
RISE, 253
RISK, 207
ROAR, 211
RUMOUR, 200
RUN, 86, 92, 216–17, 219–20, 228–30, 232–3, 252
RUSTLE, 91

SAY, 200, 251
SCORN, 196–7
SEE, 71, 75–6, 171–2, 192–3, 202–3, 231–3, 252
SEEK, 254
SEEM, 186–7, 208–9
SELL, 92, 222, 251
SEND, 205, 249
SERVE, 206
SET, 205, 249
– FIRE TO, 234–5
SEW, 252
SHAKE, 252
SHALL, 19–25, 37, 94–151 (*esp* 104–8, 113–15), 238–9, 241, 243
SHED, 249
SHINE, 251
SHOE, 248, 250
SHOOT, 250
SHOW, 91, 252
SHRINK, 250
SHUN, 205
SHUT, 249
SING, 250
SINK, 250
SIT, 211, 227, 232, 251
SLAY, 253
SLEEP, 232, 248
SLIDE, 249
SLING, 251
SLINK, 251
SLIP, 236
SLIT, 249
SMELL, 71, 73, 75–6, 203, 248
SMILE, 211
SMITE, 253
SOUND, 75
SOW, 252
SPEAK, 253
SPEED, 225, 249
SPELL, 248
SPEND, 249
SPILL, 248

SPIN, 251
SPIT, 251
SPLIT, 249
SPOIL, 248
SPREAD, 249
SPRING, 250
STAND, 196, 211, 254
START, 66, 204
STATE, 200
STEAL, 253
STICK, 251
STING, 251
STINK, 250
STOP, 204
STRIDE, 251
STRIKE, 251
STRING, 251
STRIVE, 206
STRUGGLE, 206
SUFFER, 72
SUPPOSE, 201
SURMISE, 201
SUSPECT, 200
SWEAR, 196, 253
SWEEP, 248
SWELL, 253
SWIM, 250
SWING, 251

TAKE, 200, 213, 225–6, 231–3, 252
– CARE OF, 234–5
TASTE, 71, 73, 75
TEACH, 197, 254
TEAR, 253
TELL, 84, 197
TEMPT, 197
TEND, 209, 213
THINK, 71, 200, 207, 254
THROW, 222, 253
THRUST, 249
TIDY, 219
TOLERATE, 213
TOTAL, 86
TRAVEL, 210–20
TREAD, 253
TROUBLE, 197
TRY, 193–4, 205–6
TURN, 224–5

UNDERSTAND, 197, 200, 254
UNDERTAKE, 196, 198
UPSET, 249
URGE, 197
USED, 39, 162–3, 238, 255

WAIT, 210
WAKE, 210, 253
WALK, 92, 230
WANT, 181–2, 191, 194, 208, 255
WARN, 197
WASH, 92, 219
WATCH, 203
WEAR, 253
WEAVE, 253
WEEP, 248
WEIGH, 86
WELCOME, 207
WET, 249
WHISTLE, 211
WILL, 19–25, 37, 93, 94–151 (*esp* 104–115), 154, 163–4, 238–41, 243
WILLING (BE), 109, 116, 122, 125–6
WIN, 250–1
WIND, 251
WIPE, 219
WISH, 195
WITHSTAND, 254
WORK, 232
WORRY, 197
WRING, 251
WRITE, 253

YEARN, 195–6
YELL, 211
YIELD, 213, 225

Subject index

Ability, 115–17, 125, 127, 131
achievement, *see* effort and achievement
accent, 6, 24–5, 65, 77, 132, 217, 222–3, 228–9
adjective, 174–6, 204, 235
adprep, 230
adverb, adverbial, 40–3, 49–50, 52, 54–8, 64–5, 67–70, 86, 93, 104, 108, 111, 113, 118, 189, 195, 213–221, 223, 226–9, 234
agent, 86–7, 90–2, 134
agreement, 109, 133
animate, 91
anomalous finite, 153, 156–8, 160
aspect, 8, 30–43, 50, 53–8, 64–5, 68–77, 109, 115, 136, 149, 155, 158, 170–2, 180, 190, 192–3, 195, 202–205, 225
asterisk, 8
attitude, 172–3, 179–80, 190, 196, 206–7
auxiliary, 15–150 *passim*, 152–62, 237–245
auxiliary and full verb, 39–42, 96–100

Back vowel formation, 250–2
bare infinitive, 14, 27–8, 129, 159–60, 168–71, 173–4, 190, 192, 199, 202–3, 205, 209
basic, 46, 104, 135, 167

Case, 90–2, 178
catenative, 16–17, 21, 31, 97, 108, 166–211
causative, 92, 190, 199
certainty, 135–9
characteristic, 111–12, 117–19, 128, 131
clause, 11, *see also* subordinate clause *and* main clause
code, 18, 23–4, 27, 96, 153, 160, 162, 240
collocation, 82, 212, 231
commentary, 60, 62, 72
complement, 18
completion, 57–8
complex phrase, *see* simple and complex phrase
compound, 212–36
conclusivity, 135, 138
concord, 15
conditional, 22, 47–8, 106–8, 127, 129, 131, 139–49, 163
consonant reduction, 248–9, 252
continuum, 34
current relevance, 42, 50, 52–3, 77, 87

Deductive, 113
definite noun phrase, 221, 223
deictic, 45–7, 49
demonstration, 60–2
devoicing, 247–9, 255
disapproval, 70
discourse orientation, *see* orientation
displaced, 38–9, 78–80, 107, 163

distransitive, 84
double tense, 40
duration, 35, 49–50, 53–6, 61, 63, 70–1
duty, 120–3, 132

-ed formation, 246–50
effort and achievement, 190, 205–6, 210
emotion, 210
emphatic, 33
emphatic affirmation, 18, 24–7, 96, 153, 160, 162
empty auxiliary, 25, 161.
-en form, 14, 31–4, 159, 168–71, 173–4, 199, 202–4, 246–54
epistemic, 38–40, 65–6, 68, 97, 102–3, 113, 120, 127, 135–9, 144, 147–8, 208
exclamation mark, 9

Finite, 11, 13–15, 19, 152, 154, 156, 176, 237, 243
form, 10, *passim*
form and meaning, 6–7
full verb, 16–17, 26–8, 35, 39–42, 96–100, 109, 126, 145, 152–62, 167, *see also* auxiliary and full verb
fusion, 230, 242–3
future, 34–7, 39, 42–4, 58–9, 64–8, 98, 104–8, 111, 115–16, 125, 131, 135–6, 141, 147–9, 155, 163–4, 195–6
future tense, 34–5, 37
futurity, verb, 189, 191, 195–9, 205, 208–10

Gender, 6
general possibility, 120, 127, 134
generalization, 98, 119, 125, 127, 132, 134
gerund, 14, 174–5
goal, 90–1
grammar, 4, *passim*
guarantee, 100–1, 113–14, 121, 133

Habitual, 34–5, 37, 39, 42–4, 56, 58–64, 67–8, 74–5, 124–5, 128, 136, 142, 147, 157
historic present, 44
homonym, 75–7, 192–4

Identity relations, 18, 180–8, 192, 201, 207
idiom, 213–16, 218, 225–7, 230–5
illocutionary, 101
imperative, 15, 26, 32–3, 153, 165, 203
implication, 142–3, 146–7
inductive, 64, 112
inference, 112–13, 135
infinitival, 14, 32–3, 55, 170–1, 173
infinitive, 14, 19, 174–5, 243
inflection, 1, 243
-ing form, 14, 31–4, 159, 168, 171–80, 190, 192–7, 199, 201–8, 245–6, 254
initiation, 114, 118
insistence, 111, 124, 132
instrument, 90–1
intention, 106
intonation, 4–6, 22, 65.
intransitive, 213, 223–4, *see also* transitivity
inversion, 18, 22–3, 26–7, 31, 96, 145–6, 153, 156, 160, 162, 227
invitation, 109, 120
irregular, 3, 237–8, 246–7
isolating, 1

Lexeme, 10, 16–17, 19
limited duration, 42, 50, 56, 68–9, 74, 76
locative, 91

Main clause, 11, 166, 181–8, 191, 195–196, 198–201, 203–5, 208
meaning, *see* form and meaning
mental activity, 71
modal, 6, 15–27, 31, 94–151, 169, 180, 208, *see also* auxiliary
morpheme, 9–10
morphology, 4, 39, 156, 159, 237–55
motion, 215, 224–5, 230

Native speaker, 1, 7–8
needing, 190, 208
negative, negation, 20–1, 26–9, 31, 33, 42, 96–9, 101, 103–4, 108, 111, 116, 118, 121–3, 131–3, 135, 137–9, 153, 156, 160, 162, 168–9, 206, 237–9, 254
neutralization, 119–22, 133–4
nil obstat, 118–19

non-action, 121
non-epistemic, *see* epistemic
non-finite, *see* finite
non-perfect, *see* phase
non-progressive, *see* aspect
non-progressive verb, 70–7, 193, 203
nominal, *see* noun
noun, 174–7, 179, 215–16, 218–21, 235–6
noun phrase, 10–11

Object, 18, 83–6, 175–87, 207
obligation, 113–14, 120–3, 128–9, 132–133, 158
orientation, 100–3, 113–14, 118–27, 129, 133–4, 144–5, 165
orthography, 4, 159, 162, 238–41

Paradigm, 30–4, 94–6, 170, 243
participle, 14, 174–5
participial, 14, 19, 32–3, 55, 170–3, 202
particle, 212–15, 220, 228, 234
passive, *see* voice
past, *see* tense
past-past, 41, 46, 54–5, 77
perception, 190, 192–3, 200–4
performative, 61, 121
permission, 100–2, 118–19, 121, 124, 127, 132–4
phase, 16, 30–43, 49–55, 68–9, 79–80, 88, 139–40, 146, 155, 158, 170–4, 180, 195–6, 200–1, 203
phrasal verb, 213, 220–8, 234–5
phrasal prepositional verb, 84, 234
phrase, 9–11, *passim*
pitch, 6
plan, 66, 106
plural, 6–7, 238, 242
possibility, 135–9
post-position, 219–20
predicative, 142–7
preposition, 177, 190–2, 196, 201, 205, 213–21, 223, 227–31, 233, 236
prepositional verb, 84, 213, 227–34
prepositional-adverb, 215–16
present, *see* tense
primary, 15–17, 30–93, 96–100, 104, 153, 169, 180
private verb, 71–5
probability, 37, 135–9
process, 39, 190, 204–5, 211
progressive, *see* aspect
promise, 113–14, 124
pronoun, 217
prosodic, 6
pseudo-cleft, 178
pseudo-epistemic, 39, 107
pseudo-passive, 92–3, 110
purpose, 209–10

Quasi-auxiliary, 162–5
question, 22, 100, 110, 114, 118, 122, 161
question mark, 8

Real conditional, *see* conditional
reflexive, 200, 203
relative, 232
relevance, 143, 147
remote, 48
reported speech, 38, 43–7, 107, 130–1, 139
reporting, 173, 189–90, 192–3, 199–204
request, 127–9
result, 50–4, 210, 225–6

Semi-negative, 22, 28–9
sensation, 71–3, 75–6, 117, 124, 131
sentence, 11
separation, 232
sequence of tenses, 45–6
-s form, 14, 27, 237, 245–6
secondary, *see* modal
simple and complex phrase, 16–18, 39–42, 87, 96–100, 108, 166–7, 180, 208–9, 211
simple present, 60–2
singular, 6–7
speech and writing, 3–6
speech act, 101, 115, 128
sporadic repetition, 42, 69–70, 74
statal passive, 88–9
state, 71, 73, 76, 136
stress, 4–6, 25, 239–40
strong form, *see* weak form
structuralist, 3
subject, 176, 180–1, 185–8, 191
subject complementation, 99, 169, 185–7, 190, 206, 208–9
subject orientation, *see* orientation
subject raising, 185, 190

subjunctive, 48–9
subordinate clause, 11, 14–15, 166, 169, 176–89, 191–2, 195, 200, 206–8
subordination, 11, 17–18, 46, 166
suppletive, 116, 125
syllable, 239–41, 243

Tag, 28–9, 128, 165
tense, 2, 17, 19, 30–49, 52, 97, 101, 103–4, 107, 111, 116–17, 120, 123–31, 138–42, 146, 169–74, 180, 195–6, 200–1, 203, 208–9, 246–54
tentative, 47, 109, 113, 116, 118, 120, 124, 127–8, 131, 138, 148
text, 7–9
thematization, 87
threat, 66
time, 2, 17, 34–8, 43–4, 49–50
timeless, 59, 63–4, 112
to-infinitive, 14, 19, 27–8, 154, 158, 168, 170–4, 177, 190, 193–7, 199–208, 254
transformation, 81–3
transitivity, 83–6, 179
transparent, 226, 231–2

Unreal conditional, *see* conditional
unreality, 43, 47–9, *see also* conditional

Verb class, 15–16
verb phrase, 1, 10, 13–29, *passim*
voice, 30–4, 40, 42, 81–93, 99, 101–3, 105–6, 108, 111, 116, 123, 133–6, 155–6, 165, 169–71, 181–7, 191–2, 195, 198–206, 208–9, 213, 218, 232–5
voice neutrality, 87, 99
volition, 108–11, 114, 116, 125, 127, 131, 149
vowel shortening, 247–50, 252–3

Weak forms, 153, 156, 160, 165, 237, 239–45, 254
'whenever', 142, 144, 146–7
willingness, 109, 116, 127
wish, 48, 149–50
word, 2, 6, 9–10, 243
writing, *see* speech and writing

WITHDRAWN
from
STIRLING UNIVERSITY LIBRARY